Simulated Test Marketing

Technology for Launching Successful New Products

Kevin J. Clancy

Robert S. Shulman

Marianne M. Wolf

LEXINGTON BOOKS
An Imprint of Macmillan, Inc.
NEW YORK

Maxwell Macmillan Canada
TORONTO

Maxwell Macmillan International
NEW YORK OXFORD SINGAPORE SYDNEY

Library of Congress Cataloging-in-Publication Data

Clancy, Kevin J.
   Simulated test marketing : technology for launching successful new products /
Kevin J. Clancy, Robert S. Shulman, Marianne M. Wolf.
     p.   cm.
   ISBN 0-02-9055005-9
   1. Marketing—Computer simulation.   2. New products—Marketing.
I. Shulman, Robert S.   II. Wolf, Marianne M.   III. Title.
HF5415.125.C58   1994
658.8'00285—dc20   94-17718
                                                     CIP

Lexington Books
An Imprint of Macmillan, Inc.
866 Third Avenue, New York, N. Y. 10022

Maxwell Macmillan Canada, Inc.
1200 Eglinton Avenue East
Suite 200
Don Mills, Ontario M3C 3N1

Macmillan, Inc. is part of the Maxwell Communication
Group of Companies.

Printed in the United States of America

printing number

1 2 3 4 5 6 7 8 9 10

This year we celebrate the 25th anniversary of simulated test marketing technology. Who would have guessed in those early days of trial and error that from such humble beginnings would emerge one of the most useful—and certainly most validated—tools in all of marketing research?

We dedicate this book to the pioneering innovators in our profession who made this possible: the men and women at research and consulting firms, at universities and advertising agencies, and at corporations, who invented, developed, improved, and extended simulated test marketing technology from its simple origins as a new packaged goods volume forecasting tool to its current role as the methodology of choice for improving marketing programs for new and established products and services.

Kevin J. Clancy
Gloucester, Massachusetts

Robert S. Shulman
Wesport, Connecticut

Marianne M. Wolf
Shell Beach, California

Contents

Exhibits

Acknowledgments

We are especially pleased to acknowledge the early contributions of Dr. David Learner and James K. DeVoe at BBDO Advertising, their consultants Professors Abraham Charnes and William Cooper of Carnegie Mellon University and their successors at BBDO, Dr. Lewis Pringle, Dr. Larry Light, and Edward Brody for their magnificent contributions to marketing and management science, particularly new product forecasting technology. BBDO's DEMON (*Decision Mapping via Optimal GO-NO Networks*), published in *Management Science* in 1966 and NEWS (*New Product Early Warning System*) published in *Management Science* sixteen years later represented pathbreaking efforts to model the new product introduction process.

We are equally pleased to acknowledge the seminal contributions of Florence Skelly and Robert Goldberg of the Yankelovich organization who were the creators and champions of "The Laboratory Test Market," the first and in many ways the most interesting of the early simulated test marketing methodologies. The pioneering work undertaken by Skelly and Goldberg for packaged goods clients such as Unilever and Pillsbury revolutionized the way that marketers introduced new products.

Most of today's systems could be described as a marriage of the mathematical models and the laboratory: one part DEMON/NEWS, one part LTM, and one part something new.

During the course of twenty-five years many people in the United States and abroad contributed mightily to the "something new." Indeed, the "something new" is today in many simulated test marketing systems far and away the largest part. The systems have grown and evolved so much in our lifetime that their common heritage is lost except to historians and archeologists of our profession.

We acknowledge the strong contribution to simulated test marketing made by Professors Glen L. Urban, John R. Hauser, and Alvin J. Silk, and their colleagues at Management Decision Systems, for their work on the ASSESSOR model, which represented a more theoretically grounded and methodologically sophisticated variant of Yankelovich's Laboratory Test Market.

We would also like to acknowledge Jacques Blanchard, Gerald Eskin, Louis Forte, Jane Froelich, Paul Green, Russ and Doug Haley, Philip Kotler, Peter Krieg, Lynn Lynd, John Malek, Hal Rosenbaum, Brian Shea, Al Shocker, Walker Smith, Robert Wachsler, Lynn Whitton, Gerry Wind, Joseph Woodlock, and especially Dudley Ruch for their many contributions to the field and our thinking.

We are deeply indebted to Professor Joseph Blackburn, who has consulted to us on this topic for many years and has made many contributions to the LITMUS model and this book; Professor Dale Wilson, who wrote the first drafts of several chapters in this volume while working on a consulting engagement with the authors (give Dale credit, if you like them; blame us for the editorial changes if you don't); Lisa Carter of Yankelovich Partners, whose ability to implement our ideas in an evolving system are the stuff of legend and whose gifts as a teacher of simulated test marketing technology are reflected in the independent accomplishments of her "students" including Rebecca Armstrong, Virginia Glen, and Marianne Wolf.

The client companies which used our services at one time or another over the years for simulated test marketing purposes deserve a special note of recognition. The CEOs, marketing directors, and research directors who saw promise in the emerging technology and sought our assistance in employing it to assess and improve a new product/new service marketing plan often contributed to our thinking and led to model refinements for which they received little formal recognition. These companies include (but are not limited to) American Express, Campbell Soup Co., Citicorp, Clorox, Colgate, ConAgra, Gillette, H.J. Heinz, Kraft/General Foods, Lever Bros., Lorillard Inc., McDonald's, Mobil, Norelco, Ore-Ida, Ralston Purina, Pepsi-Cola, Procter & Gamble, Sterling Drug, and Visa.

All of us would like to acknowledge the support and encouragement of our respective families during the months we researched and wrote this manuscript. Kevin thanks Kathleen for her willingness to forgo sailing and skiing weekends because of the book, while Robert recognizes that without Robin he would lose his mainspring of inspiration. Marianne is particularly appreciative of the enthusiasm and patience shown by her husband Mitch and her children, Shannon and Shane.

Finally, we would like to thank Wally Wood, a brilliant business writer and editor whose skills and spirit throughout three difficult books continue to impress us; Beth Anderson, our patient but demanding editor at Lexington Books; Lori Marvel of Copernicus: The Marketing Investment Strategy Group and Mary Ziegler of TR Productions for their help in creating the more than eighty exhibits sprinkled through these pages; Dick Clarke, chairman of Yankelovich Partners, for his support in having this book published; and Tony Hufflet, general manager of Novaction U.S., for his contributions to our discussions of the ASSESSOR and NOVACTION models.

Any errors in the manuscript are entirely our own, which will be corrected in future printings of this book.

I

Introduction to Simulated Test Marketing

1

The High Cost
of Marketing Failure

Although many business people rightly regard Procter & Gamble as one of the country's most efficient marketing organizations, even the Cincinnati giant can stumble.

In the late 1970s, when P&G began looking for fast-growing consumer products, one study suggested that the company might have an opportunity in the orange juice business.[1] The study projected orange juice sales to grow only about 10 percent a year for the next five years, but that was still better than the corporation's projected detergent growth. Furthermore, the two national juices, Minute Maid (owned by Coca-Cola Foods) and Tropicana (owned at the time by Beatrice Companies), commanded only about 30 percent of the market between them; private labels and regional brands held the rest.

Tropicana was charging a premium price for its Tropicana Pure Premium, the only national brand that was not manufactured from concentrate. P&G's management drew a reasonable inference: An orange juice that tasted noticeably better than those on the market could generate significant profits. What's more, P&G's food engineers claimed they could develop such a better-tasting juice.

Unfortunately, the inference contained a major fallacy. "If you look at consumer acceptance of orange juice," said a former member of Citrus Hill's brand management group, "the perceived difference between the best and the worst product in the category is narrower than in any other. Procter & Gamble needs to compete in categories where they can create a discernible difference and market the hell out of it. Orange juice had less room for improvement than anything."

That consumers did not see much difference between orange juices did not slow P&G's entry into the business. The corporation bought Florida orange groves and a processing plant for $19 million in 1981, and sent two brand groups to the plant. One group was to use the technology developed by P&G engineers to produce in commercial quantities a new, superior juice. The other group was to blend a conventional orange juice—the product that became Citrus Hill.

Why create a me-too product when P&G's own computer model had projected that another ordinary juice could expect to capture only an 8.1 percent market share—a share too small to cover costs?

"No one cared," said the former executive, "because we only wanted to sell it in test market to get some experience in orange juice with it. We were never going to expand it nationally."

Or that was the thinking until Procter & Gamble ran some blind taste tests. Citrus Hill scored slightly higher than Minute Maid and Tropicana—60 percent versus 40 percent. "All that means is that 10 people out of 100 can tell the difference, but everyone was running around like that was a big deal, saying, 'We have an advantage! We have an advantage! Every consumer will want it!'"

The brand group working on the conventional—if slightly better-tasting blend—put Citrus Hill into Indiana and Iowa test markets in October 1982. They ran a strong "buy one, get one free" introductory offer that persuaded 35 percent of the orange juice drinkers to try Citrus Hill, suggesting a very positive response to the new entry.

In fact, it was too high. Someone inadvertently shipped too much promotional merchandise into the test markets. As a result, Citrus Hill's Month One share of the Iowa market was 1.2 percent; a month later it was 6.7 percent; in another month it jumped to 9 percent.

As this exciting news arrived at P&G's headquarters, the group working on the new juice technology sent some bad news: The better, P&G-grade orange juice was just too expensive to manufacture.

The failure of its original strategy and the inflated results from Citrus Hill's two test markets persuaded P&G's management to expand nationally with a product it had originally intended to use only to gain some experience. As a former brand manager recalled,

"They were excited by the initial results. They felt it had the potential to be a leading brand. There had been so much published about P&G's moving too slowly on new products. The decision was, 'It appears we have a winner here. Why not expand?' That was three months into test market. We should've waited longer."

They should have. Although Citrus Hill's share had climbed as high as 17.5 percent, within three months it was becoming clear the brand would not—could not—remain at that level. Citrus Hill's strong advertising and promotion efforts may have persuaded people to try the product once, but they didn't switch from their regular brands. Citrus Hill's repurchase rate was just 50 percent, and by month six of the test, market share was back down to 11.4 percent and falling.

By the time P&G began holding sales meetings for the trade, the Citrus Hill share had leveled off at about 8.5 percent, remarkably close to the original computer model's forecast of what the brand could expect to obtain and too small for the corporation to make money. But the project, like so many others at corporations large and small, had taken on a life of its own. Procter & Gamble had announced and budgeted a national Citrus Hill rollout and went ahead anyway.

The national rollout was tarnished by several problems. A label printing error made the juice look pale and thin; a freeze damaged P&G's orange crop (so it had to buy concentrate on the open market and was not therefore even selling the same blend it had been testing); and there were difficulties with the sales force. Further, as soon as Citrus Hill achieved national distribution, Minute Maid and Tropicana doubled their ad and promotional spending and mobilized their sales forces. Frank Blod, who was vice president of marketing at Coca-Cola Foods in 1984 and 1985, recollected afterward, "Minute Maid slaughtered Citrus Hill on the beaches. They kept the product off the shelves by loading the pipeline with Minute Maid."[2]

Procter & Gamble did not give up on the Citrus Hill brand. In the middle of 1990 it replaced Citrus Hill Select with Citrus Hill Fresh Choice, "made with a new process that picks and squeezes oranges the same day,"[3] and began rolling out a three-flavor line of Citrus Hill frozen lemonade. It then ran into trouble with the Food and Drug Administration over the "Fresh Choice" name on a processed juice. P&G agreed to drop the word "fresh" after the FDA said the label misled consumers into thinking the juice was fresh.[4]

But the orange juice never became a success; estimates of the brand's losses ran as high as $200 million, and in September 1992 P&G gave up the business. "You can't make money in a business if your primary entry is a No. 3 brand, and you can't have a market leader if you don't have a competitive advantage," said Edwin Artzt, the chairman and chief executive of P&G. "We just didn't have it and couldn't get it."[5]

Watching the game films on Monday morning, almost anyone can spot the quarterback's mistakes. We are not suggesting that Procter & Gamble is a poor marketer. Citrus Hill is extraordinary only by its size and the publicity it generated. But for every Citrus Hill, NeXT computer, Polavision instant home movie system, or *Cable-TV Week* television guide there are a thousand wretched, silent marketing failures.

The High Frequency of Marketing Failure

Company managements believe that new and improved products lead to growth and profitability. *New Product News* magazine reported that companies introduced 17,571 new food and non-food products in 1993, up 4.6 percent from 1992's total.[6] While this percentage increase was down dramatically from the average 14.4 percent annual increase over the past decade (perhaps the recession had something to do with the 1993 figure), there are signs that new product introductions are heating up again. The December 1993 increase was 32 percent above that of December a year earlier.

Of course, not all of these (or even most of them) are "new" products in the sense that the world had never seen anything like them before. *New Product News* defines a new product as something the company is making for the first time, and therefore most of these are line extensions: ". . . a new Betty Crocker cake mix flavor, a new Bounty paper towel color, or a soft-moist Purina Cat Chow are included in [the publication's new-product] listings."[7] The real question is what percentage succeeds?

Unfortunately, no one knows exactly—not even the editor of *New Product News*. Industry speakers generally say that only 10 to

20 percent succeed while denying their own companies suffer such a pitiful rate. Fifty years ago, more than half of all new products introduced succeeded (by succeeded we mean the product was still on the shelf, still in distribution, two years after introduction). Products that did succeed could expect to be around fifty years or more.

Even twenty-five years ago, 65 percent of the products that companies launched succeeded. They did so for several reasons: The markets for many product categories were less penetrated and less saturated than they are today. A large part of a new product's sales came from category growth, rather than from consumer brand switching.

In 1994, no more than 10 percent of new package goods products are successful, and for those that are successful, the life expectancy is less than ten years. These statistics vary by category, but not as much as one might think. We'll have more to say about this later.

Today, almost all consumer markets are mature. Whatever real growth there is comes from population increases, which never exceed 1 to 2 percent a year. To survive at all, a new product must wrench market share away from other, established brands.

In the past, a few brands shared most of the volume in most product categories. These markets were what economists call undifferentiated oligopolies—a few dominant brands and virtually no price competition. As the markets grew, consumers eagerly looked for and companies enthusiastically provided the product diversity that new entries represented. Since the dominant brands were often slow to adapt, new brands were able to win market share.

Today, product categories are so saturated that market structures exhibit what economists call monopolistic competition. This apparent oxymoron describes a market in which no one brand dominates, where product differentiation is not so much in product performance as in brand perception, and where price competition is intense.

The trade is a new marketplace power. As recently as the early 1980s, retailers tended to be passive channels for product distribution. Today, retailers are an active, powerful marketing element. They have provoked price competition among manufacturers. They insist on slotting allowances (money to put the product on their shelves) and exit fees (money to take the product off the shelves, money that makes up what they would have earned if the product had sold properly). These fees ensure retailers against the flood of new product failures and raise the manufacturers' cost of entry. Add these costs to the high advertising and couponing expenses and it is difficult—sometimes impossible—for new product marketers to generate an adequate margin, one that will pay for the marketing program and return a profit.

Finally, marketers have watched advertising's productivity decline in the past decade, particularly advertising on network television. When the three networks reached 96 percent of all American homes, network TV was critically important in building brand awareness and in telling consumers that new products were available and desirable. Today there are four broadcast networks, scores of cable networks, and talk of 500-channel television sets. Traditional marketing communication has lost much of its effect through media fragmentation, splintered communications budgets, and the prevalence of promotional pricing.

Alvin Achenbaum, when he headed his own consulting company (he is now vice-chairman at Backer Spielvogel Bates Worldwide), analyzed SAMI/Burke data and found that fewer than 200 products of the thousands introduced in a ten-year period had more than $15 million in sales, and only a handful produced more than $100 million in sales.[8]

Marketing executives believe far more products fail than succeed, yet they also believe companies have to maintain a steady stream of new products. A majority of packaged food marketing executives said in a 1991 *Food & Beverage Marketing* survey that a minimum of 30 percent of their sales over the next five years would come from new products.[9]

The Problems with Line Extensions

Many of these executives believe that line extensions are the least risky way to introduce new products. Or they believe that because line extensions are easier to develop and introduce than completely new brands, they are the most profitable.

This may have been true once, and it may be true today in certain special circumstances. Brand extensions sometimes offer great market potential—a strong brand name can give immediate recognition to an extension, thereby saving advertising and promotion expense. Extending the brand (Liquid Tide, Listerine Cool Mint, or Gillette Sensor for Women) is a way to ensure brand/market continuity as the core brand matures, maintaining sales and profit levels.

On the other hand, a brand extension can be risky. Dangers include:

1. A product that disappoints loyal consumers and damages the core brand's reputation. The "Cadillac Cimarron" was actually a Chevrolet Cavalier with leather seats and some luxury appointments. It was not aimed at the Cadillac buyer but at the less affluent who wanted a Cadillac at a lower price. It ceased production, but not before it hurt the Cadillac image. New Coke was another example. It was an embarrassment to Coca-Cola executives, which had to hastily bring back "Classic" Coke.

For another example, take ConAgra's Healthy Choice line of frozen entrees, one of the most successful new product introductions of the 1980s. The products were well prepared, tasty, nicely packaged, and very strongly positioned. They were an instant success—with no small thanks to some very effective test marketing research—and they quickly became a major factor in the category.

Then ConAgra began slapping the name Healthy Choice on a broad range of products including desserts (ice cream), soup, pizza, low-fat ground beef—relatively few of which met even minimal standards for product success. As a result the corporation tarnished the Healthy Choice brand name and its reputation among retailers and consumers.

Other examples? Cadbury—a name associated with excellent chocolate—brought out Cadbury's Smash instant potato product, plus dried milk, soups, and beverages; these were a giant step away from the brand's key association and they failed. Woolite's Tough Stain rug cleaner conflicted with the brand's image for washing delicate clothes. Similarly, SOS Glassworks glass cleaner evoked negative associations from the brand's famous scouring pads.

2. The core name may be inappropriate for the new product (and vice–versa) even if the new product is well made and performs as intended. A good example is Toro's electric, hand-maneuvered "Toro Sno-pup," a spin-off from its line of heavy-duty snow blow-

ers. The core name should have legitimized the line extension. Instead, consumers thought the name indicated a weak, far less effective snow removal machine—as it was. But it was intended for "clean-up," light snow, walks and porches, and for the apartment or condo dweller, with its light weight and compact storage. It bombed until Toro dropped the "Sno-pup" name, made its positioning/usage clearer, and separated it from Toro's main line of snow blowers and tractors.

3. Through overuse, the core name may lose its unique positioning in the consumer's mind, leaving an apparently loosely connected bunch of brands, with the appearance of being in the same general category.

Brand extensions have run amuck. They have been turning consumers into feature shoppers and retailers into shelf space auctioneers. A feature shopper is someone who buys a product only for a certain feature. In 1980, for example, Kotex offered Maxi Pads for feminine protection. Today there are Maxi Regular; Super Maxi; Thin Maxi; Thin Super Maxi; Ultra Thin Maxi; Ultra Thin Long Maxi; Shaped Maxi; Overnites; Curved Maxi; and Curved Super Maxi.

This raises a couple of obvious problems. A big single brand is now a portfolio of smaller pieces, and that makes the company's management task much more complex. Such product proliferation means that more and more products are chasing a relatively stable amount of shelf space. As we learned in Economics 101, when demand increases and supply remains constant, prices rise. Sure enough, retailers are charging manufacturers to put new products onto the shelves and, if a product does not meet sales or profit goals, they are charging manufactures an exit fee.

Brand extensions erode consumer loyalty. Since 1975, the NPD Group, a Port Washington (New York) research firm, has maintained a data base of fifty brands that were first, second, or third in their category when the firm began its study. Joel Rubinson, the firm's chief research officer, says that although consumer loyalty (as measured by share of requirements among a brand's buyers[10]) has declined somewhat overall, it has declined significantly more for brands in categories that have increased levels of "feature segmentation." Consumer loyalty also declined significantly more for brands that reduced, rather than increased, advertising support.

Line extensions are particularly risky because they tend to cannibalize the present product as we will discuss in Chapter 7. The pattern has become common across different industries. Marketers, eager for quick success, introduce the line extension to a major brand. The "line extension manager" introduces the new entry, diverting resources away from its parent. The extension may achieve its sales objective and the manager is rewarded. Then the parent brand goes into a slow decline, however, and the diagnosis is cannibalism.

Net incremental profits—not sales—should be the criterion for evaluating line extensions. And when a company takes NIP into account, line extensions often prove to be far more risky than most marketers have been led to believe.

Marketing Failures in Every Category

But if hard figures on new product failure are imperfect, anecdotal evidence abounds. Of six major new products Colgate-Palmolive introduced in the United States in recent years, only two were successful: Palmolive Automatic dishwasher detergent and Colgate Tartar-Control toothpaste.[11] The failures included Lournay skin care products for sensitive skin; Colgate Tarter-Control mouth rinse; Dentagard anti-plaque toothpaste; and Fab 1 Shot, a single-packet detergent with fabric softener. This product took more than 4 percent of the $2.5 billion heavy-duty detergent market in its first year. Three years later its share had fallen to an estimated 0.1 percent.

In 1992 Pepsi-Cola introduced Crystal Pepsi, a line extension designed to capitalize on American's interest in clear drinks. We called the product a disaster from the start. Not only were sales well below expectations but it had a negative rub-off on the Pepsi image. PepsiCo's 1993 annual report noted, "As a result of softening trends in the Crystal Pepsi brands, the product is being refined and will be reintroduced in 1994 in a nondiet version only." With the Pepsi name deemphasized.

In 1986 Ford Motor Co. introduced the Sierra, one of its top-selling models in Germany and Great Britain, into the United States as the Merkur XR4Ti, projecting sales of 100,000 units a year by 1990. In fact, because of poor positioning, styling, advertising, pricing, and inadequate marketing support, the car never sold as many as 40,000 units in the four years between its launch and disappearance.

Miller Brewing spent $30 million to introduce Matilda Bay wine cooler in late 1987 and 1988, selling more than five million cases of the sweet, non-carbonated drink and becoming the fourth largest-selling brand in the country. However, Miller introduced the product just as wine coolers were losing their popularity and the shakeout had begun. By late 1988, Miller had stopped all TV, radio, and print ads as the brand slid into oblivion.

Bic, the disposable pen, lighter, and razor giant, introduced Parfum IBC in April 1989, four different fragrances distributed through drugstores, supermarkets, and mass merchandisers. Although it spent more than $18 million in the marketing campaign, company profits fell 22 percent in 1989, mainly due to poor perfume sales.

In the same year, Clairol introduced a home permanent product formulated for three different types of hair. It launched the line with a $25 million campaign and failed miserably.

In 1990, Sears, Roebuck & Co. closed its chain of 47 free-standing McKids children's apparel stores after a two–year test.[12] Sears, which had a licensing partnership with McDonald's Corp., opened the first free-standing McKids specialty store in August 1988. "The McKids apparel line as a whole has been successful," said a Sears spokesman, "but we've come to the conclusion that our rate of return on the free-standing McKids stores was unacceptable, so we're discontinuing them."

Wendy's International, after its memorable "Where's the Beef?" campaign, had a series of marketing failures.[13] Rather than build on the "Where's the Beef?" momentum, the company concentrated on breaking into the fast-food breakfast market. Because its entry could not be eaten on the run, the breakfast venture was unsuccessful.

Financial service companies also have high new product failure rates. "Many people have suggested the number is even higher than 70 percent for financial products," said Lynn S. Whitton, a former vice president of marketing research at American Express Company.[14] She added that new financial products fail for generally the same reasons that new cereals, toothpaste, cars, and fast-food items fail—either the company has not "identified the consumer 'hot button,' or we're too 'me-too,' or our services don't deliver versus expectations."

Whitton's observations parallel our own. The evidence that we've been quietly collecting for years suggests a financial service failure rate of approximately 80 percent. This is the same rate we've seen for new products as diverse as new television programs, inexpensive (under $300) consumer durables, and Hollywood movies.

Package goods, as we have said before, fail at an even higher rate. The 1994 mortality rate will be approximately 92 percent. Within the package goods category, of course, there are products with longer and shorter life expectancies. One failure rate estimate for new cigarettes introduced nationally is 95 percent. If that's not scary enough, consider the fast food industry where only 1 in 100 new products introduced regionally or nationally is considered to be a success.

The High Cost of Marketing Failure

The key issue here is the cost of such marketing failure. How much money do American companies waste introducing "me-too" products that do not deliver what they promise? One way to calculate that figure is to take the average cost to introduce a new product and multiply it by the number of failures.

Edward F. Ogiba, president of Group EFO Limited, a new product development consulting company, has written that the cost of introducing a national brand can easily exceed $20 million. "The going budget for creative development and market research alone now reportedly exceeds $500,000 per project, a 150 percent increase in two years."[15]

The editor of *New Product News* has written that "it probably costs $100 million to introduce a truly new soft drink nationally and it costs $10,000 to introduce a new flavor of ice cream in Minneapolis. Somewhere in between is a worthless 'average' cost to introduce a new product."[16] He added that with the help of media experts, the magazine built an "ideal" national introductory advertising/consumer promotion/trade promotion marketing plan for a major new product. The total expenditure was roughly $54 million and did not include product development, package design, sales force contribution, or brand management costs.

Rakesh Malhotra, a vice president at the Best Foods Division of CPC International, made what he believed to be several conservative assumptions and estimated that the total marketing dollars spent by manufacturers for failed new food products in a single year ranged from $9 billion to $14 billion.[17]

"Even though the $9 billion to $14 billion dollar amount is huge in an absolute sense," said Malhotra, "by itself, it is hard to judge this number. To provide a perspective, I looked up the profits of the leading companies in the food business. The total food operating profit of the top fifteen companies was $7 billion in 1989. Thus, if my assumptions are correct, the 1989 marketing spending behind failed new food items may have been twice as much as the total profits of the top fifteen companies." Even the most conservative estimate indicates that companies spent more to introduce failed products than they earned—at least $2 billion more.

Malhotra saw three probable implications from his calculations.

1. The pace of new product introductions might slow. "If wholesalers and retailers are successful in tacking on a failure fee, that could certainly curb introductions of some close-in line extensions." A failure—or exit—fee increases the marketer's cost of doing business and ultimately consumer prices.
2. Retailers increasingly recognize that new products require more testing. Malhotra quoted Michael J. Rourke of A&P as saying, "When you have a 90 percent failure rate, you know there isn't enough testing going on." In the future, Malhotra speculated, retailers will probably demand more extensive results on new products before they accept and support them.
3. Marketers themselves increasingly recognize they must do more and better new product testing before they dump items onto the market to see whether they sell. Arthur Shulze, vice chairman of General Mills, has said, "The time is rapidly passing when a manufacturer can willy-nilly introduce a product without adequate testing."[18]

To reduce the huge cost and wasted effort on products that are likely to fail, companies have tried to reduce the risk by testing their new ideas before rolling them out nationally. As we'll see in a moment, however, traditional test marketing—the way most firms go about evaluating new products prior to a national introduction—may be more hindrance than help.

2

Traditional Test Marketing

A Recipe for Failure

Until fairly recently, companies that tested new products did so by conducting a real-world experiment. Indeed, David A. Aaker and George S. Day, the authors of one popular marketing research textbook, tell us that, "In terms of providing a realistic evaluation of a marketing program, there is no substitute for conducting an experiment in which the marketing program (or perhaps several versions of it) are implemented in a limited but carefully selected part of the market."[1]

The underlying assumption is that through such an experiment a company can determine a marketing program's impact with all its interdependencies in the actual market context. This is more valid and reliable than the artificial context of concept and product tests.

A company employs a test market for two basic reasons:

1. To gain information and experience with the marketing program before committing to it totally.
2. To predict the outcome when the company implements the marketing program in the national marketplace.

Gaining Information and Experience

The test market acts as a pilot operation for the national (or regional) marketing program, just as a pilot production facility might serve to debug a manufacturing process. As we saw with the Citrus

Hill Orange Juice example, marketing programs can develop a variety of problems. Here is another example of what can go wrong.

In the late 1980s, Weyerhaeuser Co., which has manufactured private label disposable diapers since 1970, decided that it had an opportunity to take a significant share of the $3.8 billion disposable diaper market.[2] Weyerhaeuser would market its premium UltraSofts, which used a new technology to produce a softer, more absorbent diaper, as a hybrid combination of store label and national brand. In the Rochester, New York, test market where Wegmans Food Markets sold the line, for example, the package carried the name "Wegmans UltraSofts." With this strategy, Weyerhaeuser could advertise the diapers over a large territory, like a national brand, but could use packaging and promotions tailored for each retailer. Weyerhaeuser also planned to sell UltraSofts for about 10 percent less than Procter & Gamble's Pampers and Kimberly-Clark's Huggies, which together command 85 percent of the disposable diaper market.

Weyerhaeuser hired marketing researchers to conduct a consumer test and the results showed that parents preferred the new UltraSofts two to one over the leading brands. With these encouraging results, Wegmans introduced UltraSofts with a huge promotion and advertising campaign, mailing 50,000 coupons to shoppers in the Rochester area. The effort was "unprecedented," said Mary Ellen Burris, Wegmans' consumer affairs director. With the $1-off coupon, a bag of 32 large diapers sold for $8.39, or about $1.60 less than Pampers and Huggies.

Unfortunately, when Weyerhaeuser began to manufacture the new diapers in volume, it discovered production line snags. "We've got about twenty problems," reported Bobby Abraham, president of Weyerhaeuser's personal care products division. "Many are simple. Some need significant work." Because of the manufacturing problems, the factory could produce only enough product to supply Wegmans, and because it miscalculated the costs, Weyerhaeuser had to increase UltraSofts' price to retailers 22 percent, wiping out its price advantage. Wegmans did maintain the $9.39 retail price, but the retailer could not maintain the advertising and promotional support, and its profit margins declined. In addition to Weyerhaeuser's manufacturing headaches, it could never persuade other retailers in the Rochester area to stock UltraSofts because the price increase had made the brand less attractive.

Meanwhile, P&G and Kimberly-Clark spent heavily on the national rollout of their pink and blue diapers for girls and boys. Part of these efforts were thousands of $1- and $2-off coupons the companies sent to consumers.

This promotional effort made UltraSofts considerably less attractive to consumers. While neither Wegmans nor Weyerhaeuser will discuss exact numbers, Weyerhaeuser did say that ten months after introduction, UltraSofts' market share was down considerably from its peak. "It's been a disappointment," said Abraham.

Real-World Tests Have Methodological Problems

If the test market's first function is to gain information and experience with the marketing program before making a total commitment, the second is to predict the outcome when the company applies the marketing program to the total market. Although a real world test may provide a realistic measure of the marketing program's impact, as we will see, it also has methodological problems that make market prediction difficult—and sometimes impossible.

A traditional test market has at least four steps:

1. The company selects the test cities.
2. It establishes the length of the test effort.
3. It implements and controls the marketing program in each city.
4. It undertakes research to evaluate the program and to forecast how the new brand would perform nationally.

Aaker and Day point out that the company must choose cities that meet several relevant characteristics. Ideally, a test market city should represent the country as a whole in terms of characteristics that will affect the test outcome; these include product usage, consumer attitudes, and demographics. If the researchers know the idiosyncrasies of a market, of course, they can adjust the results to compensate. For example, Southerners eat more biscuits than Americans on average; teenagers drink more soda; older people buy more pharmaceutical products.

The company must have access to data. Store audit information to evaluate a test is helpful because it provides sales data adjusted for inventory changes and gives other useful information, such as shelf facings and in-store promotions. If the company must have store audit data, it must use cities that have retailers who will cooperate with store audits.

The test market communities should be isolated from contaminating media that "spills in" from nearby cities. For example, half the advertising reaching the Springfield-Holyoke, Massachusetts area originates elsewhere. On the other hand, too much media spilling out of the test market into surrounding areas is wasteful and increases the test's cost.

It may be desirable to use test market cities that do not have much "product spillage" outside the area so that it is possible to measure sales within the market. Columbus, Ohio, for example, has considerable spillage; Phoenix-Tucson has little.

After choosing the test market cities, the second major consideration is time. If possible, a test market normally should operate for one to two years. Even if after that year or two the company takes the program national, it should continue to monitor the test market to detect the impact of changes in the environment.

A market test requires an extended time for several reasons. Researchers can observe important seasonal factors only if the test continues for a full year. In addition, initial consumer interest often cannot predict a program's staying power. Finally, it is useful to allow the competition and other market factors to react to see what likely impact they will have on the new brand's performance.

The third major consideration is how the company carries out and controls the marketing program in each test city. Obviously the company wants the test cities to reflect the national program, but as we have already noted, this is never easy. The company may not have defined the national program precisely enough, or it may not be easy to apply the marketing program in selected test markets. For example, the company may not be able to translate the national advertising budget to a local level, or the test market may not be well defined in terms of scheduling television commercials. The company's sales people and retailers may give the test product special consideration—care that the product would not have in the national market. Competitors may sabotage the test, usually deliberately, but sometimes by accident. Take Procter & Gamble and its soft Duncan Hines brand cookies as an example.

Frito-Lay, with Grandma's Rich'n Chewy brand, was the first soft cookie to reach the test market stage, although P&G had been working on soft cookie technology for years. In the Frito-Lay test, Grandma's quickly captured one-fifth of the Kansas City, Missouri, cookie market, far exceeding Frito-Lay's most optimistic projections.[3] What happened?

A Frito-Lay competitor (not, ironically, P&G), concerned about Grandma's threat, had sent a research company to Kansas City to learn why people buy the product. Because consumers had to eat the cookies to talk about them knowledgeably, the researchers bought cookies to consume during the interviews. In fact, they bought so many cookies they pushed Grandma's market share higher than it would have been without the research. By chance, P&G followed Frito-Lay into Kansas City with its Duncan Hines soft cookie brand, where it achieved the same highly skewed results for many of the same reasons. Indeed, the results were so positive, P&G decided to take the product national.

Unfortunately, by the time Procter & Gamble began the national rollout, the public had lost interest in packaged soft cookies (they were overprocessed and tasted it). P&G ultimately had to write off soft cookie factories in Tennessee and Florida.

The fourth major consideration is how to monitor the test results. One traditional measure is sales based on manufacturer shipments or warehouse withdrawals. However, inventory fluctuations can badly distort the sales pattern. Moreover, manufacturer shipments and warehouse withdrawals are not a very sensitive measure of consumer response anyway. They reflect trade response to the manufacturer's marketing efforts, particularly promotion.

The company today may be able to obtain store audit data of actual sales figures, which are not sensitive to inventory fluctuations. Store audits also provide information about such variables as distribution, shelf facings, and in-store promotional activity, all factors that affect the product's sales.

Unfortunately, however, manufacturer shipments, warehouse withdrawals, and even consumer sales data tell us very little about the impact of the marketing program in building and maintaining a successful new product or service. What's required is intelligence based on a cross-section of prospective and actual buyers.

The company has to obtain measures such as consumer brand awareness, attitudes, trial, and repeat purchase from either consumer panels or surveys. Brand awareness and consumer attitudes also serve as criteria for evaluating the marketing program and can help in interpreting sales data. As Aker and Day assert, "The most useful information obtained from consumers, however, is whether they bought the product at least once and whether they were satisfied with it and have either repurchased it or plan to."[4] The Louis Rich division of Oscar Mayer (now owned by Philip Morris Companies, Inc.) used this information when it tested a line extension to its successful Breast of Turkey product, an item called Dark Roast of Turkey.[5]

Because some people in the home office "were afraid we were going to shoot ourselves in the foot anyway," said Steve Lindbloom, a Louis Rich product manager, "we didn't want to go into Minneapolis or some other major market where we stood to lose some credibility with our trade if we bombed." Instead, the company tested Dark Roast of Turkey in Eau Claire, Wisconsin, and Midland-Odessa, Texas, both markets in which Breast of Turkey sold well. "We only had one media campaign, but we split cells to see what would happen if we didn't advertise at all in one of the test groups."

Virtually nothing happened in the cell without advertising. The other cell did generate a good trial rate, but repeat sales were unacceptable. "Initial trial was 18 percent," Lindbloom recalled, "but repeat was 4 percent—and we decided that we couldn't live with that." Louis Rich also discovered that the period between initial trial and the first repeat purchase was much longer than it had expected. "That gave us some projections of the size of the idea—and it was much smaller than our assumptions had led us to believe."

Earlier in his career, Kevin Clancy, one of this book's authors, worked on a "convertible cigarette," a seemingly ordinary filter cigarette with a breakthrough, magical property. The filter contained micro-encapsulated menthol that the smoker could activate by squeezing the filter. Early returns from test markets indicated the company was enjoying tremendous success; smokers appeared to love the idea because sales during the first eight weeks rose faster than the morning sun.

Unfortunately, sales fell almost as quickly. Once they tried the product, smokers came to hate it. Sometimes a light squeeze gave a blast of menthol that was like a fist in the throat; other times it took a karate chop to release any menthol taste at all. The product enjoyed virtually no repeat sales, a fact that a tracking study clearly revealed. Without such a tracking study, the manufacturer might have mistakenly believed that it had a clear winner and geared up accordingly.

Health and beauty aids manufacturers have always found it difficult to conduct traditional test market research, said Gail A. Lanznar, director of marketing research at Helene Curtis, Inc.[6] Because drug and mass merchandise accounts represent half to two-thirds of the business in many health and beauty aids categories, the manufacturers need these retailers for their test market research. Yet many drug and mass merchandise accounts do not have scanners at the cash registers, so the manufacturer has to audit the sales. Many of these retailers are large chains, and their management's are often unwilling to permit a manufacturer to use a certain store in a certain market for an audit. Health and beauty aids marketers also compete in some categories where purchase cycles are very long. A long purchase cycle makes a test market difficult to conduct in some cases and difficult to read in others.

Test Marketing Trends

In recent years, General Foods and other packaged goods companies have been shifting much of their in-market testing activity to the newly available, small electronic markets. These are markets in which the retail stores have UPC scanner checkouts and individually targetable cable television so that the company can control what consumers see and record what products they buy.

Jane Brown, a consultant in new product development and test marketing to Kraft General Foods, noted that, on the surface, testing of both new and established products in 1990—the date of her research—looked somewhat different than it did in 1976[7]. In 1976, General Foods conducted forty-two traditional in-market tests; forty-four tests in 1986; and forty in 1990. So the number of tests had not changed dramatically. In 1976, the traditional test market took one to three years; by 1990, the company's tests—both in-market and mini-market—took four months to two years.

In 1976 General Foods selected its test markets scrupulously to replicate the average environment for a category/brand, evaluated a fully developed business proposition, and used the results for brand go/no-go decisions, considering them fully projectable. In 1976, the company would consider a mini-market only as a precursor to a full test market, since "we 'knew' it was not projectable," said Brown. She said that some of the environments in which General Foods tests today are smaller than those they considered "mini" in 1976. "The selection process is less rigid in terms of representativeness and more likely to be a function of availability and acceptability; i.e., category/brand development not less than 80[8] and enough of the characteristics to do the key analyses. We continue to evaluate a fully developed marketing plan and, despite issues of predictive accuracy, we have been making broad-scale decisions from these experiences."

Companies have not changed the type of data they collect and the key measures they use to evaluate it. What *has* changed since 1976 are the methods for capturing the data and disseminating messages. UPC scanners at the checkout, consumer data cards and individual hand-held scanners (to link individual consumers to specific product sales), and individually targetable cable television has improved test market execution and design capability. These have also led to increased experimentation with marketing variables for both new and established products.

The basics of an in-market test from a "need to know" basis have not changed. "We are still monitoring trial and repeat sales, reaction to consumer and trade promotions, looking for a fit against sourcing assumptions, market growth, etc.," said Brown. But the go/no-go decision has become far more difficult as companies learn more and more about market dynamics. To understand them adequately, the company must understand historical trends, market nuances, variable responsiveness, and more.

The Trouble with Traditional Test Markets

Test markets are fraught with problems. Often the company selects a test market because it's easy to manage, or because a retailer in the market will cooperate with the test, and not because the market represents the target the company in fact wants to reach.

Traditional test market research has four major defects:

1. *Traditional test markets are expensive.* They can cost as little as $1 million, but typically run more. "Add up the research, the media, the effort throughout the organization to control it,

check the test market, and the costs are hard to swallow," said Gail Lanznar from Helene Curtis

2. *Traditional test markets take too long.* Waiting a year, eighteen months, or two years for results is simply not competitive in an environment where the pace of change has picked up as much as it has in many product categories.
3. *Traditional test markets give away ideas.* Marketers routinely gripe, "They're not secure, and as a result we're giving our competitors free marketing intelligence."
4. *Competitors can sabotage the results.* Even modest efforts by competitors can spoil the company's ability to read the test market results. Competitors have sabotaged tests by having their sales people pull the new products off retail shelves, turn them sideways, or move them to other shelves where shoppers will not notice them. (Fortunately, what competitors do in a test market to affect a brand's performance is not what they're likely to do in the national market, which is too big and unmanageable.)

As a more extreme example—but by no means unique—take the experience we had with what we've called elsewhere "The Case of the Annihilated Brand."[9] This food product's advertising and promotion budget, projected nationally, was $70 million. The company assumed that the competition, faced with the prospect of battling a new brand, might increase its advertising and promotional spending by as much as 80 percent over the base period. Using this assumption, a model was employed that forecast the new brand would obtain a 3.6 percent market share by the end of Year One.

The company introduced the brand in test markets—where the brand failed miserably. By the end of Year One, the brand's market share was 0.7 percent—a clear disaster. Was the research and the modeling flawed? Didn't the company support the brand adequately with advertising and promotion?

An autopsy revealed that the company's advertising and promotional spending were in line with what it had said it would spend. The competition's spending, however, had not increased 80 percent in the test markets. It had increased *630 percent*. Projected nationally, this amounted to $1 billion. In effect, the competitive program "gave away" the existing product to regular buyers at a heavily discounted price. Consumers wisely responded by stocking up, which took them out of the market for months. The move overwhelmed and annihilated the new brand.

Of course the competitor who increased its spending 630 percent could not have sustained the expense for very long and not on a national scale. At that rate, the competition was losing money—certainly in the test markets. But this was not a national introduction, and the management obviously felt it was worthwhile to lose money in the test markets to prevent the new brand from establishing itself. As Frank Brod of Coca-Cola Foods said in Chapter 1, "Minute Maid slaughtered Citrus Hill on the beaches. They kept the product off the shelves by loading the pipeline with Minute Maid."

5. *Traditional test markets usually fail to tell marketers what they need to know to achieve success.* While a product failing in a test market isn't as painful as failing in the national rollout, it's often difficult to determine why. Was the problem with the way the company executed the idea or was the idea simply too small? Was the problem with the marketing program or with the competitive response? Typically, marketing managers test too few plans before introducing a new (or re-positioned) product into the real world. Most do not even realize how many plans they could test. Consider "The Case of the Escalating Sevens."

Assume we are managing the introduction of a new soft drink, Zippy Cola, a product formulated with high levels of caffeine, sugar, and carbonation. Assume further that we have to make a dozen key marketing decisions and that we have only seven choices for each—seven target groups, seven positionings, seven advertising executions, seven price levels, and so on. The first decision we have to make is the market target. Here are our seven choices:

1. Women 18-to-49-years-old, the all-time most popular target for soft drinks.
2. Health freaks, the granola and oat-bran crowd.
3. YUMMIES, a hot new target. Young, Urban, *Moneyed*, and Single. These are the yuppies with high school teachers excluded and $100-an-hour plumbers included.

4. Friends of Ponce de Leon, the people looking for the fountain of youth, virtually all of whom belong to a health club.
5. Kids 6-to-12-years-old.
6. Folks who need a sugar and caffeine fix regularly.
7. Aging athletes, the people who relive their days as a high school football player or tennis star. This group is heavily represented by middle-aged men.

If there are a dozen ingredients in the marketing mix and exactly seven options for each, how many different plans might a marketing manager develop?

Not twelve times seven, but seven to the twelfth power: thirteen billion, eight hundred forty-one million.

Given such a staggering number of possibilities, how do modern marketing managers handle the problem? Most companies do a little research—six to eight focus groups, some concept, product, and copy testing. And then management uses its experience and best judgment to pick the best options from the different possibilities and puts together the best plan it can. This is the plan it takes into the traditional test market. But what are the odds of picking the best plan out of fourteen billion when the company does so little research? Not even one in a billion.

Our example is based on the assumption of a dozen marketing mix ingredients and exactly seven options for each. In the real world there may be many more than this or fewer, but our point is the same. Managers seem to select the marketing plans they take into test markets impulsively, and as a result marketplace failure abounds. Worse, little information flows back to the manager on how the marketing program could be improved. If a company actually tested three or thirty or three hundred of the plans it might develop, managers would have a wonderful basis to discover the factors that led to success or failure. Yet, traditional test marketing is simply too complicated and too expensive to permit such an analysis.

Managers are not the only people unhappy with traditional test marketing. Retailers are not happy either. Ronald Frost of the Fleming Companies, the country's largest food wholesaler, has been quoted as saying, "We are in effect paying the cost of market research. They are putting it out there and seeing what happens. We don't feel that's an appropriate approach to market research."

As a way to deal with the situation, some wholesalers and retailers are introducing a "failure fee" in addition to the slotting allowances, the fees manufacturers pay to retailers to gain shelf space for new items. The manufacturers pay the failure fee if a new item does not sell as well as agreed upon. It is, in a sense, "a guarantee of sorts to reduce the retailer's financial risk" while increasing the manufacturer's.[10]

A Brief for Simulated Test Marketing

What can marketers do to improve the likelihood of new product success in an age of promotion and unprecedented competitive response levels? How can companies anticipate defensive competitive response and develop and test offensive strategies designed to overwhelm those defenses? And how can companies do this without costly, time-consuming real-world test marketing?

A well-done simulated test market reduces risks that include not only lost marketing and sales dollars but also capital—the expense of installing production lines or building a new factory to manufacture the product. Why would a company spend $2 million or $3 million and wait a year and half to learn of a failure about which it can do little when it can spend $100,000 or $150,000 and take three to six months to learn how to fix any problems?

A simulated test market study increases efficiency. If a company has, say, three new-product development projects underway, and one seems to offer more volume and greater margins, sagacious management would promote that project rather than the others. The STM can indicate the project offering the greatest return. An STM can also optimize the company's marketing efficiency in a new product it does go ahead with—to see the effect, say, of shifting a budgeted $1 million from television advertising to a coupon or vice versa. (We discuss optimization in detail in Chapter 11.)

A simulated test market study maintains security. As soon as a company puts a product into a real-world test, everyone who cares knows about it, starting with the competition's sales people. Several years ago, Procter & Gamble began testing a ready-to-spread Duncan Hines frosting. General Mills saw the test and rushed its own Betty Crocker brand introduction, which now dominates the category.

A simulated test market can save the company time. The STM can give you results in three to six months where you may have to wait more than a year for the same results from an in-market test.

Time, as an element of competitive advantage, is only beginning to gain currency. But as a strategic weapon, time is the equivalent of money, productivity, quality, even innovation. George Stalk, Jr., a vice president of the Boston Consulting Group, wrote in *Competing Against Time*, "The ways leading companies manage time—in production, in new product development and introduction, in sales and distribution—represent the most powerful new sources of competitive advantage. While time is a basic performance variable, management seldom monitors its consumption explicitly—almost never with the same precision accorded sales and costs. Yet time is a more critical competitive yardstick than traditional financial measurements."[11]

A company that builds its strategy on flexible manufacturing and rapid-response systems is a more powerful competitor than one with a traditional strategy based on low wages or manufacturing cost efficiencies. "These older, cost-based strategies require managers to do whatever is necessary to drive down costs," Stalk wrote, "move production to or source from a low-wage country; build new facilities or consolidate old plants to gain economies of scale." These all do reduce costs, but at the expense of responsiveness— and in the 1990s, customers will be more interested in response than in price.

Time-based marketing allows companies to serve key customer needs quickly, which in turn creates more value. In this era, the total time required to produce a product or service—not cost—defines a firm's competitive advantage. "Early adopters report that actions modeled on just-in-time—simplified flows, waste reduction, reduced setup times and batch sizes—can also dramatically reduce time in product development, engineering, and customer service," says Dr. Joseph Blackburn, a professor at the business school of Vanderbilt University and a long-time friend and consultant to the authors. "Firms able to achieve faster response times have reported growth rates over three times the industry average and double the profitability. Thus the payoff is market dominance."

Today's better simulated test markets capture every important component in the marketing mix and assess the effect of any plan on product awareness, trial, repeat rates, market share, profitability, and more. These STMs test any plan the marketer wants to consider—even a competitor's. The marketer simply enters the plan into the computer and the model forecasts what is likely to occur month by month in the real world.

Some simulated test marketing methodologies are even smart enough to help recommend a plan and we have never seen a plan a sophisticated STM recommends that does not beat the one submitted by the product manager. Sometimes the margin is modest; sometimes the difference is overwhelming.

Simulated test marketing is the single best validated tool in all of marketing research. For a new packaged goods, the better STMs can forecast what will happen in the real world, plus or minus 15 percent.

This is not to say, however, there are no cases when an STM result goes awry. Perhaps the biggest failures come about because the assumptions on which the model made its forecast were flawed. If a company estimates a distribution level of 90 percent and obtains only 60 percent, the volume forecast can be off substantially because, in some product categories, distribution corresponds almost a one-to-one with volume.

But not only may the assumptions be mistaken, the market's dynamics may change between the STM and the actual test market. The company may have a new competitor, one it did not know existed when it began the simulated test market research.

Sometimes the company's commitment changes between the STM and the real-world market test—and we believe a company *should* do a real-world test, but only after a STM. Or, to put it another way, in most simulated test markets, companies assume adequate marketing support, support that may disappear by the time the firm begins the product's national introduction. For a simulated test market study it's easy to say that you're going to spend $24 million on advertising because no one has to write a check. It's something else to spend real money.

Discrepancies also arise between the simulated test market performance and the actual test market because the real world is messier than a STM. But discrepancies also arise between the test market and the national performance. Companies routinely obtain test market distribution levels that are much higher than they ever see again because the sales force is excited by the new product and the sales people work harder than usual. This sensitivity to the product's success brings results the company never repeats.

But suppose the real-world test results are significantly worse than the simulated test market research results. We ask the client, "What's happening in the test market? What are the shelf facings ... the distribution? What is the trade activity ... consumer promotion ... your share of voice? What is the competition doing?" With these new inputs, the STM can virtually always match what's going on in the market.

At that point we can ask different questions: "Given what's happening, is there anything we can do, anything we can learn from the simulation that would produce a better plan? Given that the competition has increased its promotional spending in our test markets by 630 percent, can we add markets until it becomes just too expensive for them to continue?"

Today the goal of simulated test marketing research is not to obtain a simple volume forecast. The objective is to provide diagnostic insights that will help improve the likelihood of product success. Telling marketers they will obtain a 5 percent share or a 10 percent share doesn't satisfy them. They want insight from the study that will help them build plans with an even lower risk of failure.

A good STM will tell you not only how you're doing but what to do differently. A sophisticated decision support system combines simulated test marketing with mathematical modeling of the marketing mix. Such a system goes beyond forecasting first-year volume potential to providing insights into improving the advertising, the concept, the product and packaging, and the marketing plan itself.

Marketers can ask a state-of-the-science STM model to evaluate every ingredient in the marketing plan in terms of effects on sales or profits or both. The model will run hundreds—in some cases thousands—of simulations to identify those factors that contribute most to marketing success.

But what is the source of simulated test market research? How did this methodology get its start and what is its status today?

3

A Short History of Simulated Test Marketing Research

Given the problems of cost, time, and security connected with traditional in-market tests and the development of the computer, which allowed people to manipulate vast amounts of data inexpensively, researchers began looking into simulated test marketing more than twenty years ago. Many of the marketing research ideas (such as research design and measurement issues) that were later incorporated into simulated test markets were initially developed in the mid- to late-1960s.

At the beginning, these efforts followed two separate paths that eventually converged. We call the first the "mathematical modeling" path, the second the "laboratory experiment" path. The first started with the idea that researchers could take historical data—advertising and promotional spending, distribution, market share, and much more—and build a series of equations that would forecast new product sales.

The second started with the idea that if the researchers could "simulate" experimentally in a laboratory setting the process by which consumers learn about and buy a new product, it would be possible to project the real-world results from such an experiment.

By the 1970s, simulated test marketing research models had become a major force in the marketplace. The 1980s saw a number of major refinements in the STM procedures themselves and saw literally thousands of applications. During this decade, the major STMs underwent quite a bit of evolution and convergence—that is, they

31

are far more similar today than they were a generation ago—and now may resemble their original specifications only slightly.

The Origins of Mathematically Modeling New Products: DEMON

In 1966 Dr. David Learner, who was research director of BBDO Advertising, and James DeVoe, an associate research director at BBDO, and two Carnegie-Mellon professors, Abraham Charnes and William Cooper, published a pioneering paper titled "DEMON: Decision Mapping via Optimal GO-NO Networks—A Model for Marketing New Products."[1] They described a very sophisticated mathematical model of the new product marketing process that BBDO was testing with several clients at the time.

For the first time the DEMON model examined very complex relationships including those between advertising spending and consumer awareness and between promotion and new product trial. With DEMON, a researcher could forecast brand awareness, trial, repeat purchase, and sales using techniques that were the state of the science in the new and emerging discipline of management science.

The problem with the DEMON model was that it could estimate none of the other necessary market parameters such as trial and repeat purchases *prior* to an actual test market. Typically in a DEMON consulting engagement, a marketer would introduce into markets a new product; collect data on awareness, trial, repeat, usage rate, and other factors at a three or more points in time; and then use this data to estimate the parameters of the model. DEMON would then tell the company how the product would do at the end of the year.

This meant a marketer could use a mathematical model to make national projections from the test market experience and could, theoretically, use DEMON to improve the marketing plan before going national—a revolutionary concept at the time.

After three years of experimentation, which was accompanied by growing excitement in the industry concerning this new technology, the model fell into disuse. It was simply too complicated and too sophisticated. There were too many input parameters, the computing technology at the time was slow, and management found it difficult to understand what DEMON could do for them.

DEMON's future was not helped when David Learner, its developer and champion, left BBDO to become president of a high-technology firm in Pittsburgh.

Edward I. Brody, a senior vice president at BBDO New York, points out that advertising agencies such as Leo Burnett, DDB Needham, and NW Ayer, as well as BBDO, were also pioneering the development of new product forecasting models during the 1960s.[2] Two young management scientists at BBDO, Drs. Larry Light and Lewis Pringle, picked up Learner's work and took the best of DEMON to create a newer, simpler, stochastic model of the new product introduction process, a model called NEWS, an acronym for New Product Early Warning System.[3] NEWS, however, like its predecessor was also limited by its inability to make valid predictions before an actual new product test market experience.

BBDO developed NEWS as an independent model designed to provide an accurate and easily understood input to a marketing manager's new product decisions. Companies initially used NEWS only with early test market data (typically obtained from the first two or three months of an in-market test) to provide a forecast and certain diagnostic information for the remainder of the test market period. This became NEWS/Market, and the agency used it exclusively until years later when BBDO's Pringle and Brody had accumulated sufficient validation to develop another version of the model called NEWS/Planner. The only difference between the two versions is that the input for NEWS/Planner came out of consumer research the company conducted before introducing the product into test market.

A Competing Vision: The Laboratory Test Market

Learner and his associates were barely aware at the time of what Yankelovich Skelly & White were doing to create the Laboratory Test Market that YSW introduced in 1968—an example of independent, almost simultaneous inventions. The Laboratory Test Market measured consumer trial in a laboratory environment by making prospects aware of the new product through advertising.

Yankelovich Skelly & White exposed a group of about 500 consumers to advertising for a new product and its competitors. They then brought these people into a store and gave them an opportunity to buy anything they wanted, but clearly the store's focal point was the new product. People who bought the product took it home and used it. Later (the time varying by product and purchase cycle), YSW researchers phoned the consumers who had bought the product, asked their reactions, and asked if they'd like to re-order. Their responses gave YSW the probability that a consumer would re-purchase the product if he or she found it in a store.

Based on the answers to these and other questions, Yankelovich Skelly & White had an estimate of trial (or, more technically, an estimate of awareness-to-trial conversion given distribution), an estimate of trial-to-repeat conversion, and the usage rate. If consumers were to purchase the new product just as frequently as other products in the category, YSW would assign a usage rate index of 1. On the other hand, if heavy users were going to buy this product or if consumers were going to buy it more frequently than other brands in the category, its usage index would be greater than 1—1.1, 1.2, 1.3, or more.

The Yankelovich Skelly & White researchers would then apply a factor they called "clout." YSW used this variable to account for the effects of advertising spending, sampling, couponing, and the manufacturer's overall power. A small, obscure, weak manufacturer had less clout than a large, well-known, powerful corporation. A YSW committee based its clout figure on historical experience, and these estimates—and they were simply estimates—ranged from 0 to 100.

To develop a final forecast, Yankelovich Skelly & White would take the consumer trial figure, multiply it by the client's estimated distribution at the end of the year, multiply that by the estimated clout, multiply that by repeat purchase, multiply that by the index of usage rate, and the final result was an estimate of what YSW called "on-going market share" in units.

As an example: say that 40 percent of the prospects bought the new product in the laboratory store. Yankelovich Skelly & White, recognizing that people's behavior in the laboratory was generally overstated, developed norms by which they reduced the 40 percent to a number the firm felt more closely reflected what people would do in the world. Assume that in this case the researchers multiplied the 40 percent by .75, so the trial figure becomes 30 percent.

The 30 percent was affected by product distribution, so assume the manufacturer estimated that it would have 67 percent distribution at the end of the year. Multiply the 30 percent by .67 to obtain

20 percent. YSW now multiplied the 20 percent by the clout factor. If we assume a clout of 0.5, the trial figure becomes 10 percent.

YSW further reduced the trial rate by repeat purchase, and let's assume that half the people who originally bought the product will buy it again.

Multiplying the 10 percent by 0.5 reduces the repeat figure to 5 percent. Finally, assume that the people who were buying this product were either light users—80 percent of average—or were going to be using this product to fill 80 percent of the normal requirements. In either event, YSW multiplied the 5 percent by 0.8, which yields a 4 percent year-end share of market.

The system, though primitive by today's standards, worked remarkably well. Over its first ten years, the Laboratory Test Market proved to be accurate plus or minus 10 to 15 percent about 90 percent of the time in forecasting a new product's first year sales.

The Pillsbury School of Simulated Test Marketing

The work that ultimately led to today's ESP and BASES simulated test marketing systems began at the Pillsbury Company in the early 1960s. Gerald J. Eskin, who became one of the founders of IRI but was then at Pillsbury, has said that his marketing research mentor, Dudley Ruch (in our view, one of the most brilliant, innovative, and supportive people in the marketing research profession), asked him to work on the following problem: Suppose the company has three to six months of data from a test market. Suppose the data included some diagnostic information on purchasing patterns— who's buying the new product and how many times they buy it. From this information, said Ruch, forecast the product's first year sales and the likelihood that the product will grow or decline thereafter.[4]

Eskin says that he started with trial/repeat modeling. He went back to work that Joseph Woodlock had done at MRCA in the 1950s with Louis Fourt. "I took the Fourt Woodlock Model and expanded it," says Eskin. "I studied each repeat level separately. First repeat. Second repeat. Third repeat, etc. I also looked at repeat in a new way, one that took account of the amount of time that a person had to make a repeat purchase. These, we called 'true repeat curves.'"

These curves described both the probability that an individual would repurchase a product and the distribution of time until the next purchase. The Pillsbury researchers called the finished model "PanPro" for Panel Projection.[5]

In one sense, as Eskin freely acknowledges, PanPro was a kind of sales accounting model. It described how people go through the process of first buying a new product, waiting a time, deciding to buy the product again, then perhaps waiting a time again, and if they decide to repurchase, making a third purchase, and so forth. PanPro was not a model that would forecast the outcome of a test market. It was *not* a pretest market simulator.

When Gerald Eskin finished the PanPro project at Pillsbury, John Malec visited Pillsbury and asked Eskin if he would be interested in developing a model that would work *prior* to the test market—a simulator.[6] At the time Malec was working at the NPD Group, Port Washington, New York. Eskin reports that he did develop such a model, but not by building it from scratch. Rather, he collected concept test data and product test data for a wide range of products and tied these measures into the PanPro model, which produced the ESP (for *Estimating Sales Potential*) model. The NPD Group has been marketing the ESPN model since 1975. The company introduced versions of the model designed specifically for line extensions and for product re-stagings in 1980 and 1983, respectively, and the model is known now as Simulator ESP.

Eskin says that shortly after ESP was developed, Lynn Y. S. Lin, who was also working at Pillsbury, inspired by the same Dudley Ruch, developed an interest in simulated test marketing research. "Lynn was exposed to my early work at Pillsbury and had knowledge of the PanPro model and the NPD work for that matter," Eskin reports.[7] After leaving Pillsbury to go to Burke Marketing Research, in Covington, Kentucky, Lynn developed a simulator model along lines similar to the ESP model. This became the BASES model, which Burke introduced in 1978, a model that went on to become the most widely used laboratory simulation model in the world.

It's interesting to note that BASES became successful despite its modeling simplicity and attitudinal rather than behavioral foundations. In the Yankelovich Laboratory Test Market, as we've said, consumers were exposed to advertising for the new and for competitive products in a laboratory environment; they were brought into a store where they used their own money to buy the product; and after they tried it at home, they were asked if they wanted to re-order it. The BASES approach simply called for presenting the new product in concept form to consumers and asking them how likely they would be to buy. Their answers were on a five-point purchase probability scale—from "definitely would buy" to "definitely would not buy." BASES then multiplied each point on the scale by a conversion weight (for example, the "definitely would buys" scores might have been hit by a weight score of 90 percent and the "probably would buys" by, say, 75 percent.

Following a period of in-home use, BASES gave consumers the same rating scale and asked them how likely they would be to buy the product again. BASES then applied a second set of weights. BASES then multiplied a string of figures to estimate the volume sales at the end of the first year following launch: the client-provided year-end awareness figure, times the projected trial number, times distribution, times Nielsen ACV distribution estimates, times the forecast repeat purchase figure, times the purchase rate. For more than fifteen years this simple, but very successful, model has demonstrated a satisfactory level of validity and has gone on to become the market leader in terms of number of new products tested and sales.

The Academically Grounded STM Systems

Management of Decision Systems, Inc. (MDS) introduced the ASSESSOR model in 1973 after initial development work by Professors Alvin J. Silk and Glen L. Urban of the Sloan School at MIT. Unlike all previous laboratory methods, ASSESSOR received an academic imprimatur when two seminal papers based on the model were published in the *Journal of Marketing Research* and presented at numerous conferences.

The ASSESSOR model conceptualized awareness and based the awareness figure on estimates developed between the client and the client's ad agency. The ASSESSOR researchers measured trial in the laboratory setting, much like Yankelovich, but instead of measuring trial by buying behavior—the Yankelovich approach—ASSESSOR researchers gave prospects vouchers they could use to buy any product they wanted in a model store; the coupon-induced trial behavior coupled with a sophisticated constant-sum-based preference model were the ASSESSOR analogs to Yankelovich laboratory buying behavior and the BASES five-point purchase probability scale.

Like its predecessor, the Laboratory Test Market, the ASSESSOR model called for contacting "buyers" of the test product a few weeks after the purchase to gather information about attitudes toward the new product and re-purchase intentions and plans. The ASSESSOR model used a constant sum model to estimate what proportion of on-going sales a brand could obtain. They told prospects, "If you could divide eleven chips among the leading brands in the category, how many chips would you give to the different brands?" In other words, they employed two different approaches for estimating trial and repeat, one was behavioral, the other was attitudinal.

As a consequence, ASSESSOR had an awareness-to-trial conversion estimate, just as Yankelovich had its clout-to-trial conversion estimate. ASSESSOR multiplied that figure by on-going distribution, multiplied that by an estimate of repeat purchase and by a usage rate, and that gave them an on-going share estimate.

Any comparison of the leading laboratory STMs circa the late 1970s cannot help but give high marks to the Yankelovich Laboratory Test Market, in contrast to most other models because (a) it was based on actual spending behavior as opposed to coupon redemption methodologies or attitudinal responses (or both), and (b) Yankelovich Skelly & White consultants had more years of experience in estimating clout than ASSESSOR or BASES researchers had in working with the awareness numbers provided by clients and their ad agencies.

In fact, clients and their ad agencies almost always inflated the awareness numbers by a considerable margin. Given that a linear relationship exists in all these models between where they start and where they end, to the extent that someone exaggerates an awareness estimate, every other figure will also be exaggerated—most significantly the year-end share estimate. Marketers praise the modeling intricacies of ASSESSOR, however, and the simplicity and relatively low cost of a BASES study, thus explaining in part the strong success of these methods.

In 1979, Malec and Eskin started Information Resources Inc. (IRI), which acquired MDS in the mid-1980s. "As you might expect," says Eskin, "we couldn't resist the temptation to try to improve on our earlier work. But as you might also expect, the ASSESSOR model also has some of the flavor of those earlier PanPro-based models." Assessor's preference structure models were merged with IRI's FASTRAC in-store scanning system database; and the model became known as ASSESSOR-FT in 1985.

The M/A/R/C Group of Irving, Texas, bought the rights to the ASSESSOR model in July 1989. Before that M/A/R/C had ENTRO, its own simulated test marketing system, with which it had been successful. M/A/R/C established a new subsidiary company, MACRO Strategies Inc., to provide marketing consulting and modeling services, including simulated test market research studies. MACRO Strategies merged the ASSESSOR and ENTRO models, which it currently offers as MACRO ASSESSOR. We, however, will call the model simply ASSESSOR.

The Development of DESIGNOR

In the early 1970s, Jacques Blanchard was sent to MIT's Sloan School of Management by a major European management consulting firm. The firm wanted him to develop a market modeling business in Europe, and he worked as an MBA student of Glen Urban's. Blanchard worked with Urban on the European implementation of SPRINTER (an early model similar to DEMON in design that made predictions on the basis of early in-market tests) and on PERCEPTOR, which was introduced in Europe in 1973.

PERCEPTOR is a tool to understand consumer preferences for different products as a function of their competitive positioning and buyer perceptions. It relates preferences to buying behavior. Blanchard says in fact that some of the findings of ASSESSOR came from earlier work done on PERCEPTOR. "There already was a trial and repeat mechanism in PERCEPTOR which was a new concept for ASSESSOR. We already had a lot of experience in the evaluation of concepts and how people react to perception before launch, and we also had a lot of work using market response modeling on in-market data for new products, both in the US and in Europe."

The ASSESSOR was developed, and Blanchard and his associates tested ASSESSOR's micro-structure in Europe before it was released there in 1975 (and in Japan shortly afterward). At the time they were using the PERCEPTOR technology to evaluate concept-use placement tests and make projections. Blanchard did some micro-structure validation of the trial and repeat model in ASSESSOR that they had used in developing PERCEPTOR. In 1979, his firm, Novaction, headquartered in Paris, introduced the PERCEPTOR/Concept test system based on ASSESSOR, and in 1983 introduced several new modules covering line extensions, relaunches, and price elasticity.

Novaction introduced DESIGNOR in 1986, in which the emphasis is heavily on diagnosis and optimization, rather than simply volume forecasting. DESIGNOR was a combination of PERCEPTOR, ASSESSOR, and several new modeling tools, including price optimization and an awareness forecasting subsystem, designed to make forecasts in a unique way not available through MDS in the United States.

Today's DESIGNOR forecasts trial using a combination of the voucher methodology and the sophisticated preference model that made ASSESSOR famous, integrated with repeat purchase, usage rate, and awareness forecasting approaches that are entirely its own. These tools coupled with a third forecasting methodology, an analog model, which forecasts new product performance based on the IDQV (impact, differentiation, quality, and value) of the new product compared to the IDQV of other products with similar market structures whose sales performance is known, provide DESIGNOR with a powerful arsenal of modeling tools and make it a formidable competitor in the STM industry.

At the Interstices of Mathematical Modeling and LTM: The Origin of LITMUS

In 1977 Florence Skelly, one of the Yankelovich Skelly & White principals and a pioneer in the field of marketing research, met Kevin Clancy, who she knew was interested in mathematical models. She also knew that he had worked on the NEWS model at BBDO Advertising. Concerned that ASSESSOR was having a negative impact on Laboratory Test Market sales, Skelly asked Clancy if he could combine the Laboratory Test Market method and data bases with a mathematical model of the new product process to improve the Laboratory Test Market system's capabilities. Clancy thought he could, and he and Professor Joseph Blackburn spent the next year working on a model they eventually called LITMUS. Robert Shulman, a vice president and sales manager for LTM at the time, became their in-house consultant and most enthusiastic supporter, constantly pressing them to improve the capabilities of the evolving model.

To test the LITMUS model, Skelly and Robert Goldberg, a Yankelovich Skelly & White new products guru who had been working on the Laboratory Test Market for more than ten years, gave Clancy and Blackburn twenty marketing plans for which YSW already knew the real-world results. They asked Clancy and Blackburn to run a forecast through the LITMUS model that they could compare to the actual national introduction.

At the meeting to discuss the results, each group had twenty envelopes. Clancy's envelopes contained the forecast of what the product would do based on the marketing plan input, laboratory response, and LITMUS's calculations; the Laboratory Test Market veterans' envelopes held the products' actual results. The veterans expected major differences between the forecasts and the actual results because they found it difficult to believe that a mathematical model could equal the intelligence and expertise of a group that had been making new product forecasts for years.

In fact, the LITMUS model's forecasts were virtually identical to the actual results in seventeen of the twenty cases. The results were so close that Clancy and Blackburn decided to write up the results for publication[8] and Yankelovich began to market the program in 1981.

One of the three cases in which LITMUS produced a result that was quite different the real world experience was for a new peanut chip (a peanut equivalent of the chocolate chip, an essential ingredient in chocolate chip cookies). LITMUS factored its trial estimates by expected Nielsen All Commodity Volume (ACV)[9] estimates and produced a sales forecast which was just about half what the manufacturer actually achieved in the real world.

In analyzing the differences between the model and the actual experience, it was found that the model didn't take into account the fact that many housewives, pushing their carts down supermarket aisles, would reach out to grab a package of chocolate chips to quiet a restless child. They would see the new peanut chip product beside chocolate chips on the shelf and take it for the novelty or— in some cases—by mistake. As a result, the usual effect of product distribution was considerably different (and greater) for this product than for most others. Real-world sales were terrific.

LITMUS had a number of properties that were unique at the time. Its submodel for forecasting awareness, as an illustration, contained thirteen different determinants of what awareness should be for a new product—including advertising impact and gross rating points by time period, media impact, and forgetting coefficients. This differentiated LITMUS from the original LTM, which didn't have a formal awareness function at all, and from the ASSESSOR model and other simulated test marketing models introduced later, which called for advertising agencies and clients to estimate awareness.

In addition to the awareness submodel, the evolving LITMUS enjoyed some other technological breakthroughs, among them that the model did not assume (as all models did at the time) a linear relationship between distribution and sales—an innovation inspired by the peanut chip case. Research had discovered that the more involved consumers are in the product category, the more likely they are to shop in several stores to find the product. One can imagine a situation where consumers are so involved that they will go from store to store to find a new entry until they do find it. Hence, in those categories, for those consumers, a 10 percent distribution level might act in the same way that an 80 or 90 percent distribution level might perform for a very low involvement product. LITMUS took this into account by estimating each consumer's involvement level and correcting distribution by that knowledge to estimate the real distribution effect.

Among the many differences between LITMUS and other models at the time, we should mention a third. For the first time in an STM model, LITMUS took into account the product's purchase cycle, differentiating between a product that a consumer might buy once or twice a year and one a consumer would buy weekly. Because LITMUS was able to provide weekly or monthly estimated sales and accumulate them over time, the model needed to know the amount of advertising and level of distribution in every month. Other models, ignoring these issues altogether, could not differentiate between time periods when a corporation might have very high advertising spending levels and no distribution or periods when the firm had high distribution and no advertising.

The methods and models discussed here are, of course, not the only simulated test marketing approaches available today. The published academic literature discusses two other simulated test market research programs: Elrick & Lavidge's Comp[10] and BBDO Worldwide's NEWS/Planner.[11] In addition to the STMs that the academic literature has examined, a variety of other simulated test market research services are available commercially: Leo Burnett Model by Leo Burnett (Chicago); and Adopter by Data Development Corp. (New York), Tele-Research's Micromarket, ASI Market Research's Purchase Action, Market Simulation Inc., and Robinson Associates' Speedmark.[12] The literature does not explain them in detail, however, and it is therefore impossible to know from the outside how these models work.

What has been observed over the passage of time is both the evolution and the convergence of all the different systems available. The systems have both been improved, in terms of their capabilities, and they have converged in the sense that they have become more similar to one another.

As an illustration, when Yankelovich Skelly & White launched LITMUS it was the first simulated test market methodology to model awareness. Although the LITMUS awareness subfunction is arguably the most sophisticated in the industry even today (and the only one that's been examined by academics), other simulated test marketing services are forecasting awareness as well. ASSESSOR, BASES, and DESIGNOR all have their own awareness forecasting approaches, which appear to work quite well.

Another area in which LITMUS played a revolutionary role was in optimization technology, not only the formal optimization routines, which we describe later in this book, but in terms of the general use of this new and emerging technology to evaluate many different marketing plans prior to an actual test market introduction to discover which plan, or combination of plans, appears to work best. Today all of the services appear to be taking a similar approach to this problem such that there is now a blurring of the distinctions between the commercially available technologies.

Who Uses Simulated Test Market Research?

Given this history of the development of STM models, how are corporations actually using them? The Advertising Research Foundation has conducted two surveys to gather industry-wide data on simulated test market research. A 1988 study established the STM market size and trends, how and when manufacturers use STM, how valid they perceive the results, and the benefits and limitations.[13] The 1990 study's objectives were to gather information and set directions.[14]

The 1988 study found that among the six research firms reporting (which represented 80 percent or more of all simulated test market research in America), there were an average of 680 tests in 1986/87, the latest figures available. The average test cost $45,000, and the total market for simulated test market research was approximately $30,500,000.

The survey found that the majority (64 percent) of simulated test market research in 1987 was for new products; line extensions accounted for a third of the tests, and the remaining 3 percent was for established brands. Further, the STMs were being conducted almost exclusively for packaged goods manufacturers. More than half (56 percent) were for food products, with health and beauty aids (21 percent) and household products (16 percent) making up most of the remainder. The "all other" category includes not only tests for such things as financial services and consumer durables, but includes many tests for packaged goods, such as pet foods and beverages.

In surveying marketers, the ARF found that a few large manufacturers seemed to account for a disproportional high share of STM activity. "The most active 20 percent of the 42 responses we received, accounted for about two-thirds of the STM's conducted by this sample," said Allan L. Baldinger, senior vice president and director of marketing research at the ARF. "In fact, I believe that the slowdown in overall activity since 1985 is largely due to a few manufacturers who are cutting back from their peak levels, whereas most smaller advertisers are still on an upward growth curve."[15]

What Companies Do with STM Results

The 1988 survey also looked at what manufacturers do with the simulated test market research. A company can do five major things, said Baldinger: "You can go national, if your proposition looks good enough, or if the fear of preemption is great. You can go to test market, and, given consistently positive results, *then* go national. You can go to test market, get poor results in test market and then discontinue the product. You can use the STM for product optimization, by identifying some fixable weaknesses in your concept or product and recycle the concept for further testing. Or, finally, you can use the STM to reduce your test marketing risk, by discontinuing poorer performing ideas."

Exhibit 3–1 shows the results of almost 600 tests, in total and comparing companies that run many tests versus companies that use relatively fewer. Baldinger pointed out that the seven companies that use STM's heavily—spending several hundred thousand dollars a year on such tests—"were much more likely to be using

Exhibit 3–1

Results of Simulated Test Market Research

Results	Percent of All Tests	Percent Among Heavy Users	Light Users
#1: Go National	14	8	25
#2: Test Market, Then Go National	12	7	19
#3: Test Market, Then Discontinue	14	16	10
#4: Recycle	16	12	21
#5: Discontinue Project	45	54	25
(Base: Total Completed 1985-1987 Tests)	(589)	(381)	(208)
(Base: Companies)		(7)	(35)

Source: Advertising Research Foundation, "Trends and Issues in STM's: Results of an ARF Pilot Project."

STM's to screen out poorer performing ideas than were the selective users. This seems to suggest that the heavier users are using STM's to broaden their scope of new product investigation, to widen the mouth of the new product funnel."

Results of Simulated Test Market Research

The survey also found that the lighter, more selective users, were much more likely to spend more money per test than the heavier users. Also, almost two-thirds of the tests conducted by the heavy users were based on concepts *only*, said Baldinger, while a similarly high proportion of lighter users' projects involved a product use phase.

Finally, this survey asked the manufacturers, based on the tests they conducted between 1985 and 1987, how many the market confirmed, how many generated higher results in the market than the research predicted, and how many generated lower results. "We gave them no definition of how close the final volume estimate had to be to the original estimate to be validated. We asked only for their perceptions of validity."

According to the manufacturers, slightly more than half (52 percent) of the in-market results confirmed the simulated test market research; a few (8 percent) of the in-market results were higher than the STM predicted; and the rest (41 percent) were lower. More than half (55 percent) of these 42 manufacturers said the single most important benefit of STM research was risk reduction; a third said the most important benefit was the diagnostics/what if capability. Other benefits included confidentiality (mentioned by 14 percent), cost effective (10 percent), product optimization (7 percent), and speed (7 percent).

This 1988 questionnaire asked simulated test marketing's single most important limitation, and more (40 percent) manufacturers named validity, with a typical complaint that STM's don't "reflect highly complex situations accurately." Although this may be true, the fact remains that simulated test marketing research is the single most validated tool in marketing research. Other limitations included analytical/diagnostic issues (mentioned by 31 percent of the manufacturers), methodological limitations, particularly when they involve estimating long-term repeat rates and products with long purchase cycles (mentioned by 24 percent); category appropriateness/experience (17 percent); while the rest (12 percent) were generally negative.

The study found that companies frequently use natural sell-in tests for new products, and seven in ten manufacturers use them to test line extensions. "This could easily be due to the fact that trade acceptance is a critical component of line extension tests," said Baldinger, "and hence the need for a real-world reading, including the trade as a test vehicle."

The study found that manufacturers seem to be using simulated test market models for new products (94 percent of the respondents cited this reason) and line extensions (78 percent). These respondents are not using STMs extensively for other purposes; for example, few said they use STMs to test advertising spending/weight or copy strategy (13 percent), consumer promotion (12 percent), trade promotion (11 percent), or other marketing issues (16 percent).

Although we have briefly described the differences in simulated test marketing models in this chapter, how do the major simulated test marketing systems compare in their methodologies and outputs? The next chapter covers them in depth.

4

How the Major Simulated Test Marketing Systems Compare*

All the major STM research models—ASSESSOR, BASES, DE-SIGNOR, LITMUS, and Simulator ESP—are similar enough that they exhibit some common strengths and weaknesses. One of the things that they do best is to quantify topics that were mostly qualitative before the models were invented. For example, concept tests and product tests now have more meaning than they had before the models existed. A product marketer now has more to work with than, say, a 3.2 score on a "probability of buying" scale. Today, through modeling, the computer can combine knowledge of the relationship between consumer self-reports of likely behavior with actual behavior and other data (such as retail distribution and marketing plans) to develop sales estimates with reasonable levels of predictive validity.

The models allow marketers to take more factors into consideration when making forecasts. The earliest models focused primarily on the product itself. Over time, researchers paid more and more attention to such marketing variables as distribution, advertising, trade and consumer promotion, and as a result models today include most marketing factors.

---

*This chapter is based heavily on R. Dale Wilson's "Test Market Simulation Systems: A Review of Four Major STM Methodologies," Working Paper, The Eli Broad Graduate School of Management, Michigan State Universty, 1992.

Basically, however, all simulated test marketing models have consumer inputs and marketing assumptions that the research company feeds into the "model." The model uses sophisticated mathematics (we'll see some in the next chapter) with judgment and logic checks to produce the output.

This chapter explores some of the features of simulated test market research methodology and discusses the marketing research procedures different companies use to collect the data that serves as STM input.

We focus on the five simulated test marketing research programs that are the most popular in the commercial marketplace—ASSESSOR, BASES, DESIGNOR, LITMUS, and Simulator ESP. We present some of the major features of these simulated test market research methodologies, emphasizing their similarities and differences. This discussion focuses on six major elements:

1. What information the research requires from the new product marketer.
2. How the research company designs the "shopping" environment.
3. How the company selects respondents.
4. How the company collects data.
5. How consumer reaction to the new brand is measured.
6. What diagnostic information and sales forecasts are provided.

We compare each simulated test market research methodology's approach, and we focus on the specific details associated with each.

The ASSESSOR Model. According to information provided by the company, ASSESSOR has been applied to over 1,300 new product introductions. While the vast majority of ASSESSOR applications have been in consumer packaged-goods categories, the model has also been applied to consumer durables, restaurant and fast food services, and financial services.

ASSESSOR currently has five components or phases, designed to guide management at various product development stages: Phase I, Concept Evaluation and Screening; Phase II, Product Positioning (with volumetrics); Phase III, Positioning and Product Evaluation (respondent callbacks and volumetrics); Phase IV, Total Proposition Evaluation (with laboratory store); and Phase V, In-Market Evaluation (post launch or multiple callbacks, or both). Our analysis will focus on Phase IV.

The volumetric projections for the various phases are derived and converged from three independent models in a "check-and-balance" forecasting procedure. Discrepancies in the forecasts from any one module force analytical re-examination of the parameters used for all. ASSESSOR uses a behavioral decision (choice) model; a modified, attitudinal preference model; and a period-by-period (Markov) depth-of repeat model.

Documentation for many different aspects of ASSESSOR's original specification and measurement tools can be found in Silk and Urban (1978), Urban and Hauser (1980, pp. 393–417), Urban and Katz (1983), and Urban et al. (1983). Also, Shocker and Hall (1986) include a discussion of how the former ASSESSOR-FT model worked. Of all of the STMs available commercially, the initial details of ASSESSOR's approach to simulated test marketing are documented most thoroughly in the published literature. This chapter, however, is based on the literature and on information supplied by David Lipson, Director of MACRO Strategies, Las Colinas, Texas.

The BASES Model. The BASES approach to STM modeling is one of several separate procedures used at different stages of the new product planning process. Like ASSESSOR, BASES has separate models for everything from concept evaluation to in-market testing. The most widely used model BASES III and it combines a concept test with an in-home use test with a proprietary, unpublished mathematical model for diagnosing and forecasting new product trial and repeat purchasing. We will refer to it simply as BASES. The research tells clients how well a product fulfilled triers' expectations and the likelihood that triers will remain loyal customers. Since 1989, the BASES Group, a division of BBI Marketing Services Inc., Covington, Kentucky, has marketed the BASES group of procedures.

Although market share figures are not available, BASES appears to be the clear market leader in STM procedures. Company brochures indicate that the firm has conducted over 4,000 BASES studies in the United States, with additional studies overseas. Of these BASES studies, approximately 50 percent have applied to food products, about 30 percent have applied to health and beauty aids and household products, and about 20 percent to other types of consumer products.

Unfortunately, the BASES procedures have not been well documented in the published academic literature; although an article by Lin et al. (1980) provides some sketchy information on how BASES data are collected. But precise information on measurement techniques and model specification used by BASES has not been made available. Review articles on a variety of STMs by Robinson (1981) and Shocker and Hall (1986) provide additional information on BASES and describe some its features. Nonetheless, BASES remains more of a "black box" approach to simulated test marketing than any of the four other STMs we review here. Our information about BASES comes from company literature and discussions with our clients.

The DESIGNOR Model. Since its introduction in 1972, DESIGN-OR has been applied to over 200 product and service categories in forty countries. According to company literature, more than 2,000 studies have been conducted in hundreds of product categories including fast-moving consumer goods, consumer durables, services, and pharmaceutical products.

DESIGNOR was developed from the ASSESSOR model, which, at the time, was a model to evaluate market share for a new product entering a well-defined category and which needed finished marketing mix materials (advertising, package design, promotion responses, and the like) in order to function. DESIGNOR evaluates volume sales for a new product and works equally well on a product that does not belong to a well-defined category. Marketing mix materials used in the test do not need to be in final form. DESIGN-OR will estimate the volume potential of a new brand, a line extension, or a re-launch. The firm offers four main simulation services that address the major steps in the marketing process. DETECTOR is an entry strategy and brand mix evaluation tool to help assist decision makers with share/volume forecasts; PERCEPTOR obtains data on critical success factors in a market; and BRAND HEALTH CHECK optimizes the use of allocated marketing resources for both new and established brands.

This chapter is based on literature supplied by Novaction's General Manager in the United States, Tony Hufflett, who is headquartered in South Natick, Massachusetts.

The LITMUS Model. The LITMUS procedure has evolved greatly since Yankelovich Skelly & White introduced the Laboratory Test Market, which contained some of the original ideas, in 1968. Since the first LITMUS introduction in 1981, procedures for simulated test market modeling have evolved substantially. Yankelovich Partners Inc., Westport, Connecticut, currently markets the LITMUS model. According to information provided by the firm, the LITMUS model and/or its predecessor LTM have been applied in approximately 3,000 studies of new product introductions. Approximately half of these studies have been conducted in food product categories, with the remainder applied to health and beauty aids, household products, consumer durables, consumer soft goods, consumer services, and financial services.

The documentation for the LITMUS model has been provided by Blackburn and Clancy (1980, 1982, 1983), and Blackburn, Carter, and Clancy (1984), and Blackburn, Clancy, and Wilson (1989, 1991). Additional information on LITMUS is included in Shocker and Hall's review article (1986). Interested readers may consult articles discussing aspects of the LTM model (Robinson 1981; Yankelovich Skelly and White, Inc. 1981) and the NEWS model (Pringle, Wilson, and Brody 1982) to obtain additional perspectives on how LITMUS works. An on-going research and development program has been conducted on the LITMUS model since its introduction, and this book contains some of the unpublished research.

The Simulator ESP Model. The STM procedure currently known as Simulator ESP (for *Estimating Sales Potential*) has been marketed by the NPD Group, of Port Washington, New York, since 1975. The company introduced versions of the model designed specifically for line extensions and for product re-stagings in 1980 and 1983, respectively.

Documentation for the ESP approach to simulated test marketing can be found in Eskin's original work on PanPro (Eskin 1973) and Eskin and Malec's extension of PanPro to pre-test marketing situations (Eskin and Malec 1976). Narasimhan and Sen (1983) published a critique of the PanPro model (as well as of eight other test-market models); it provides a good analysis of some of the Pan-Pro model's features. Interested readers should also see an article by Kalwani and Silk (1980), which presents some of the hypotheses on the structure of repeat buying used by Eskin (1973) as well as some of interesting aspects of the PanPro/ESP model parameter estimation process.

While the early work on PanPro and ESP appeared in the published literature, little on the ESP approach to simulated test marketing has been published since 1976. According to information obtained from the NPD Group in Port Washington, New York, well over 2,000 studies have been conducted using ESP and Simulator ESP. The ESP approach has been applied only to consumer packaged goods, with 65 percent of the applications conducted in food product categories.

Because the company has unique access to NPD/Nielsen Purchase Panel data bases, which it uses to estimate purchase cycles and buying rates for new products entering established categories (it recommends sales waves for innovative products), it argues that its estimates are more accurate than survey data. Further, the firm uses purchase panel data to update ESP model parameters to incorporate recent category sales trends; this keeps the model current and minimizes "model" bias. It also uses purchase panel data for on-going model development such as Line Extension ESP, Restage ESP, and Subline ESP.

Typical Design of STM Research Methodologies

It is important to understand the general approach that all simulated test market research procedures take. In many ways, most STMs are similar in their inputs, the approach they use for data collection, and their outputs. Reviewing the similarities between simulated test market research procedures will help clarify each procedure's specific details that we discuss later. Note that here we refer to the marketer of the new brand or service as the *client* and the marketing research organization that owns the simulated test market procedure and coordinates the STM methodology as the *STM consulting firm*.

Before the STM consulting firm can begin to collect data, the client must provide a stock of the test product. Preferably, the client has packaged the test product with the finished logos and graphics that it will use when it actually introduces the product into the market.

The client also must provide test product advertising, preferably in finished form. If necessary, however, the test product advertising can be in rough or even concept-board form. This is certainly the case for BASES, which is based on exposure to a concept, not to advertising. In addition, for ASSESSOR, DESIGNOR, LITMUS, and Simulator ESP, the client must provide advertising for the top competitors in the product category in which the new brand will compete.

If a client supplies finished advertising for competitors and rough advertising or concept boards for the test product, however, the difference may alert respondents to the fact that the STM consulting firm is interested primarily in reactions to the test product, thereby skewing the test results. For this reason, the simulated test market research should use finished (or rough) advertising for all brands so that respondents cannot easily guess which is the test product.

In addition to the test product, test product advertising, and competitive product advertising, the client must supply key information from the test product's marketing plan. A simulated test market study typically requires the following information for the test and competitive brands:

1. The market's size, stated in terms of the number of target consumers, households, dollars, or all three.
2. The advertising budget in dollars and gross rating points allocated by time period, e.g., monthly and media type.
3. Results of the test product advertising's copy tests. Generally, a client can use any one of the many copy testing techniques, as long as the STM consulting firm can compare the results to a norm or data base of advertising effectiveness relative to other brands in the same product category.
4. The types of promotional techniques planned and the budget for each.
5. The test product's price and the prices of the major competitive brands in the product category.
6. The expected distribution build over time, measured as Nielsen All-Commodity Volume (ACV).
7. The expected margin contribution as well as the total costs budgeted for marketing the new brand.

Design of the "Shopping" Environment

The laboratory environment that simulated test market research consulting firms use to collect data varies somewhat, depending upon the specific methodology. There seem to be three major types of "shopping" situations that consulting firms use to simulate a real test market.

1. People are exposed to advertising in a laboratory environment, either in a rented space in a shopping mall or in a traveling laboratory van, and then are given the opportunity to "buy" the test product and competitive product—and in some cases products in other categories as well—from a mock supermarket/drug store shelf, which is set up in the laboratory environment. One could think of this type of shopping environment as a mini 7-11.

2. Similar to #1 insofar as it involves a rented space in a mall or in a traveling van. However, there is no shopping experience per se. Researchers show people a concept board and ask how interested they are in buying the test product, typically on a five-point rating scale. The researchers then give consumers the new product to take home, so there's no buying involved at all.

3. Consumers are exposed to the new product in a facility adjoining a supermarket. They then go into the supermarket and actually buy the test product (or not).

   Given the wide variety of types of shopping environments that STM consulting firms use, it seems there is a wide range of opinions on the "best" way to simulate the shopping experience that might occur in an actual market.

Respondent Selection. The STM consulting firms recruit participants at shopping malls, grocery stores, or by telephone. They sometimes screen potential respondents for product usage (or potential usage). In all cases, they collect basic demographic characteristics and use this data in defining the sample. To control for security and bias, they do not permit consumers who are employed by competitive organizations (for example, ad agency employees) to participate in an STM study. Average sample size ranges from a low of 250 to 300 respondents to a high of 1,500 to 2,000.

Data Collection Procedures. Major STM methodologies employ a wide range of data collection procedures, depending primarily upon the type of shopping environment the STM consulting firm uses. The typical STM data collection methodology is the following:

1. The consulting firm conducts an initial interview, using either a self-administered questionnaire or a personal interview, to measure brand awareness, brand attitudes and preferences, and product usage for the product category's major brands.

2. The consulting firm then exposes respondents to advertising for the test product and some of the leading competitors. Typically, the consulting firm shows the advertising in the context of ordinary programming (in the case of television commercials) or within editorial material (with print advertising). In some cases, the consulting firm will use concept boards in lieu of finished or rough advertising.

3. Immediately after the advertising exposure, the STM consulting firm administers a short interview or self-administered questionnaire to determine respondent reaction to the advertising. Depending on the simulated test marketing research methodology, the consulting firm will take a variety of measures from respondents.

4. The typical simulated test market research study provides some mechanism for giving the respondent the opportunity to "purchase" the test brand, depending upon the shopping environment's exact set-up. The specific type of "purchase" opportunity depends upon whether the STM uses a simulated or an actual store. In the case where the study employs an in-home usage test rather than a simulated or an actual store, a purchase experience is not available to the respondent. Purchase intent serves as a starting point for trial forecast.

5. Those STMs that use a simulated store or an actual store to allow respondents to purchase the test brand typically employ a purchase incentive. These incentives can take several forms: a coupon for the test brand, a cash payment that can be used to purchase the test product, and a price discount on the test brand and competitive products, among others.

6. For STMs that employ a simulated store, the consulting firm may conduct a post-purchase evaluation to determine the respondents' reactions to the test and competitive brands and to determine why the respondents did or did not buy the test product. The interview may ask a variety of questions, depending upon the

client's interests. Researchers may gather this data through focus group interviews, a personal interview, a self-administered questionnaire, or all three. Rather than interview the entire group of participating respondents, researchers typically complete in-depth interviews with only a sample of respondents who tried the product and a sample of those who did not try it.

7. Respondents who select the test product in the actual or simulated store (or rate it high in terms of purchase intent) are considered to be "triers," and the STM consulting firm asks them to use the brand at home as they normally would use any brand in the product category. In some cases, to assure that both triers and non-triers have the opportunity to use the test brand, the consulting firm may give some of those who did not buy the product a sample and ask them to use it at home as well.

8. Once the respondent has had an opportunity to use the product, the consulting firm conducts a follow-up interview over the telephone to determine respondent reactions and the respondent's anticipated future usage of the test brand. The consulting firm may, depending upon the client's specific interests, also collect respondent evaluations of specific product attributes. The STM consulting firm uses data from these follow-up interviews to estimate, among other things, repeat purchase probabilities and the purchase cycle.

9. In some simulated test market studies, the consulting firm conducts a so-called "sales wave" phase as part of the follow-up interview. For some methodologies, consulting firms consider sales waves to be an optional add-on to the basic STM design and are thus available at an additional cost to the client. They are, however, very useful for estimating second repeat purchase and loyalty. Moreover, after an extended use period, consumers have a better estimate of the new product's purchase cycle. If the consulting firm uses this response measure as part of its research design, it gives respondents the opportunity to buy additional units of the test product at the full retail price; the results provide a measure of continued consumer interest in the brand or continued repeat purchase.

It is important to note that different situations may be more or less suited to a data collection methodology. The most important thing, however, is making sure the model/modeling is compatible with the client's inputs—that is, the adjustments the STM model makes are generally more important than the data collection method per se.

Sales Forecasts and Diagnostic Information

Once the STM consulting firm has collected all of the information, the model generates sales forecasts and provides diagnostic information. Some STMs deliver forecasts of consumer awareness, and all provide forecasts of the trial rate, the repeat purchase rate, and market share or sales volume (or both). Each STM uses its own mathematical or statistical model, combined with the use of the STM analyst's judgment and a data base of norms from previous new brand introductions to estimate the new brand's sales and market share. The consulting firm may provide other forecasts—such as sales forecasts geared to alternative sets of marketing plans or forecasts of market share in the "steady state" or "equilibrium" market—depending upon the specific STM. Diagnostic information may include a variety of tools, depending on the approach the STM uses and the options the client buys. Other information available includes diagnostic reports structured to provide feedback on advertising effectiveness, profiles of the triers and non-triers of the test product, brand attribute analyses, and competitive draw analyses.

In addition to including sales waves as an add-on to the basic simulated test market research design, other STM features are typically available at an additional cost to the client. These additional features include a positioning analysis of the test product and competitive brands (some STMs include perceptual maps), additional reports on information obtained from triers and non-triers, and the evaluation of alternative marketing strategies and tactics.

A Comparison of the Major Simulated Test Market Procedures

While most STMs have characteristics similar to others, each has its own unique "personality," due to its differences. We have been focusing on the similarities among the major STMs. We now consider the unique features of the five major STMs available to marketers.

In addition to the articles cited earlier, we consulted review articles published by Robinson (1981), Shocker and Hall (1986), and

Wilson and Smith (1989). Other academic treatments of STMs are also available in textbooks on new product development, product management, and marketing modeling.[1]

Another major source of information is a variety of brochures that STM consulting firms have prepared, published, and distributed. But, despite these sources, the specific details on certain aspects of some of the STMs are still somewhat incomplete. Nevertheless, whenever possible, we will provide enough information on the various STMs to indicate the differences among them.

Test Product and Packaging Requirements

As we've said, the client must provide the STM consulting firm with the test product, test product advertising, and competitive product advertising. Since all STMs judge consumer responses to a test product, their forecasts can only be as accurate as the test product is representative of actual production. It should be as close as possible to the way it would appear on the shelf in a national rollout. This means that many aspects of the product design, such as the logo, labels, packaging, packaging graphics, and directions for preparation and use, must be finished. Also, it is important that the test product be of production-line quality (especially food products, which often taste better when prepared in small quantities in a test kitchen than when in full production).

ASSESSOR's first two phases, Concept Evaluation and Screening and Product Positioning, do not require test product. Later phases do require it.

BASES can use packaging prototypes that include the brand name, logo, and directions for preparation and use. The test product must be production-line quality.

LITMUS can use a shelf mockup unless the packaging is critical to the test's success (as in the case of cosmetics products), when it must be in its most finished form.

Simulator ESP uses the product in its most finished form (as close as possible to the way it would appear on a shelf nationally).

Advertising Requirements

The test product advertising applied during simulated test market research should be as close as possible to the actual introductory advertising campaign. The further the advertising is from the finished design, the less accurate the forecasts.

ASSESSOR's lab store simulation requires that respondents be exposed to test product advertising in a competitive context and therefore requires finished commercials and competitive ads. Several studies have used print-only advertising.

BASES works with a finished concept board that has a photograph of the package or of the product (or both) along with a product description and the key selling messages. It may also use rough or finished commercials as well as animatics.

DESIGNOR works with a concept board, print ad, TV animatic, or final television commercial.

LITMUS uses the methodology that employs print-only advertising in those cases where the client plans a print campaign.

Simulator ESP model prefers finished commercials but frequently uses concept boards.

These five major STMs handle the inclusion of competitive commercials quite differently.

ASSESSOR, DESIGNOR, and LITMUS require competitive commercials if the client plans to use television advertising. The form of the competitive clutter depends on the form used in the test product advertising.

BASES does not use competitive advertising at all.

LITMUS and Simulator ESP also run commercials for non-related products as clutter commercials.

Other Information Required

While these five STMs share many similarities in the information they need from the marketing plan, there are also some key differences depending upon the specific study design. With regard to brand awareness, for example, ASSESSOR projects total in-market awareness from client plans for marketing support and expenditures. It does not require an awareness estimate from the client.

Similarly, LITMUS, DESIGNOR, and BASES do not require awareness data to be input since the models generate awareness forecasts as part of their output.

Simulator ESP does not deal with awareness at all since it uses actual advertising and promotion spending dollars (media equalized to reflect effectiveness of GRPs, daypart, and timing) input into the model. There is no need to make an estimate (trial) based upon the estimate of another intermediate variable (awareness).

Each of the five requires estimates of the advertising budget's total dollars and gross rating points. BASES and LITMUS also require a copy of the media plan, and LITMUS requires estimates of total advertising dollars for both the test product and its competitors to generate share-of-voice inputs.

For promotional spending, ASSESSOR, BASES, and LITMUS require estimates of the total dollars to be spent, as well as the number and kind of consumer events to be used. In addition to these data, BASES and LITMUS require a schedule of the timing of these events. Simulator ESP requires estimates of total spending as well as specific details on the product sampling plan to be used (if applicable), such as the percentage of households sampled and the definition of the sampled population.

For distribution build data, all five of the STMs require estimates of all-commodity volume (ACV). Simulator ESP requires "steady state" estimates, while the other models require estimates of ACV in relevant channels at four-week intervals (BASES) or at one-month intervals (LITMUS). ASSESSOR models both distribution and awareness on a period-by-period basis throughout the first year.

LITMUS requires a measure of the total size of the product category, usually generated from Nielsen store audit data. ASSESSOR says that it is helpful to have a client's estimate of total category volume, but it uses the data primarily to check the correctness of the model parameters. (The original ASSESSOR was a share-based model, but this is no longer true. ASSESSOR directly estimates product volume.) BASES and Simulator ESP do not require any estimate of the size of the market for the product category.

Design of the "Shopping" Environment

The shopping experience can be structured in many different ways to simulate a real shopping trip. In fact, each of the five stimulated test market research methodologies approaches the design of its "laboratory" differently.

ASSESSOR generally uses mall-intercept; sometimes it pre-recruits. It may or may not use a simulated store laboratory.

DESIGNOR uses a simulated shopping shelf (mock-up store) or photos showing each product with its price. The firm gives customers a voucher they can use to buy a product or redeem for cash. Any difference between the product's purchase price and the value of the voucher is either refunded or made up by the customer.

LITMUS also uses a simulated shopping environment with all research conducted in central locations in appropriate markets.

The simulated store environments used by ASSESSOR and LITMUS, whether located in a traveling laboratory or in a central location facility, are designed as mock, mini-stores having grocery-store shelving, refrigerators, or frozen-food cases. The mini-store is designed to resemble a supermarket or drug store in which the STM consulting firm can control shelf facings, shelf position, and price. In this way, the company can simulate either expected in-store situations or alternative marketing strategies. With central location facilities, both ASSESSOR and LITMUS offer clients multiple cities in which to collect data. They can use these to gauge reaction to the new brand in various parts of the United States (as well as internationally).

BASES uses no shopping experience at all. Rather, the approach uses consumer reactions in the form of purchase intent, purchase frequency, and the like as the starting point in the sales estimate. The researcher exposes respondents to the test product (or a test concept) in interview facilities in large shopping malls in major markets. After the consulting firm interviews respondents, it gives those who express purchase interest the test product to try at home.

Simulator ESP focuses on an actual in-store shopping experience in a real store (such as Kroger's or Walgreen's). It conducts the testing over a three- or four-day period. Trial purchase of the test product is typically in at least three supermarkets in three different cities. In tests for products such as health and beauty aids or over-the-counter drugs, Simulator ESP may add drug stores to the supermarket outlets. In each store used in the test, the consulting firm sets up a temporary research facility near the store entrance to expose respondents to the advertising and to conduct interviews.

Recruiting Procedures

All five STM methodologies collect a number of demographic characteristics along with product usage information and security measures. Typically, the sample group's final characteristics match as closely as possible the characteristics of the product category's users or the overall U.S. population. To assure adequate coverage of all demographic groups, STM consulting firms commonly resort to quota sampling. Samples may include primary adult buyers (both men and women), other adult buyers, teenagers, or children (or both), depending upon the test product's market characteristics.

ASSESSOR and BASES employ mall intercepts to screen respondents using a personal interview.

LITMUS methodology recruits product category users or brand decision makers over the telephone.

Simulator ESP also uses personal interviews, but the interview is conducted using a store-intercept rather than a mall-intercept technique.

Typical Sample Sizes

The size of the typical sample used in simulated test market methodologies varies widely, depending upon the specific STM.

ASSESSOR sample size is a function of the number of "cells" in a study—variations in the product or its positioning, for example. The sample is larger if a study requires multiple callbacks since respondents drop out at each wave. The company generally wants about 300 respondents per cell and it expects to recontact 80 percent for follow-up.

BASES—an initial interview with 400 or more respondents, with callback data collected from 190 triers.

DESIGNOR—250 to 400 respondents

LITMUS—400 to 500 respondents initially.

Simulator ESP—approximately 1,500 to 2,000 respondents interviewed in the store with at least 300 triers included.

The Initial Interview

ASSESSOR interviews are person-to-person, using computer entry. The exceptions are self-administered questionnaires following advertising exposure in simulated-store studies. The company conducts most studies in person; it has used telephone (e.g., phone-mail-phone) interviews for selected situations.

BASES conducts a brief initial interview as part of the mall-intercept procedure. Questions pertain to category and brand usage for several product categories, including the test brand category.

DESIGNOR conducts an initial interview in a central location among target consumers for the new product (usually users of its category of products).

LITMUS respondents complete a self-administered questionnaire regarding their current product category and brand usage. Questions also include information on attitudes and preferences about various brands in the category. Attitude measures include specific important attributes for both the test brand and the leading competitive brands. The consulting firm later analyzes these attribute measures to provide guidance on product positioning issues.

Simulator ESP takes a similar approach to that of BASES. During the store intercept interview, the consulting firm questions each respondent briefly concerning brand and category usage for the test product as well as several other products.

Exposure to Advertising

ASSESSOR respondents, after the initial interview, view advertisements for the test product and for the leading competitive brands in the product category. Respondents view these advertisements individually. If the study uses television commercials—now the exception—the commercial for the test product is embedded among four or five competitive spots. If the study uses print advertising, the consulting firm gives a brochure containing the test advertisement plus four to five competitive ads to each respondent.

BASES respondents are not generally exposed to advertising. They are exposed to a concept board describing the new product with no competitive context.

DESIGNOR respondents are exposed to advertising for the new product among advertising for competitive products in the category. The method depends on the quality of the communication available for the new brand. A lower-quality TV ad (e.g., animatics), for example, is shown in isolation, followed by exposure of a reel of competitive TV ads. A high-quality print ad is inserted in a folder of print ads.

LITMUS respondents view the commercials in a theater-like setting in the context of a television program (usually a situation comedy, with normal commercial breaks). Commercials are shown for the test brand, for the leading brands in the product category, and for non-related products (i.e., clutter commercials) as well. If the client plans to use print advertisements, the STM consulting firm gives a portfolio containing the test ad and four or five competitive ads to each respondent. If rough or finished ads are not yet available, respondents might see a concept board.

Simulator ESP respondents typically view a series of television commercials without other programming. Alternatively, respondents see a concept board for the test product. These commercials or print ads are viewed independently.

Reaction to the Advertising or Concept

Immediately following exposure to the advertising, the STM consulting firms interview respondents to determine their reaction to it.

ASSESSOR uses a short, self-administered questionnaire to measure respondent reactions. The questionnaire includes measures of brand recall as well as recall of the advertising's major messages.

BASES uses a short personal interview to determine reactions to the concept and the respondents' intent to purchase.

DESIGNOR uses a short in-person interview to measure advertising impact, differentiation, and quality. The questionnaire includes measures of brand recall, advertising themes recalled, uniqueness, and relevance scores.

LITMUS uses a short questionnaire that focuses on measures of advertising intrusiveness.

Simulator ESP includes no post-advertising questioning except in the case a Communication Evaluation option is added to the design (available at an additional cost to the client, and depending upon the redemption rate of the coupons provided to the group of respondents). In this case, the consulting firm surveys 100 coupon redeemers and 100 non-redeemers by telephone regarding advertising recall, reaction to the advertising, product category and brand usage, and demographics.

The Shopping Experience

After exposing respondents to the advertising and administering a brief post-advertising questionnaire, the consulting firms give respondents the opportunity to shop in the "store" environment used by the particular STM.

ASSESSOR respondents shop in the simulated store using coupons of sufficient value to permit respondents to make any reasonable purchase.

BASES does not use a store shopping simulation per se. Instead, it uses consumer buying intentions to model trial.

DESIGNOR respondents shop in the simulated store using coupons of sufficient value to permit any reasonable purchase.

LITMUS respondents shop in a store designed to simulate a real-world shopping occasion. They shop as part of a small group and complete an order form for their purchases, a procedure designed to ensure that respondents are making a purchase decision independently of other respondents. The purchase is made at a regular cash register, and the respondents use their own money to pay for it.

Simulator ESP uses real stores, and respondents conduct their shopping "as usual" in their regular supermarket. The STM consulting firm places the test product on the shelf in the appropriate section of the store with other brands in the product category.

The Purchase Incentive

Those STMs that include a "shopping" experience also offer a purchase incentive to encourage respondents to buy the test or a competitive product in the store. The purchase incentive does not apply in the BASES approach since respondents have no opportunity to shop in a BASES study.

ASSESSOR respondents use coupons to purchase a product in the simulated store.

LITMUS respondents are given a discount—generally 30 percent—on all products purchased. While respondents may choose to buy the test product or competitive products or both, they are also told that they do not have to purchase any product (thus simulating a real-world buying situation).

Simulator ESP gives respondents a coupon worth 20 percent off the test brand. For other brands in the category, there generally seems to be no purchase incentive.

Post-purchase Evaluation

ASSESSOR, DESIGNOR, and LITMUS use a post-purchase evaluation to question the respondents about their reactions to the test and competitive brands. Also, the post-purchase evaluation attempts to determine why respondents bought the test product or why they did not buy it. This post-purchase interview takes place immediately following the shopping experience.

ASSESSOR interviews roughly 10 percent of the respondents who bought a brand in the product category other than the test brand (i.e., non-triers of the test brand) individually to determine why they bought a brand other than the test product. Also, if the client chooses to purchase perceptual mapping as part of the AS-SESSOR study, the consulting firm asks all respondents to rate the brands in the category on a set of attributes.

LITMUS has approximately 5 to 10 percent of the total sample (both purchasers and non-purchasers of the test brand) participate in post-purchase focus groups. Here, the discussion centers on the respondent's "in-store" experience. To gain insight about the shopping experience, questions probe why respondents did or did not purchase the test brand as well as their reactions to the advertising, the packaging, the price, and so forth. All other respondents (that is, the remaining 90 to 95 percent of the total sample who do not participate in the focus groups) complete a self-administered questionnaire that focuses on the advertising, the packaging, and the price of the test brand and competing brands. Also, this questionnaire assesses pre-usage product positioning by asking respondents to rate the test brand vis-à-vis competitive brands on critical attributes.

Simulator ESP conducts no post-purchase questioning in the store.

Home Usage Experience

Since respondents who buy the test brand in the store are considered to be "triers" of the new brand, the STM consulting firms typically ask them to use the brand at home as they normally would use any brand in the product category.

ASSESSOR provides respondents who do not buy the test product with a sample of it so that they can use it at home.

BASES identifies only those who indicate a positive purchase intent in response to the new product concept as triers and gives them the test brand for in-home use.

LITMUS also identifies test brand purchasers as triers. The triers take the product home as they normally would after a normal shopping experience. To avoid bias, LITMUS researchers do not inform them that it will be calling about the product. As an additional feature of the LITMUS approach (available as an option at an additional cost), some of the respondents who do not buy the product may be given the test product for trial at home. This simulates the distribution of samples for the new product. This additional cell is then used to provide an estimate of the impact of sampling on trial sales. In other words, a multi-cell study can forecast the test brand's incremental sales due to the sampling program.

Simulator ESP study identifies those respondents who redeem their 20-percent-off coupons for the test brand as triers. Simulator ESP will add as an option "Non-trier Diagnostics" to the design; this asks a sample of non-triers to use the test product in their homes.

The Follow-up Interview

After enough time has elapsed to allow the respondent to try the test product in a normal usage situation, a telephone follow-up interview determines reactions to the test product to estimate repeat purchase probabilities. Also, the STM consulting firm may also collect information regarding specific product attributes during this interview.

ASSESSOR conducts this phone interview long enough after the simulated shopping experience to allow product usage. This period varies by the nature of the product and can be as little as three or four days. The consulting firm asks respondents for their general reactions to the test product and their after-use acceptance. Respondents also provide their attitudes regarding the test product as well as their preference ratings for the test product relative to a set of competitive products. ASSESSOR measures repeat purchase probabilities as well. As an option available at an additional cost, ASSESSOR will arrange focus groups among different groups of respondents to obtain qualitative feedback on certain issues relevant to the client.

BASES surveys triers by phone within an appropriate usage period (two to four weeks) regarding future buying intentions and intended frequency of purchase. BASES also obtains data on price/value considerations and on product satisfaction evaluations. The interview may also include other questions, dealing with respondents' reaction to the test brand on specific product attributes.

DESIGNOR follows up by telephone a few days or weeks after the customer's shopping experience to check product usage, repeat purchase opportunities, purchase intent, purchase frequency, comparison to usual brand/expectations, preference of test product after use versus evoked set, PERCEPTOR attribute ratings of product after use, and other questions.

LITMUS uses a phone study one to six weeks (depending on the product category's purchase cycle) after the simulated shopping experience. The questionnaire is designed to ascertain respondents' reactions to the test product, their repeat purchase probability, their anticipated quantity purchases and usage frequency, and their comparisons of the test brand with other competing brands. In addition, the study collects respondents' ratings on critical product attributes.

Simulator ESP uses a follow-up phone interview (conducted several weeks after the in-store experience), with a base sample of triers. The firm questions triers about their test brand usage, likes and dislikes regarding the test brand, the likelihood of their buying the test brand as a substitute or a replacement for their current brand(s) in the product category, and ratings for several specific product attributes. If the "Non-trier Diagnostics" option is being used as part of the study, the firm surveys a sample of 100 non-triers by telephone within twenty-four hours of the in-store shopping experience. Questions attempt to ascertain advertising recall and reactions, brand and product category usage, reasons for non-purchase of the test brand, and basic demographics.

The Sales Waves Phase

When the STM consulting firm conducts sales waves as part of the follow-up interview, respondents have the opportunity to buy additional units of the test brand at the full retail price. Respondents spend their own money for the product, and multiple sales waves can measure likely depth-of-repeat for the test product. A positive response provides a measure of continued interest in the brand.

STM brochures discuss sales waves, but only briefly. Each of the five STM approaches considered here uses sales waves as an option that can be included in the study design at an additional charge. Additional information is available in the material made available by ASSESSOR, Simulator ESP, and LITMUS.

ASSESSOR includes multiple sales waves in the design when extended use of the test product is an important issue faced by the client. An example would be the client who is concerned the users may lose interest in the test product after the first few usage occasions.

LITMUS usually recommends at least one sales wave for food products and innovative or novelty products.

Simulator ESP has three or more sales waves in 10 to 20 percent of its new product studies. These are used primarily for innovative or novelty products where repeat purchase or frequency of purchase (or both) are hard to predict. In such cases, a series of sales waves can be used to determine the purchase cycle length or to identify potential depth-of-repeat problems.

Sales Forecasts and Diagnostic Information

Once the stimulated test market research consulting firm has obtained all the input data from the respondents participating in a STM study, the consulting firm generates sales forecasts and other variables and prepares diagnostic information. Each model generates parameter estimates using a combination of methods. These include:

1. A mathematical or statistical model designed to provide unbiased estimates of the quantitative relationships that serve as the basic structure of the model.
2. The judgment and experience of the STM analyst.
3. A database of norms from previous new brand introductions (which is often sorted and used on a category-by-category basis).

While it is clear that these three all serve as important contributors to the process of developing each STM's forecasts and diagnostics, the mathematical or statistical model is generally the most important contributor.

As we mentioned above, the academic literature has disclosed much of the model specification and measurement procedures for the ASSESSOR, Simulator ESP, and LITMUS models. These details have also been published for NEWS/Planner, another solid, but less widely used, simulated test market model. However, such disclosure for BASES does not exist.

Sales (and Other) Forecasts

Brochures and other information sources for the five major simulated test marketing research models provide insight into the array of forecast measures that they provide.

ASSESSOR makes the following available:

- First-year sales volume or market share potential or both.
- Projected selling rate at the end of the first year.
- On-going sales potential after the first year.
- Projections for alternative marketing plans and programs.
- Projected sales impact of alternative competitive response scenarios.

The model also projects sources of business for the new product/service, line extension, or restaging, including:

- Cannibalization of the company's existing business—i.e., contributions from the company's existing products or services.
- Projection of incremental business—i.e., contributions from sources other than the company's existing products or services.
- Projection of business contributions from demographic groups, behavioral segments, attitudinal segments, and retail trade segments.

BASES output includes:

- Sales volume in the first year (with an option for the second year).
- The trial rate (for the first year).
- The repeat rate (for the first repeat purchase).
- Repeats per repeater.
- The average time between purchases.

- The average number of units per trial and repeat purchase occasions.
- Awareness.

DESIGNOR output includes:

- The trial rate.
- The adoption rate (or retention).
- The share of choice (or share of purchases).
- Year 1 and Year 2 volume sales build-up.
- Long-term stabilized share (Year 2 and beyond)
- Price elasticity
- Cannibalization/draw estimates.
- Awareness modeling. Cross-checking/correcting client assumptions.

LITMUS provides:

- Monthly awareness (for the first year with an option for the second year).
- Monthly market share or sales volume or both (for the first year with an option for the second year).
- The trial rate.
- The repeat purchase rate.

Simulator ESP provides:

- Sales volume (for the first year).
- Monthly trial rate, repeat purchase rate, and sales volume.
- The percentage of the target market who will "ever" repeat the purchase.

Diagnostic Information

The diagnostic information that these simulated test market research models generate include a variety of different items, depending on the STM's approach and the options the client purchases. Accordingly, some of the diagnostics available for each STM are provided below.

ASSESSOR is capable of providing the following:

- An evaluation of advertising or concept communication, covering major selling points: differentiation versus competitive products or services; perceived advantages and disadvantages versus major competitors; and reasons for trial motivation or rejection.

- Product/service fit with the advertising or concept, covering perceived delivery versus expectations; reasons for satisfaction or dissatisfaction.
- Product/service acceptance, covering perceived advantages and disadvantages of the product overall and relative to existing competitive alternatives; importance of product delivery dimensions on acceptance and adoption of the product; preference and intensity of appeal relative to competitive products.
- Consumer adoption diagnostics covering trial potential; first repeat purchase potential; on-going repeat purchase potential; purchase/usage cycle; quantities purchased per occasion; average purchase price.
- Impact of the marketing plan and program in creating awareness; generating trial/first purchase; and developing repeat purchase and adoption.

BASES diagnostic information includes:

- Respondent likes and dislikes of the concept.
- Profiles of triers, focusing on demographics, product categories and brands used, and brands on hand.
- Profiles of the test brand, centering on respondents' likes and dislikes, areas for improvement, attribute ratings, and product usage and directional ratings.

DESIGNOR diagnostic output includes:

- Measures of the brand's IDQV—impact, differentiation, quality, and value. Impact is the brand's capacity to create strong identification with the target consumer via advertising and packaging. Differentiation is the brand's capacity to create a dominating position of both uniqueness and some perceived consumer benefit via the brand's mix. Quality is measured by the product's pre-use perception, importance, and usefulness to the consumer; the anticipation of the quality performance; the positive expectations generated by the product's positioning; and the post-use performance when the customer judges the product against the promise. And value is the relationship of total quality and price in the competitive environment.

LITMUS's diagnostic output includes:

- Advertising effectiveness, including brand recall from the post-advertising (but pre-shopping) period, brand recall and main message communication measures from the post-purchase questionnaire, and brand recall and main message communication measures from the focus group discussion.
- Target market guidance, including demographics, category and brand usage, and measures of brand preference measures for the test brand and leading competitors.
- Product guidance, including respondents' usage, likes and dislikes, repeat purchase intentions, and reactions to the test brand's name, label, package, and price.
- Marketing plan diagnostics, including a sensitivity analysis to changes in the various marketing plan input levels, a "source of volume" analysis, and marketing mix optimization plan.

Simulator ESP's diagnostics include:

- Measures of advertising effectiveness (available as an option).
- Profiles of triers, including demographics, categories and brands used, and a definition of the "interested universe" or target market.
- Profiles of non-triers (available as an option).
- Profiles of the test brand, including respondent usage patterns, likes and dislikes, repeat purchase intentions, post-usage attribute ratings, and likely replacement or substitution for the current brand(s) purchased.
- A report on the introductory spending level necessary to achieve sales objectives.

Additional Features that Are Available

In addition to including sales waves as an add-on to the basic simulated test market research design, other STM features are available at an additional cost to the client.

ASSESSOR and BASES clients, for example, can obtain a forced-trial report, which focuses on ways to encourage concept rejectors to try the test brand (for example, through couponing or sampling).

LITMUS and DESIGNOR include any of the following at an extra cost: cannibalization analysis, competitive response analysis, price sensitivity, and market share optimization.

Simulator ESP can make available a report on non-trier diagnostics (using a sample of 100 respondents). Also, a Communication Program report is available, which estimates the impact of a free sample (instead of the coupon that a Simulator ESP study typically uses) on the trial and repeat purchase rates.

Validity

Each of these five simulated test marketing research methodologies provides an indication of the predictive validity of its studies. The claimed accuracy for each of the models is as follows:

ASSESSOR forecasts in Phases III, IV, and V have been within plus or minus 10 percent in approximately 90 percent of the cases where product/services were evaluated with the consumer having the opportunity to experience the product or service. In earlier stages of development where consumers respond only to a concept or advertisement, accuracy has been plus or minus 20 percent approximately 80 percent of the time.

BASES reports that in-market sales have been within an average of 10 percent of predicted sales in 250 validated cases.

DESIGNOR says that in-market sales have been on average less than 9 percent of forecast sales. In the United States, almost two-thirds have been within 10 percent deviation.

LITMUS says that in-market sales have been within 10 percent of predicted sales in nine out of ten of the approximately 200 cases that have been validated.

Simulator ESP says that for forty-eight verified cases, in-market sales have been within 10.5 percent of the model's forecasts.

Timing and Cost Estimates

These five consulting firms indicate the following timing—from field start to final presentation—and cost estimates at the end of 1993:

ASSESSOR: Phase I and II, six to eight weeks; Phase III, eight to ten weeks; Phase IV, nine to twelve weeks; and Phase V, three to five months. Costs vary with the phase, the number of cells in the study, the effective incidence for qualified respondents, and whether or not extended use is incorporated. Costs can range from $45,000 up.

BASES: approximately $50,000 to $60,000. The consulting firm provides a volume estimate eight weeks from the field start, and a final report ten to twelve weeks from the field start.

DESIGNOR: approximately $80,000 for a concept test to $150,000 for a full DESIGNOR test. Typically a study takes eleven weeks from commissioning to presentation.

LITMUS: approximately $175,000, plus $15,000 per sales wave. Timing is twelve weeks from the field date.

Simulator ESP: approximately $50,000 to $60,000, plus $12,000 for three sales waves, plus $5,000 for each set of non-trier diagnostics, plus about $500 for each additional model run to address the appropriate level of introductory spending. Timing is twelve to fourteen weeks from the field date. The consulting firm provides top-line forecasts approximately six weeks from the field date.

Management Implications

In systematically comparing the five major STMs, several conclusions can be drawn. Some of the more salient are the following:

ASSESSOR (and, by extension, DESIGNOR), Simulator ESP, and LITMUS have all been documented in the academic literature, where the focus of several articles on each has centered on issues such as the structure of each model and measurement issues. Unfortunately, this type of information is not available for BASES; virtually none of its details have been published for industry scrutiny.

There are major differences among the five methodologies regarding how the consumer's in-store experience is "simulated." These differences may be important in obtaining high-quality results from the STM study.

The details of the collection of data from respondents vary widely, depending upon the STM. Marketing managers must consider these differences carefully before they select an STM procedure since some introduce a large amount of artificiality into the study and thus may limit the results and conclusions that may be drawn from them.

Simulator ESP does not deal with brand awareness data. On the other hand, BASES, DESIGNOR, and LITMUS generate brand awareness forecasts and consider these forecasts to be an important outcome of the modeling process.

ASSESSOR and Simulator ESP provide forecasts for a "steady state" or "equilibrium" period. LITMUS and BASES, however, provide forecasts for Year One (and sometimes Year Two) quantities and are dynamic models of market event timing. This approach more clearly allows managers to assess the incremental effects of advertising, sales promotion, and distribution on consumer awareness, trial, repeat purchasing, sales, and market share.

The ASSESSOR model seems to be primarily a "market share" model. This means that, in many cases where the product category is ill-defined, ASSESSOR has difficulty in predicting unit or dollar sales.

A major difference between the systems is in terms of their diagnostic capabilities. DESIGNOR, as an illustration, employs interesting technology for identifying the perceptual dimensions that determine brand preference; Simulator ESP can readily assess the effects of in-store promotion better than alternative systems; LITMUS enjoys a "sensitivity analysis" and optimization technology that are unique.

The remarkable thing about the five STMs described here is that despite their differences they appear to perform similarly—assuming that we accept the claims of the research companies—in terms of predictive validity. This is not unlike a situation in medicine today where different types of treatment for, say, back pain (treatments ranging from drugs to chiropractic therapies to surgery) appear to yield comparable levels of success.

II

Detailed Analysis of Simulated Test Marketing

5

The Marriage between Mathematical Modeling and Simulated Test Marketing*

S imulated test marketing technology, as we discussed in Chapter 3, has evolved over time to reflect the gradual convergence of two different approaches to forecasting: mathematical modeling and laboratory experimentation. Mathematical modeling involved the use of statistical and mathematical equations to predict real-world sales performance from detailed marketing plan inputs. Laboratory experimentation involved the exposure of the new product concept to a cross-section of prospective buyers to gauge their reactions to the idea and to the product itself under at-home usage conditions.

The first system to incorporate *both* approaches was LITMUS, initially introduced as a diagnostic tool by Yankelovich Skelly & White in 1981, formally introduced as a stand-alone new product forecasting system by Clancy Shulman Associates in 1982, and successfully employed since 1986 by Yankelovich Clancy Shulman, which is now known as Yankelovich Partners.

During the past decade, a number of simulated test marketing systems have made great progress in incorporating both mathematical modeling and laboratory experimentation in their methodologies. DESIGNOR, as an illustration, represents a powerful example of modeling and laboratory approaches while ASSESSOR,

---

*This chapter is co-authored by Professor Joseph Blackburn of the Owen School of Management at Vanderbilt University, a co-developer of the LITMUS model and a consultant to the authors for more than a decade.

81

BASES, and Simulator ESP have all taken enormous strides to improve their methodologies, reflecting the best of the modeling and experimentation paths to new product forecasting.

In this chapter we will use the LITMUS system to describe in detail how a marketer may employ a simulated test marketing system to forecast a new product introduction's success or failure. This chapter describes the kinds of forecasts that the system generates for a new product, and it details the development of the mathematical model used to do them.

As we pointed out in the last chapter, the specific types of forecasts that simulated test marketing research provide vary by system. All simulated test marketing systems provide volume forecasts. The LITMUS system generates a variety of different forecasts on a monthly basis for up to twenty-four months following the introduction of a new or re-staged product or service. In particular, the system forecasts:

1. Total brand awareness for a new product or campaign awareness in the case of a re-staged brand.
2. Penetration (percent of consumers purchasing at least once).
3. Repeat buyers.
4. Unit sales.
5. Market share in units and dollars.
6. Profitability—if the marketer provides detailed information on the cost of the marketing program, manufacturing, packaging, and distribution.

The Infrastructure of an STM Model

To forecast accurately a new product's launch or an existing brand's restaging through simulated test market methodology, a simulated test marketing system must model the marketing environment that will exist at the time of the launch or re-staging. A smart system models the entire marketing mix (Exhibit 5–1), and the system requires three kinds of intelligence: market response information, product category data, and marketing plans (we cover these in detail in the next chapter).

Market response is the consumer response to the test product; the laboratory experiment provides this information. The key con-

Exhibit 5–1

A Model of the New Product Introduction Process

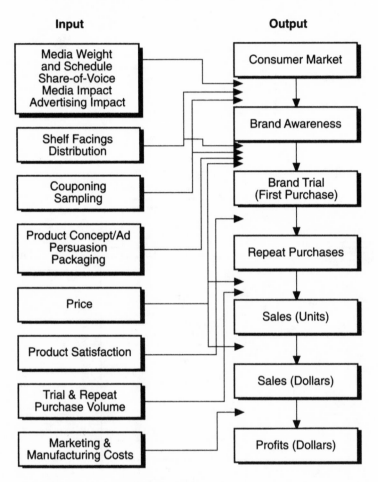

sumer response components include trial probability, repurchase probability, usage rate, and preliminary estimates of the new product's purchase cycle.

The company's marketing management provides the product category data and marketing plans as we discussed in the last chapter. These are necessary to establish the general framework for doing the forecast and the competitive environment that will exist during the launch or re-staging.

Exhibit 5–2

Model Structure Through the First Trial State

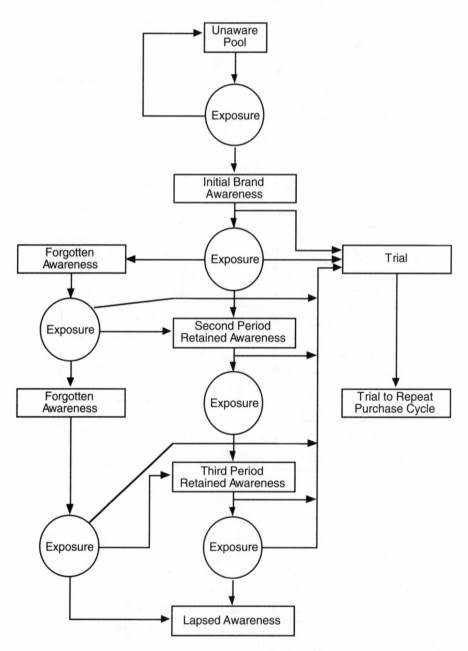

The LITMUS system characterizes the new product model by a Markov process with trial and purchase probabilities that change over time. Exhibit 5–2 shows the model's basic structure through the first trial state. The model allows a company to begin with some initial awareness, initial trial, and even initial repeaters (at levels set by the user). The rectangles and circles show general state categories that the company can achieve over the product introduction period. They denote points in the process at which the consumer's behavior is subject to chance effects that can alter the consumer's awareness of the product.

Model Development and the Purchase Cycle

As with other new product models, notably NEWS (BBDO 1971) and TRACKER (Blattberg and Golanty 1978), Clancy and Blackburn originally built LITMUS around a time period that corresponded to the product's normal purchase cycle. Researchers had observed that the product's purchase cycle works quite well for packaged goods that people purchase frequently, when, for example, the consumer buys the item once a month or more often.

However, such a purchase cycle does not work well for the infrequently purchased new product, when, for example, the consumer buys the product only once or twice a year.

To illustrate, consider a real-life situation: a new solid room air freshener whose real-world performance was wildly overstated by a simulated test market for reasons we will explain. Category data suggested that the expected purchase cycle would be every four months. The company built its marketing plan on a monthly basis although consumers would purchase the product on average only three times a year. The marketing plan provided, as customary, month-by-month gross rating points by media type, couponing, sampling, distribution figures, and all other marketing information.

There are two obvious "solutions" to this conflict between purchase cycle and marketing plan. Each solution leads to a different and incorrect conclusion concerning the plan's performance. The first solution is to treat input and output data as if there are only three periods during the year. This was the original NEWS model formulation. Consider this the every-four-months approach. In this construction, the company adds media and promotional figures into three periods of four months each while it averages distribution figures for each of the periods. Taking this approach, however, overstates performance. Awareness, trial, and sales forecasts far exceeded actual real-world achievement.

This first approach generates a "hyper-forecast" for two reasons. First, the same level of gross rating points, *ceteris paribus*, produces different awareness levels depending on the exposure period's duration. One thousand GRPs, for example, yield considerably less awareness when spread over four months rather than over four weeks. Yet the model was not able to recognize this difference. Because the model overestimated awareness, it overestimated trial as a function of awareness.

Second, the short time—three four-month periods during the launch year—did not permit the decay function for repeat purchasers to play a role in determining sales. In other words, there was not enough time for consumers who tried the product to drop away from it. The model assumed that everyone who tried the product would continue to buy it, which never happens.

The second solution is a two-year approach: base the model on six periods, or, in this case, two years. Increasing the number of periods permitted the company to observe the anticipated decay in repeat purchases. Moreover, the company adjusted the awareness forgetting coefficient upward to compensate for the longer-than-usual time periods between "bursts" of gross rating points. In other words, since the period between advertising bursts was longer than usual, the advertiser expected more consumers than usual to forget about the product between the advertising exposures.

The result was that the model showed awareness down considerably by the end of the six periods. The model still overestimated trial—in contrast to awareness—because it never declined. Sales decelerated rapidly because the model increased the proportion of consumers who did not repeat their purchases. The total repeat forecast was less than half the original plan's forecast. The sales estimates generated by these two solutions were very different, and they could not be reconciled with the need for a one-year forecast of a product that has an annual purchase cycle of three. It was clear the model required a new approach.

In working with marketing managers who used the system, Clancy and Blackburn encountered a number of these infrequently purchased new product applications. These were situations in which the managers needed both the marketing plan inputs and awareness and sales projection outputs on a month-by-month basis. Thus, Clancy and Blackburn found a basic inconsistency between the input and output time period definitions and the model's internal time clock.

Clancy and Blackburn considered another alternative to solve this problem (which was not used in the room air freshener case). In this approach, they applied monthly time periods in the model while reducing the trial and repeat probabilities. In the LITMUS experience, this solution has also proven unsatisfactory because there is no consistent way to compensate for the lower trial and repeat rates that result.

Ultimately, a solution was found by making the time interval units equal to the time period defined by the marketing plan. In other words, if the marketing input is weekly, the model provides for transitions from one awareness and purchase state to another on a weekly basis. The model then defines the purchase cycle as the number of time periods between purchases, which can, of course, be virtually anything.

To accommodate a purchase cycle that may be several months long, the system superimposes the purchase process onto the model's time increments (Exhibit 5–3). For example, if the time

Exhibit 5–3

**Opportunities to Try and Repeat
as a Function of the Purchase Cycle**

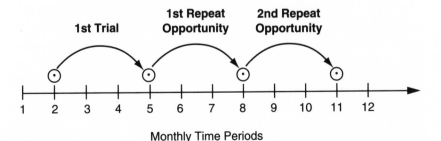

Monthly Time Periods

between purchases is three periods, a consumer who makes a transition from awareness-to-trial in Period Two will not make another transition until Period Five, when she has consumed the product and may make her first repeat purchase. If she does so, and becomes a regular purchaser, subsequent repeat opportunities would occur in Periods Eight, Eleven, Fourteen, and so on.

Although this change in the model complicates the Markov chain representation, it provides the flexibility necessary to predict accurately what will happen when a company introduces a product that consumers buy infrequently as well as one they buy frequently.

Awareness Probabilities

Over the years, researchers have found that the more determinants of awareness they include in the forecast, the smaller the error range in the awareness estimates (Exhibit 5–4). Therefore, the system employs four basic factors to forecast awareness: (1) advertising, (2) couponing, (3) sampling, and (4) distribution.

We discuss the inputs for these factors in Chapter 6, but it is important to note that in each purchase period, prospects who do not know of the product (the members of the unaware pool) have the potential to become aware of the new product through advertising, couponing, sampling, distribution, or some combination of all four. As a result, a certain fraction of these prospects moves into an awareness state—awareness prior to trial. They know the product exists.

We assume exposure to the product through advertising or through couponing or sampling or distribution to be independent effects. We define the following probabilities:

$P_A(t)$ = unconditional probability of awareness due to advertising in time period t;

$P_C(t)$ = unconditional probability of awareness due to couponing in time period t;

$P_S(t)$ = unconditional probability of awareness due to sampling in time period t;

$P_D(t)$ = unconditional probability of awareness due to distribution in time period t.

Exhibit 5–4

To Hit the Bullseye Requires a Complex Model

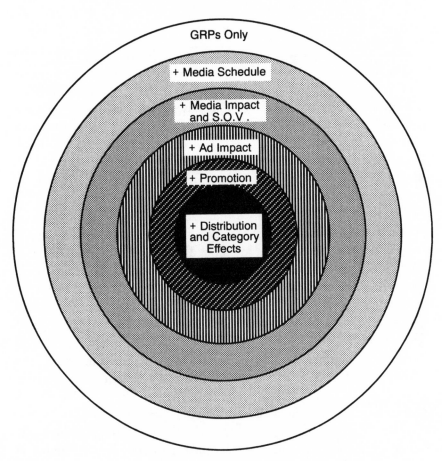

GRPs Only

+ Media Schedule

+ Media Impact and S.O.V.

+ Ad Impact

+ Promotion

+ Distribution and Category Effects

Modeling Advertising Awareness

In early versions of LITMUS, the model used a simple exponential relationship between advertising gross rating points and brand awareness patterned after the function used in the NEWS system (News 1971):

$$P_A(t) = 1 - e^{\alpha GRP(t)}$$

We define the components of the awareness function as:

$P_A(t)$ = probability of advertising generated in period t;
$GRP(t)$ = gross rating points, period t;
α = a parameter to be estimated.

Case histories show this simple model's shortcomings. A leading manufacturer of plastic trash bags employed the system to forecast a new bag's performance, one supported by a $15 million advertising effort. The marketer allocated advertising dollars to daytime television (approximately 40 percent), prime time television (35 percent), and print (25 percent). Following the forecast, the marketing manager wanted to know the proper mix of dollars by media and requested a sensitivity analysis, one that would show the effects of gross rating points, by media, on sales and profits.

A major tobacco company's manager made the same request at about the same time. The company's advertising budget was much larger, $50 million, and the media choice was unusual, and included outdoor, news magazines, shelter magazines, and newspapers. In both cases the clients wanted to know what effect different spending levels in different media would have on consumer brand awareness and, ultimately, on product sales.

As a result of these and other requests, we used the system to generate a number of simulations. We examined the impact of adding variables that account for the media schedule, the media impact, the share of voice, and the advertising impact. We found that adding the media schedule—versus using gross rating points only—reduces the forecasting error by 29 percent (Exhibit 5–4). When we included the media schedule, media impact, and share of voice, we reduced the error by 55 percent. And when we included the media schedule, media impact, share of voice, and advertising impact in the forecast, we reduced the forecasting error from 28 percent to 9 percent—a 68 percent improvement.

Because including the media schedule, media impact, share of voice, and advertising impact significantly improved the system's awareness forecasting power, we revised the advertising awareness submodel to include them. The relationship the system uses to forecast advertising awareness is:

$$P_A = 1 - \exp[\alpha\Sigma_i(\beta_i\gamma_i GRP_i(t))]$$

We define this function's components as:

$GRP_i(t)$ = gross rating points in media type i, period t;

α = a parameter to be estimated;

β_i = attention-getting power of media type i, the norm = 1;

γ_i = w_i (attention-getting power of advertising) + $(1 - w_i)$ (sov) where $0 \leq w_i \leq 1$;

sov (share of voice) = test brand advertising spending in dollars relative to total advertising spending in the category.

This change increased forecast accuracy, and it allowed marketing management to test the media mix's effectiveness. The trash bag manufacturer, for example, learned that the dollars the company spent on daytime television were more effective than the dollars it spent elsewhere. The cigarette company discovered that outdoor advertising outlays did little to advance brand awareness or, consequently, sales.

Modeling Couponing and Sampling Awareness

Since many new product launches involve extensive promotions that include coupons and samples, systems that have inadequate models of these elements of the process are seriously handicapped. With heavy promotional activity, a danger exists that the model will inflate the predicted aggregate awareness. This can have the counter-intuitive effect of underestimating the predicted trial rate in subsequent periods. To see how promotional activity can distort the process, consider the following.

A decade ago, a major health and beauty aids marketer used the system to forecast and diagnose a new toothpaste's sales. Although the system indicated initially that the launch would be successful, the marketing manager asked us to test eighteen different marketing plans. Many of these employed heavy promotional activity—sampling and couponing. Other plans employed low promotional levels. Moreover, the client requested a sensitivity analysis of the projected effects of each marketing input on sales. Since the sensitivity analyses were easier to produce than the eighteen forecasts, we provided the sensitivity analyses first.

These analyses and simulations revealed discrepancies. The sensitivity analysis of some marketing plans, for example, showed that sales were very responsive to gross rating point changes. The plans simulation results suggested precisely the opposite: on average, plans with high advertising levels failed to produce sales significantly higher than plans with lower advertising levels.

These discrepancies, of course, did not please the marketing manager, who called for an immediate "autopsy" of model failure. We traced the problem to the promotion-to-awareness function built into the original LITMUS model and into several other simulated test marketing models, including NEWS. These models treated coupon and sample recipients as consumers who are "Brand Aware." Given "normal" promotional activity levels, the deleterious effects of such treatment are minor. Given massive promotional activity, however, especially promotion that is "front loaded" as was the case for the new toothpaste, the effects can be calamitous. As more and more consumers become aware of the product due to promotion, the proportion remaining to become aware due to the advertising becomes smaller and smaller. Promotional awareness stops only at 100 percent or, in the case of original LITMUS and NEWS, a maximum figure, which, as set by the model's designers, was less than 100 percent.

In the real world, of course, not every prospect who receives a sample or a coupon becomes "Brand Aware." A company mails many samples prospects never receive; many prospects ignore or discard the samples they do receive; and some prospects notice the sample but do not use it for whatever reason. This is even more true for coupons. When the original LITMUS assumed that everyone who receives a sample or a coupon is aware of the product, it and other models exaggerated awareness and mistakenly reduced the pool of unaware consumers. As a consequence, the model erroneously reduced new awareness and trial in future periods, which attenuates the likely sales forecast and, simultaneously, the model's predictive accuracy. In this case, we learned that instances occur when advertising is more efficient than promotion. When advertising is more efficient and the marketer applies strong promotional pressure early, models that assume every coupon and sample recipient is aware of the product will suppress advertising's "true" effects.

To deal with this situation in the LITMUS system, we added a stage to the promotion process that provides a closer approximation to reality. First, the model calculates a sample's reach by time period and inputs it to obtain the fraction of the market the company has scheduled to receive the sample. Second, the model estimates the probability of sample awareness given a sample receipt and uses this figure to compute the awareness fraction. The model computes a trial estimate from the sample awareness-to-trial probability. Adding this stage to the calculations improved the consumer awareness estimates and ultimately sales and market share forecasts. We formulated a similar process to deal with coupon promotions.

During the late 1980s, promotion budgets became a larger and larger portion of marketing budgets. As corporations spent more and more on promotion, they used multiple coupon events throughout the year and during the same period. Although the system improvement corrected for the hyped awareness, it did not account for the interaction effects of different coupon events. In many cases, multiple free-standing inserts, run-of-paper ads, cross ruffs, and samples will yield a reach of over 200 percent.

Since such a reach is not possible, we modified the system again to account for the interactions. First, we put the reach for each coupon event into the system separately and matched it with the appropriate couponing awareness-to-trial-figure. Second, we put a maximum coupon reach constraint into the model. The model accordingly adjusts the reach of each event in each time period. These improvements have enhanced the system's capability to handle heavy promotions with multiple events and to provide keener diagnostic capabilities at any promotional activity level.

Modeling Distribution Awareness

A major durable goods marketer used the system to diagnose sales for a new product. Although initial indications were positive, the marketing manager believed that the awareness forecast was lower than forecasts observed for similar new product introductions and spending plans. After we compared awareness levels achieved by other plans and reviewed all other marketing parameters, we realized that awareness generated through distribution was an important factor missing from the awareness equation for a product in this category. In this category, shelf presence is an important factor in generating awareness.

The system generated accurate forecasts without distribution awareness for low-involvement products with high advertising expenditures such as packaged goods. In product categories that have traditionally lower advertising levels and higher involvement, however, distribution awareness becomes more important. The system therefore evolved once again to include awareness due to distribution. The probability of awareness due to distribution is a linear function of the all-commodities-volume (ACV) distribution during each time period. The parameters of the equation vary based on the level of involvement of buyers in the category.

Sixteen Awareness States

In Month One there are sixteen awareness states resulting from the possible combinations of advertising, couponing, sampling,

Exhibit 5–5

Sixteen Awareness "States" in Month 1

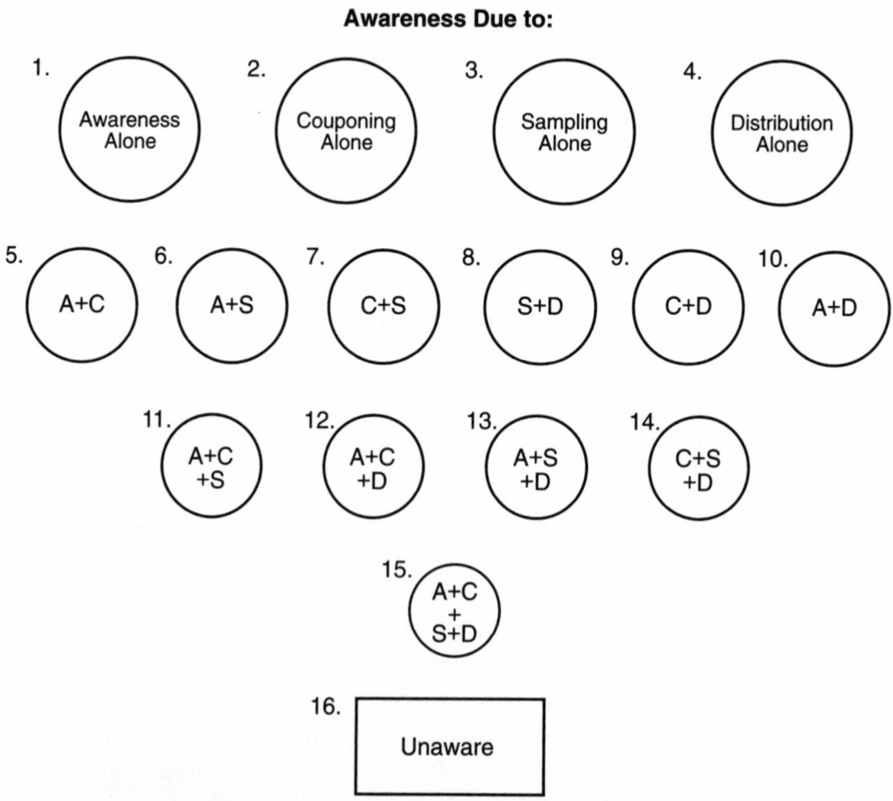

Awareness Due to:

1. Awareness Alone
2. Couponing Alone
3. Sampling Alone
4. Distribution Alone

5. A+C
6. A+S
7. C+S
8. S+D
9. C+D
10. A+D

11. A+C +S
12. A+C +D
13. A+S +D
14. C+S +D

15. A+C + S+D

16. Unaware

and distribution. These include advertising alone, advertising plus couponing, advertising plus sampling, and so forth (Exhibit 5–5). By Month Two, the number of possible awareness states has increased to 256. By Month Three, the number of possible awareness states has increased to 4,096 (16 x 16 x 16), which the LITMUS system considers (Exhibit 5–6).

The system determines the probability that a consumer is in a particular awareness category in Month One from the unconditional probabilities of awareness due to advertising, $P_A(t)$; couponing, $P_C(t)$; sampling, $P_S(t)$; and distribution, $P_D(t)$. Using these unconditional probabilities and assuming independence, the probability of advertising awareness only is:

$$P_1(t) = P_A(t) - P_5(t) - P_6(t) - P_{10}(t) - P_{11}(t) - P_{12}(t) - P_{13}(t) - P_{15}(t)$$

Exhibit 5–6

Escalating Number of Awareness "States" by Month 2

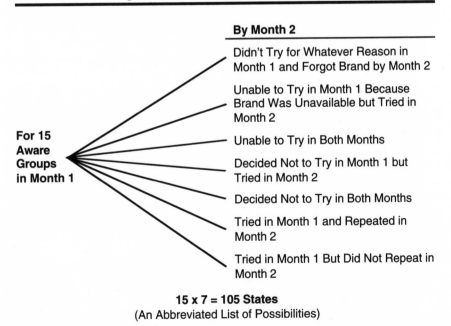

By Month 2

Didn't Try for Whatever Reason in Month 1 and Forgot Brand by Month 2

Unable to Try in Month 1 Because Brand Was Unavailable but Tried in Month 2

Unable to Try in Both Months

Decided Not to Try in Month 1 but Tried in Month 2

Decided Not to Try in Both Months

Tried in Month 1 and Repeated in Month 2

Tried in Month 1 But Did Not Repeat in Month 2

For 15 Aware Groups in Month 1

15 x 7 = 105 States
(An Abbreviated List of Possibilities)

The probability of couponing awareness only is:

$$P_2(t) = P_C(t) - P_5(t) - P_7(t) - P_9(t) - P_{11}(t) - P_{12}(t) - P_{14}(t) - P_{15}(t)$$

The probability of sampling awareness only is:

$$P_3(t) = P_S(t) - P_6(t) - P_7(t) - P_8(t) - P_{11}(t) - P_{13}(t) - P_{14}(t) - P_{15}(t)$$

The probability of distribution awareness only is:

$$P_4(t) = P_D(t) - P_8(t) - P_9(t) - P_{10}(t) - P_{12}(t) - P_{13}(t) - P_{14}(t) - P_{15}(t)$$

The joint probability of couponing and advertising awareness is:

$$P_5(t) = P_C(t) * P_A(t) * (1 - P_{12}(t)) * (1 - P_{11}(t))$$

The joint probability of sampling and advertising awareness is:

$$P_6(t) = P_S(t) * P_A(t) * (1 - P_{11}(t)) * (1 - P_{13}(t))$$

The joing probability of couponing and sampling awareness is:

$$P_7(t) = P_C(t) * P_S(t) * (1 - P_{14}(t)) * (1 - P_{11}(t))$$

The joint probability of sampling and distribution awareness is:

$$P_8(t) = P_S(t) * P_D(t) * (1 - P_{14}(t)) * (1 - P_{13}(t))$$

The joint probability of couponing and distribution awareness is:

$$P_9(t) = P_C(t) * P_D(t) * (1 - P_{14}(t)) * (1 - P_{12}(t))$$

The joint probability of advertising and distribution awareness is:

$$P_{10}(t) = P_A(t) * P_D(t) * (1 - P_{13}(t)) * (1 - P_{12}(t))$$

The joint probability of advertising, couponing, and sampling awareness is:

$$P_{11}(t) = P_A(t) * P_C(t) * P_S(t) * (1 - P_D(t)).$$

The joint probability of advertising, couponing, and distribution awareness is:

$$P_{12}(t) = P_A(t) * P_C(t) * P_D(t) * (1 - P_S(t)).$$

The joint probability of advertising, sampling, and distribution awareness is:

$$P_{13}(t) = P_A(t) * P_S(t) * P_D(t) * (1 - P_C(t)).$$

The joint probability of couponing, sampling, and distribution awareness is:

$$P_{14}(t) = P_C(t) * P_S(t) * P_D(t) * (1 - P_A(t)).$$

The joint probability of advertising, couponing, sampling, and distribution awareness is:

$$P_{15}(t) = P_A(t) * P_C(t) * P_S(t) * P_D(t).$$

In addition to the awareness probabilities defined, the probability of not being exposed in the current period is $P_{16}(t)$. The probability of forgotten awareness is $P_{17}(t)$.

New Awareness

For each of the fifteen states in which the prospect is aware (in $P_{16}(t)$ the prospect is unaware; in $P_{17}(t)$ the prospect is no longer aware), the fraction of people who are newly aware in the current purchase period, $A_i(1)$, where $i = 1. \ldots , 15$, is the product of the unaware fraction in time period t, μ, and the probability of new awareness in category i, $P_i(t)$:

$$A_i(1) = P_i(t) * \mu(t)$$

To update the unaware fraction at the beginning of the next purchase period, we use the following:

$$\mu(t + 1) = \mu(t)(1 - \sum_{i=1}^{15} P_i(t)).$$

That is, we reduce the pool of consumers who are unaware of the product by the fraction of those who become aware of it during period t.

Awareness-to-Trial Probabilities

Once the product achieves consumer awareness, the system assumes a person has as many as three time periods to try the product, that is, to move from an awareness state to a new-trier state. The probability of purchase diminishes over this time interval, but the probability also depends on the number and type of exposures. For example, a consumer may see the advertising in Period One, experience no exposure in Period Two, and clip a coupon and see an in-store promotion in Period Three. The model then bases the trial probability in Period Three on the consumer's entire exposure history.

The probability of trial in time period t, therefore, depends on the consumer's awareness states in the three most recent time periods, t, t-1, and t-2. We describe the trial probabilities for prospects newly aware first, followed by the two-period aware consumers, and finally consumers who first achieved awareness in period t-2, the third period. The current system, incidentally, employs a much larger number of states of nature to capture the richness and complexity of the awareness-to-trial process than the original LITMUS, and especially its precursors, NEWS and TRACKER.

Trial Probability of New People Aware of the Product

Newly aware consumers have a trial probability τ_i, where i denotes the consumer's particular awareness state:

τ_1 = awareness-to-trial due to advertising, or probability of trial given awareness due to advertising alone;

τ_2 = awareness-to-trial due to couponing, or probability of trial given couponing awareness alone;

τ_3 = awareness-to-trial due to sampling, or probability of trial given sampling awareness alone;

τ_4 = awareness-to-trial due to distribution, or the probability of trial given distribution awareness alone.

The probability of trial given advertising and couponing awareness is:

$$\tau_5 = \tau_1 + \tau_2 - (\tau_1 * \tau_2).$$

The probability of trial given advertising and sampling awareness is:

$$\tau_6 = \tau_1 + \tau_3 - (\tau_1 * \tau_3).$$

The probability of trial given sampling and couponing awareness is:

$$\tau_7 = \tau_2 + \tau_3 - (\tau_2 * \tau_3).$$

The probability of trial given distribution and sampling awareness is:

$$\tau_8 = \tau_3 + \tau_4 - (\tau_3 * \tau_4).$$

The probability of trial given distribution and couponing awareness is:

$$\tau_9 = \tau_2 + \tau_4 - (\tau_2 * \tau_4).$$

The probability of trial given distribution and advertising awareness is:

$$\tau_{10} = \tau_1 + \tau_4 - (\tau_1 * \tau_4).$$

The probability of trial given advertising, couponing, and sampling awareness is:

$$\tau_{11} = \tau_1 + \tau_2 + \tau_3 - (\tau_1 * \tau_2) - (\tau_1 * \tau_3) - (\tau_2 * \tau_3) + (\tau_1 * \tau_2 * \tau_3).$$

The probability of trial given advertising, couponing, and distribution awareness is:

$$\tau_{12} = \tau_1 + \tau_2 + \tau_4 - (\tau_1 * \tau_2) - (\tau_1 * \tau_4) - (\tau_2 * \tau_4) + (\tau_1 * \tau_2 * \tau_4).$$

The probability of trial given advertising, distribution, and sampling awareness is:

$$\tau_{13} = \tau_1 + \tau_3 + \tau_4 - (\tau_1 * \tau_3) - (\tau_1 * \tau_4) - (\tau_3 * \tau_4) + (\tau_1 * \tau_3 * \tau_4).$$

The probability of trial given distribution, couponing, and sampling awareness is:

$$\tau_{14} = \tau_2 + \tau_3 + \tau_4 - (\tau_2 * \tau_3) - (\tau_2 * \tau_4) - (\tau_3 * \tau_4) + (\tau_2 * \tau_3 * \tau_4).$$

The probability of trial given advertising, couponing, sampling, and distribution awareness is:

$$\tau_{15} = \tau_1 + \tau_2 + \tau_3 + \tau_4 - (\tau_1 * \tau_2) - (\tau_1 * \tau_3) - (\tau_1 * \tau_4) - (\tau_2 * \tau_3) - (\tau_2 * \tau_4) - (\tau_3 * \tau_4) + (\tau_1 * \tau_2 * \tau_3) + (\tau_1 * \tau_2 * \tau_4) + (\tau_1 * \tau_3 * \tau_4) + (\tau_2 * \tau_3 * \tau_4) + (\tau_1 * \tau_2 * \tau_3 * \tau_4)$$

We base these estimates of trial probability on an assumption that the joint effects of different awareness forms act independently. For example, in the expression for τ_6, if the prospect is aware of the product because of the advertising and having received a sample, then the model assumes trial to occur as a result of one of these two effects. Let event A denote trial due to advertising awareness and event S denote trial due to sample awareness; then

$$\tau_6 = P(A \cup S) = P(A) + P(S) - P(A \cap S)$$
$$= \tau_1 + \tau_3 - (\tau_1 * \tau_3)$$

under the independence assumption. We derive the other trial expressions similarly.

Essentially, the model assumes no interaction between the different forms of awareness and, as such, satisfies the following inequalities:

$$\max(\tau_1, \tau_3) \leq \tau_6 \leq \tau_1 + \tau_3.$$

Although some might hypothesize a positive interaction exceeding that suggested by τ_6, no empirical evidence supports this hypothesis. Experience with the LITMUS simulated test marketing model and with consumer test marketing suggests that the interactive effect is negligible.

Multiple-Period People Aware of the Product

Two additional factors complicate computing trial probabilities for prospects who have maintained awareness for two purchase periods. Since these prospects have failed to try the product during one purchase period, their probability of trial should be less than those of newly aware prospects. In addition, the marketer has exposed these prospects to new advertising or a promotion in the current period and this will alter the degree of their awareness and, as a result, trial probability. To account for this latter factor, the system denotes the awareness state by two components (i,j) where

$i =$ one of the sixteen possible awareness states in time period t, including unaware, and
$j =$ awareness state in time period t-1.

For example, (1, 6) is the initial awareness due to advertising (State 1) in period t, and initial awareness due to advertising and sampling (State 6) in period t-1.

State 16 indicates no new awareness in the current time period. So (16, 1) indicates a consumer who was initially aware of the product due solely to advertising and then, since there was no new exposure, simply retained the awareness in period t.

Since State 17 indicates forgotten awareness, (2, 17) denotes a consumer who became aware in period t-1, forgot the product, and then had renewed awareness achieved due to couponing in period t.

The model expresses trial probability as $(\tau_{ij})^2$ for consumers who are aware for two periods. The model squares the probability to show the failure-to-purchase effect during period t-1, the period of initial awareness:

$$\tau_{ij} = \tau_i + \tau_j - (\tau_i * \tau_j),$$

where $\tau_1, \ldots \tau_{15}$ are defined for prospects who are newly aware of the product, and thus τ_{ij} depends on the mix of exposures over the previous two time periods. Also, $\tau_{16} = \tau_{17} = 0$.

Three-period people who are aware of the product first achieved awareness in period t-2 and have failed to try the product in the two time periods prior to t. Developing the consumer states analogously to the two-period people who are aware of the product, the model denotes this state by a triplet (i,j,k), where

i = awareness state in time period t,
j = awareness state in time period t-1,
k = awareness state in time period t-2;
   $i, j, k = 1, \ldots 17.$

The trial probability is given by $(\tau_{i,j,k})^3$ for consumers who are aware for three periods and

$$\tau_{i,j,k} = \tau_i + \tau_j + \tau_k - (\tau_i * \tau_j) - (\tau_i * \tau_k) - (\tau_j * \tau_k) + (\tau_i * \tau_j * \tau_k).$$

As before, $\tau_1, \ldots, \tau_{15}$ are the awareness-to-trial probabilities for new people who are aware of the product and $\tau_{16} = \tau_{17} = 0$.

Updating Awareness and New Trier Fractions

Consumers who first achieve awareness in period t, $A_i(1)$, where i = 1, \ldots, 15, can be in one of the three states in period t+1:

1. new trier,
2. retained awareness, but did not try in preceding period, or
3. forgotten awareness.

In calculating the fraction of new people who try the product, the effect of imperfect distribution in period t is to diminish the probability of trial by a factor, $D(t)$, which denotes the probability that the product is available to a prospective purchaser. The trial fraction from new people who are aware of the product in period t is:

$$T_1(t) = \sum_{i=1}^{16} A_i(1) * \tau_i * D(t).$$

The last expression, $(A_i(1) * (1 - \tau_i D(t)))$, is the fraction of the newly aware prospects who did not try the product in period t. Of the prospects who do not buy the product (the non-triers), a fraction will retain awareness and the remainder will not. The retention coefficient, $r_c(i)$, denotes the probability that a consumer in awareness state i will retain awareness in the succeeding purchase period. The fraction of consumers in two-period awareness state (j,i) in period $t+1$ is given by

$$A_{ji}(2) = P_j(t + 1) * r_c(i) * A_i(1) * (1 - \tau_i * D(t)),$$
$$i = 1, \ldots 15;$$
$$j = 1, \ldots 16.$$

A prospect who fails to retain awareness of the product can still become a trier, given that renewed exposure regenerates awareness within two periods of initial exposure. Otherwise, the model assumes that the prospect will not try the product. In the event of regenerated awareness, the probability of trial will, of course, be lower than that for a prospect who is newly aware of the product.

The fraction of consumers who fail to retain awareness is

$$\sum_{i=1}^{15} (1 - r_c(i) * A_i(1) * (1 - \tau_i D(t))$$

These consumers can achieve new awareness states in period $t+1$:

$$A_{j17}(2) = P_j(t + 1)[\sum_{i=1}^{15} (1 - r_c(i) * A_i(1) * (1 - \tau_i D(t))],$$

where $j = 1, \ldots 16$.

We use an analogous process to update two-period awareness in period t. The trial fraction $T_2(t)$ is given by

$$T_2(t) = \sum_{j=1}^{17} \sum_{i=1}^{17} A_{ji}(2) * \tau_{ji}^2 * D(t)$$

Awareness in t+1:

$$A_{kji}(3) = P_k(t + 1) * r_c(j,i) * A_{ji}(2) * (1 - \tau_{ji}^2 D(t)),$$

where i = 1, . . . 17; j = 1, . . . 16; k = 1, . . . 16.

We may express the new awareness created from the pool of consumers who had failed to retain earlier awareness by:

$$A_{k1717}(3) = P_k(t + 1) \sum_{j=1}^{15} \sum_{i=1}^{15} [(1 - r_c(j,i) * A_{ji}(2) * (1 - \tau_{ji}^2 D(t))]$$

Consumers who have been aware of the product for the past three periods either become people who try the product during the period or have a negligible probability of trial thereafter. This group of consumers, called lapsed people who are aware of the product, remains in this state for the study's duration. The trial fraction, $T_3(t)$, is:

$$T_3(t) = \sum_{k=1}^{17} \sum_{j=1}^{17} \sum_{i=1}^{17} A_{kji}(3) * \tau_{kji}^3 * D(t).$$

We compute the lapsed awareness fraction, $L(t)$, as follows:

$$L(t) = \sum_{k=1}^{17} \sum_{j=1}^{17} \sum_{i=1}^{17} A_{kji}(3) * [1 - \tau_{kji}^3 * D(t)].$$

The Trial-to-Repeat Purchase Process

The fraction of consumers who are new people who try the product in period t is

$$NT(t) = T_1(t) + T_2(t) + T_3(t).$$

Once a consumer has tried the product, in each succeeding purchase period there is an opportunity to make a repeat purchase. The probability of a repeat purchase increases with the number of prior purchases and decreases whenever a consumer fails to purchase during a period.

Exhibit 5–7

Markov Model of the Repeat Purchase Process

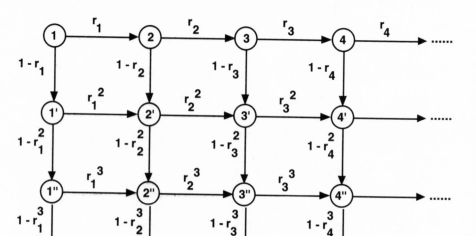

Exhibit 5–7 shows the repeat purchase process schematically. The nodes represent repeat purchase process states and the arrows denote the probability of moving from one state to another between purchase cycles. Primes indicate the number of purchase periods in which a consumer has failed to make a purchase since trying the product. For example,

1 = a new trier, one who first tried the product in the preceding time period;

2 = a consumer who made a second purchase in the preceding purchase cycle;

1′ = a new trier who failed to purchase last period;

1″ = a new trier who has failed to purchase in the preceding two periods;

2′ = a consumer who has made two purchases, but has failed to purchase in one purchase cycle;

$r_1 =$ the trial-to-repeat purchase probability; and
$r_2 =$ the loyalty factor where $r_2 \geq r_1$.

For $k = 1, \ldots$, the kth repeat purchase probability is
$$r_k = r_{max} - [((r_{max} - r_2)^{k-1})/((r_{max} - r_1)^{k-2})].$$

Therefore, $r_1 \leq r_2 \leq r_k \leq r_{max}$. The repeat purchase probabilities increase and approach maximum awareness, r_{max}, asymptotically, that is, continually increasing until it reaches the limit.

The consumer who fails to repurchase during a period is less probable to repurchase in the next time period than the consumer who does repurchase. The first failure reduces the probability of repeat purchase from r_1 to $(r_1)^2$ and the second missed purchase reduces it by another factor of r_1. After three purchase periods without a repurchase, a consumer's repurchase probability drops to zero; these consumers move into the lapsed purchaser state.

Calculating Unit Sales

We symbolize the volume of an initial purchase in a given package size as VF. We index the product category's most common package size at 1.0. If the average package size is sixteen ounces, a sixteen-ounce purchase VF equals 1.0; an eight-ounce package in this category would have a VF equal to 0.5. Therefore, the standardized fraction of units purchased by people who try the product in a period is NT(t) * VF, where NT(t) denotes the fraction of people who try the product in period t.

Similarly, repeat purchasers may buy the product in the same or a different size. VS indicates this repeat purchase's size or volume. Thus, the standardized fraction of units purchased by a repeat purchaser in a period is R(t)*VS. The total fraction of buyers in the period is NT(t)+R(t), and the total fraction of units sold, the market share in units, or U, gives:

$$U = NT(t) * VF + R(t) * VS.$$

Here we assume that the new product's purchases essentially do not affect the total market's size in units. Exhibit 5–8 shows a simplified summary of the process used to generate sales and share.

Exhibit 5–8

Simplified Overview of a Sophisticated STM Model

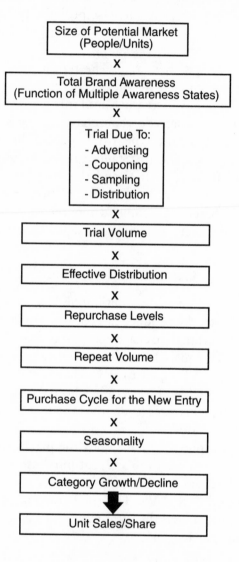

Size of Potential Market
(People/Units)

X

Total Brand Awareness
(Function of Multiple Awareness States)

X

Trial Due To:
- Advertising
- Couponing
- Sampling
- Distribution

X

Trial Volume

X

Effective Distribution

X

Repurchase Levels

X

Repeat Volume

X

Purchase Cycle for the New Entry

X

Seasonality

X

Category Growth/Decline

Unit Sales/Share

Some Applications of Awareness, Penetration, and Share Forecasts

Marketing managers use the Year One awareness, penetration, share, and volume forecasts in their decisions whether to continue in the development and launch of the new or re-staged product. Management uses the month-by-month forecasts to aid in inventory planning. Moreover, they use the month-by-month forecasts diagnostically to decide how to schedule marketing plan expenditures.

Awareness Forecast

The awareness forecast is the key to the volumetric forecast. The company must make prospects aware of a new product before they will buy it. After they become aware of the product, consumers will buy if they have decided they want it and if they can find it.

Marketing management can use the awareness forecast from simulated test market research to evaluate a marketing plan's effectiveness. Marketing managers who test a number of marketing plans usually compare the awareness forecasts generated by the different plans. They often use the awareness forecast diagnostically by comparing it with other marketing factors such as seasonality and distribution.

Exhibit 5–9 is an example of the month-by-month forecasts the system generated. The Exhibit 5–9 forecast reveals that awareness peaks in Month Three and continues to fall thereafter. If this forecast is for a product with high seasonality, and Month Three is the month every year with the greatest sales, then the marketing plan may be appropriate. If the product's seasonal sales are relatively flat, however, or if it is a seasonal product but the peak month falls later during the launch year, management should examine a marketing schedule that is more consistent with the product's seasonal performance.

It is also useful to compare the awareness build with the all-commodity-volume distribution build, which is the percentage of the category's total volume reflected in stores that carry the new brand. In other words, if the stores that initially carry the new product account for only 5 percent of total category volume, the new product could not obtain more than a 5 percent total share of market even if it replaced all other brands. If a product attains peak awareness early in the launch year, but the distribution build is slow, the product may lose those people who would try the product because it is not available on the shelf when they are aware of it.

Exhibit 5–9

Example of a Monthly STM Forecast

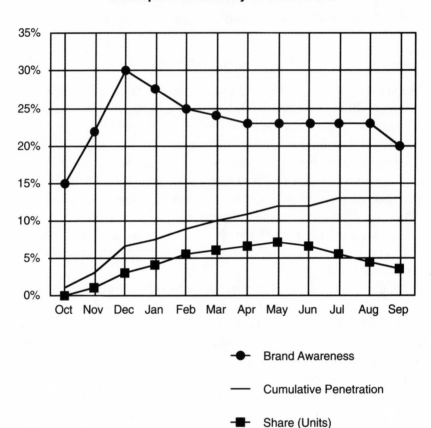

Penetration Forecast

The month-by-month penetration forecast generates a cumulative penetration rate and a net (incremental) penetration rate based on the sample represented by the study. The cumulative penetration rate is the projected cumulative percentage of potential purchasers who have bought the product in each month. The net penetration rate represents the projected incremental percentage of potential purchasers who have bought the product in each month.

If the sample used to generate the forecast illustrated in Exhibit 5–9 is representative (all households are potential purchasers), the

14 percent year-end penetration indicates a prediction that 14 percent of all households will buy this product at least once during the introductory year. If the sample is a user-based sample that represents, say, 75 percent of total households (for example, if a potential purchaser must own a microwave oven to use the product, oven ownership limits the market), then the figure indicates that 14 percent of this smaller market will buy the product, or a 10.5 percent penetration among total households.

The marketing manager who analyzes the month-by-month penetration forecast can diagnose the link between awareness creation and the generation of people who try the product. The Exhibit 5–9 forecast indicates that the product's net penetration increases with awareness during the first three months. After Month Three, however, awareness falls and net penetration declines with it, except in Month Eight in which both awareness and net penetration increase.

By Month Four, the product has achieved 55 percent of its Year One penetration and 20 percent of its sales. Such a rapid build in penetration combined with a subsequent decline in net penetration and awareness levels may signal the marketing manager to test marketing plans with different media and promotion flights and schedules. Since the awareness and penetration build is rapid in the first three months, followed by a decline, testing plans with less activity in the beginning (are less front-loaded) may yield an increase in projected sales and penetration.

Volume and Share Forecasts

The system generates its volume forecast in the measurement units most useful for the client: packages, standard packages, or cases. The number of units sold each month reflects both trial and repeat units.

The forecast the system generates for a line of items is the total line volume. The model further provides the distribution of items within the line based on consumer preferences at the trial and repeat stages. The model derives the monthly share figure by dividing the sales volume projected for the product by the total category sales each month.

The share and volume forecasts interest marketing managers because they most often base the decision to continue development toward launch on a volume or share goal. The test product's profitability is a function of the market share it obtains.

The monthly sales build is key in achieving distribution. If the product does not move off the shelf as quickly as retailers anticipate for that product category, they may not restock and the product thereby loses distribution. Marketing managers are familiar with the requirements of their category, and they compare the annual and monthly forecast figures with these retailer requirements for movement.

Together with the awareness and penetration forecasts, marketers use the month-by-month share and volume forecasts to adjust the marketing plan. For example, monthly total sales and share peak in Month Ten and decline thereafter (Exhibit 5–9). It appears that the repeat generated by the consumers who try the product early is not enough to maintain the market share.

The share drop may result from the reduction in the awareness and net penetration or the product's performance or both. If the estimated repeat sales figure is strong and other post-usage diagnostics are positive, it is likely that the monthly share decline is a result of the drop in awareness and net penetration.

This example shows that the forecasts generated by simulated test market research are helpful not only in making the decision whether to launch a new product or not, but in evaluating the effectiveness of the marketing plan used to launch it.

Management Implications

The purpose of this very technical chapter was to describe the evolving marriage between mathematical modeling, one of the two paths to simulated test marketing we discussed in Chapter 3, and laboratory experimentation.

In it we described how one contemporary model combines the mathematical elegance and construct validity of BBDO's NEWS model and its parent, DEMON, with the pioneering laboratory simulation work of Florence Skelly and her colleagues at the Yankelovich organization in the late 1960s. Once joined, the two approaches grew significantly in sophistication and complexity to become an "ideal type" for simulated test marketing in the mid-1990s.

The chapter showed the key parameters underlying a sophisticated STM system and how each can be modeled today. The chapter also described in detail procedures for modeling awareness, the effects of promotion and sampling, and the purchase cycle, four critical but missing ingredients in some commercially available simulated test marketing systems.

Finally, we presented examples of the types of forecast a smart system can generate and how this forecasting capability can be employed by marketing mangers to build better plans.

6

Marketing Plan and Market Response Inputs for a Simulated Test Marketing Model

The last chapter described in detail a sophisticated test marketing model used to generate a volume forecast. Three types of information fuel any model including the LITMUS model described in Chapter 5: product category data, marketing plans, and research-based estimates of market response. Marketing management provides the category data and the marketing plan for the introductory year of the new product's life. The simulated test market consulting firm designs and implements the study to measure market response.

Product category data describes the size and nature of the category in which the new brand will compete. The new product's marketing plans indicate in detail how the company proposes to generate awareness and trial for the new product. Advertising, promotion, distribution, and other issues need to be covered. And finally, by market response we mean consumer reaction to the new product at the trial and repurchase stage; simulated test marketing research provides this information. This chapter describes the inputs that consultants use to do a simulated test market and make a valid forecast.

The Category Data Required

The marketing manager sets the stage for the simulation with secondary data pertaining to the new product's category. The category data that provides the background for a volume forecast includes:

1. The potential market's size in millions of buyers.
2. The market's size in dollar sales and in millions of units or cases.
3. The average standardized price of the product sold at retail. (e.g., price per ounce).
4. The market's seasonality.
5. The category's growth or decline trend.
6. Total advertising spending in the product category.
7. The brands in the category that account for 80 percent or more of category sales and the market shares for each.
8. The nature and magnitude of promotional activity.
9. Insights into likely competitive response to a new product.
10. New developments taking place in the category (e.g., other introductions, packaging changes, pricing changes, and the like).

A critical part of the forecast is the response of buyers to the new product. This requires research undertaken among a specific group of consumers. The sample may represent all households or it may be a subset, such as buyers in a given product category. When the sample is a subset of total households, the potential market's size is that group's incidence in the general population. If, for example, only microwave oven owners are potential consumers, microwave ownership defines the market's limit. If the sample includes only microwave oven owners, and if 20 percent say they would buy the product, the total sales potential can be no more than 20 percent of some fraction of all households, that fraction being the incidence of microwave ownership.

The marketing manager provides this incidence figure. Since a model generates its volume forecast based on the size of the buyer group, the incidence figure directly affects the volume forecast. It is the forecast's cornerstone. If the marketing manager gives an incorrect incidence figure, the resulting volume forecast may be wrong by the same percentage. In one recent case, which resulted in a lawsuit, a marketer overstated the incidence of product category users by 100 percent. The research firm, basing its forecast on that estimate, overstated the sales potential for the new product. The unhappy marketer, facing the prospect of another major new product failure, turned on the research firm and blamed the model for the problem when the model, in fact, produced an accurate forecast when adjusted by the— later to be discovered—correct category incidence figures.

Take as an example a company launching a new frozen meat product. The marketing manager assumes that the potential buyers will be consumers who have bought a frozen meat product during the past year. To determine the market response from such a sample, the forecast depends on the number of frozen meat product buyers. The marketing manager has several data sources, but suppose that one indicates that fifty million American households purchased frozen meat during the past year. Another source indicates that forty million households purchased frozen meat during the past year.

Assume that the research forecasts a 10 percent Year One penetration of American households. Such a forecast means that, when the model uses a base of fifty million households, five million will try the product during the launch year. If the model uses a base of forty million households, however, the forecast will be for four million purchasers of the new frozen meat product during Year One. The potential buyer base reduction produces a 20 percent reduction in the number of purchasers forecast during the launch year. Category data must be accurate, therefore, for the eventual forecast to be accurate. Nowhere is "mindless input/vapid output" more true.

To generate market share forecasts, the model uses the market's size in millions of cases provided by the marketing manager. In addition, the model uses the category buyer data to generate an average category purchase rate. When the model uses seasonality factors, it increases or decreases the buying population's size on a month-by-month basis to account for this real-world change.

As in the case with seasonality, a smart system adjusts for total category growth or decline. The model adjusts the buying population's size to account for an increasing or decreasing number of people in the target universe who are likely to try the product.

The system needs additional category data when it is to generate a forecast for a re-staged (re-positioned, re-launched) product versus a new item. The LITMUS system and other sophisticated simulated test marketing models such as DESIGNOR recognize the brand's history by incorporating the brand's "going-in" sales share as well as the brand's annual growth or "erosion rate." A smart model obtains the latter information by a trend or regression analysis of brand sales over the past five years. The re-staged brand must strive to surpass whatever sales level is projected by this analysis.

The Marketing Plan's Role in the System

The marketing plan is a key component in successfully launching a new or re-staged product. The marketing plan's elements describe how the product will obtain awareness and distribution and encourage trial. The simulated test marketing research model therefore simulates the marketing environment through a month-by-month procedure that details advertising, couponing, sampling, and distribution (shelf presence).

Advertising

To generate an awareness forecast a sophisticated model incorporates at least ten advertising plan components, including:

1. Total Gross Rating Points (GRPs) or target group rating points.
2. GRPs allocated by month (i.e., the media schedule).
3. GRPs allocated by media type (e.g., prime time network television, newspapers, drive time radio, outdoor).
4. Share of voice.
5. Attention-getting power of the advertising.
6. Attention-getting power of media by medium type.
7. Initial brand awareness.
8. Maximum likely brand awareness.
9. The probability that a buyer will remember the brand in the absence of subsequent advertising exposures.
10. The proportion of the target market aware of the new brand before the advertising breaks.

Simulated test marketing researchers can conduct surveys among media experts to obtain a consensus estimate of the attention-getting power of various media vehicles ($ß_i$ in Chapter 5). The results of such work show that attention-getting power varies by medium. For example, surveys indicate that a commercial shown on prime time network television has more attention-getting power than the same commercial shown on daytime network television. The gross rating points for vehicles (GRP_i in Chapter 5) that differ in attention-getting power are put into the model separately so the model can account for the differences. Exhibit 6–1 reproduces the advertising information form.

Exhibit 6–1

Advertising Input Form

Month 1: Start of Advertising

Allocation by Month:

A.	1 GRPs	2 GRPs	3 GRPs	4 GRPs	5 GRPs	6 GRPs	7 GRPs	8 GRPs	9 GRPs	10 GRPs	11 GRPs	12 GRPs	Total GRPs
B. Network TV:													
i. Prime	___	___	___	___	___	___	___	___	___	___	___	___	___
ii. Day	___	___	___	___	___	___	___	___	___	___	___	___	___
iii. Early Fringe	___	___	___	___	___	___	___	___	___	___	___	___	___
iv. Late Fringe	___	___	___	___	___	___	___	___	___	___	___	___	___
v. Early Morning	___	___	___	___	___	___	___	___	___	___	___	___	___
C. Spot TV*													
i. Prime	___	___	___	___	___	___	___	___	___	___	___	___	___
ii. Day	___	___	___	___	___	___	___	___	___	___	___	___	___
iii. Early Fringe	___	___	___	___	___	___	___	___	___	___	___	___	___
iv. Late Fringe	___	___	___	___	___	___	___	___	___	___	___	___	___
v. Early Morning	___	___	___	___	___	___	___	___	___	___	___	___	___
D. Cable TV:													
i. Prime	___	___	___	___	___	___	___	___	___	___	___	___	___
ii. Day	___	___	___	___	___	___	___	___	___	___	___	___	___
iii. Early Fringe	___	___	___	___	___	___	___	___	___	___	___	___	___
iv. Late Fringe	___	___	___	___	___	___	___	___	___	___	___	___	___
v. Early Morning	___	___	___	___	___	___	___	___	___	___	___	___	___
E. Magazines	___	___	___	___	___	___	___	___	___	___	___	___	___
F. Newspaper	___	___	___	___	___	___	___	___	___	___	___	___	___
G. Radio	___	___	___	___	___	___	___	___	___	___	___	___	___
H. Total GRPs	___	___	___	___	___	___	___	___	___	___	___	___	___

* Spot GRPs should be equivalent to national - not merely GRPs in designated spot markets, but expressed on a national basis.

Most new product introductions employ a combination of television and print advertising. Companies also frequently schedule radio and outdoor advertising. Television advertising includes network, spot, and cable vehicles. Daypart further differentiates these television vehicles; these include early morning, day, early fringe, prime, and late fringe. Before a company even considers program content, the combination of vehicle and daypart offers fifteen media placement options for television alone.

Studies have shown that commercial length (thirty seconds versus five, ten, fifteen, or sixty seconds) also affects its attention-getting power. When a company employs different-length commercials, a smart model differentiates each spot's gross rating points by length and by each daypart to forecast consumer awareness.

Likewise, print vehicles differ in their attention-getting power. Typically, magazine advertisements show greater attention-getting power than do newspaper ads. Moreover, full-page four-color ads typically attract more consumer attention than do half-page color ads in the same publication. A good model considers such differences and adjusts accordingly.

LITMUS also applies a share-of-voice factor (sov in Chapter 5) to account for the advertising spending variation between categories. For example, in the plastic wrap category, a $20 million advertising expenditure during Year One will yield a relatively large share of voice because the companies in the category spend relatively little on advertising and therefore the category generates less clutter.

In the laundry detergent category, however, a $20 million Year One expenditure obtains a relatively small share of voice since laundry detergent advertisers spend so much. The plastic wrap $20 million will generate greater awareness than the same $20 million in the more highly advertised laundry detergent category because it is easier to be heard in the category with lower spending. A good model includes a share-of-voice parameter to account for such differences, the way the same expenditure levels generate differential awareness in different product categories.

The advertising's attention-getting power by media type (a function of γ in Chapter 5) reflects the recall score generated through copy testing using ARS, ASI, Burke, McCullum-Spielman, or similar methodology. The model expects an advertisement that scored below average on a copy test to generate less awareness than one which scores at the norm. Conversely, a smart model expects an advertisement that scores well above the norm to generate higher awareness levels. Simulated test marketing systems apply the copy test recall score to the norm in the category to reflect the advertisement's awareness-generating power.

Over time, the better simulated test marketing systems have developed historical data bases to estimate initial brand awareness, maximum likely brand awareness, and the probability that a prospect will remember the brand in the absence of additional advertising exposure.

Couponing

Chapter 5 discussed why it is important to enter the planned coupon event for each month. Often, a company will plan multiple free-standing inserts and run-of-press ads for the new or re-staged product during the launch year. The researchers enter each event separately to allow a model to account for interaction effects between events. Exhibit 6–2 illustrates the coupon plan information form.

The marketing manager supplies the reach and anticipated redemption rate for each event for every month, and LITMUS researchers input these figures to the model. Reach is the percentage

Exhibit 6–2

Couponing Input Form

	1	2	3	4	5	6	7	8	9	10	11	12
Coupon Events:	(Indicate if Purchase is Required Before Coupon Can be Redeemed - i.e., On-pack Coupon, Bounce Back)											
i. Type	—	—	—	—	—	—	—	—	—	—	—	—
ii. Value	—	—	—	—	—	—	—	—	—	—	—	—
iii. Projected Reach (Millions)	—	—	—	—	—	—	—	—	—	—	—	—
iv. % Reach	—	—	—	—	—	—	—	—	—	—	—	—
v. Projected Redemption Rate (Net of Misredemptions)	—	—	—	—	—	—	—	—	—	—	—	—

of potential prospects who will receive a given coupon. For example, if the marketing manager expects that 10 million of the 30 million dog food purchasers will receive a new dog food coupon, the reach is 33 percent. The marketing manager also furnishes the anticipated redemption rate (adjusted for misredemptions). The redemption rate is the percentage of coupons consumers actually redeemed for the product. If consumers redeem 250 thousand of the 10 million coupons distributed for the new dog food, the redemption rate is 2.5 percent.

Sampling

Direct mail sampling, on-door sampling, trial size samples with coupons, free in-store sampling, and taste sampling are marketing tools that companies often use in new product introductions. When they do employ such events, the researchers add the trial due to sampling and the corresponding reach to the system for each month of the launch year. Exhibit 6–3 illustrates the sampling plan information form.

The sample reach is the percentage of the potential buyers who receive the sample. If 300,000 of the 30 million dog food purchasers receive a new dog biscuit sample through the mail, the reach is 1 percent. The sample conversion rate is the awareness-to-trial *due to sampling*. When sampling is a small part of the marketing plan, the marketing manager estimates this figure based on his

Exhibit 6–3

Sampling Input Form

	1	2	3	4	5	6	7	8	9	10	11	12
Sampling:	(Indicate if Sample is Purchased or Given Away)											
i. Type	—	—	—	—	—	—	—	—	—	—	—	—
ii. Number	—	—	—	—	—	—	—	—	—	—	—	—
iii. Projected Reach (Millions)	—	—	—	—	—	—	—	—	—	—	—	—
iv. Anticipated Rate of Conversion	—	—	—	—	—	—	—	—	—	—	—	—

or her experience in the category. As we discussed in Chapter 4, all of the major STMs employ marketing research methods to estimate the conversion rate when sampling accounts for a large portion of the marketing budget.

Distribution

The trial information generated by laboratory research reflects "ideal" marketing conditions: 100 percent awareness and 100 percent distribution. As we will discuss later, one role of distribution for any new product is to generate awareness of the brand. Even in the absence of advertising, couponing, and sampling, some consumers will become aware of the new entry due to distribution alone. The higher the distribution level, the greater the distribution-induced awareness level.

The most important function of month-by-month distribution in a test market simulation model, however, is to temper ideal trial in order to create a "real world" shopping environment. All models employ ACV distribution information to reflect the probability that a consumer will be able to find the new or re-staged product if he or she wants it. In most new product simulation models, distribution has a powerful, almost linear impact on the volume forecast. The wider and deeper the distribution, the greater the sales. If marketing management gives the model an ACV distribution figure 10 percent higher than what the product actually achieves during each month of the launch year, the model's forecast will be approximately 10 percent too high.

Take, as an example, a new salad dressing. Historical data indicated that the corporation had achieved an 80 percent average Year One ACV distribution for the last three new salad dressings it had introduced. Since the corporation planned to spend more on advertising and promotion for the *new* dressing than it had budgeted for the last three introductions, the marketing manager believed that she would achieve even higher levels of distribution. The number she decided to go with was an 85 percent average Year One distribution. This became the basis for a first year forecast and the new brand was launched.

At the end of Year One, however, faced with lower sales than expected, an autopsy revealed that the dressing achieved only a 77 percent average ACV distribution, 10 percent less than the level anticipated. This meant that, contrary to the forecast's assumption, 10 percent fewer potential consumers who would try the salad dressing were able to find it in stores. Since all other factors remained constant, the product's actual sales at the end of Year One were 10 percent lower than the sales forecast.

Distribution Search

One of Blackburn and Clancy's discoveries in developing and implementing the LITMUS model was that the typically assumed linear relationship between distribution and sales is a myth in many cases. Under some conditions, a low level of distribution can "work" as well as a very high level of distribution for a different product. The key to understanding the true effect of distribution is to know how involved consumers are in the product category, the new product in particular, and how many stores they will shop to find it. The more stores they will shop in, the less important the absolute level of distribution will be.

LITMUS addresses this issue with a distribution search feature for those product categories in which consumers shop in more than one store to buy the item. Typically, such categories contain many high involvement consumers who will shop in multiple stores until they find what they want. Consider a new cosmetic guaranteed to remove wrinkles overnight, an R&D breakthrough supported by $100 million in advertising and minimum distribution. This product would be a success even if it meant that people had to shop ten stores to find it.

The laboratory research study includes measures of the level of involvement of consumers in the product category and self-reports of the number of stores they would shop in to find the new product. This enables researchers to estimate the percentage of consumers who will shop in only one, in two, three, or even more stores to find the new product. Model input. as a consequence, calls for "effective distribution" as opposed to simple ACV distribution. To illustrate: if every consumer would shop in two stores to find the new entry and if the stores were independent of each other, then a 50 percent ACV distribution level would represent an effective distribution of 75 percent (50% plus 50% minus 50% times 50%).

Marketing Program Costs

Marketing program cost data that marketing management supplies for profitability analysis includes:

1. Average cost per thousand GRPs by medium.
2. Average cost per coupon by promotion type.
3. Average cost per sample by promotion type.
4. The cost of distribution.

The analysis can also include manufacturing costs, research, and other costs.

Depending on the marketing manager's needs, the profitability analysis can range from the gross margin level to an operating profit level. Not only will this information improve the value of a volume forecast, but it can also be used in a sensitivity analysis to determine the relative efficiency of each of the marketing mix components.

Simulated Market Response

Market response measures consumer reaction to the new or re-staged product after advertising, couponing, sampling (or all three) makes them aware of it. The three market response components essential to forecasting a new product's sales are the item's (1) trial, (2) repeat, and (3) purchase cycle. The researchers measure these components of market response through survey research and electronically in test markets, regional introductions, and national introductions. The simulated test market research's interview process generates consumer response to a new or re-staged product in a simulated test market. We will first describe the interview process that collects the market response information and then describe how a system such as LITMUS forecasts each of the measures.

Simulated test marketing systems use different methodologies depending on the test product's development stage. One methodology is employed when the marketer is limited to a product concept description and test product for the consumers to use at home. The BASES method represents this approach.

An alternative methodology is employed when the marketer has advertising for the new product and competitors and sufficient quantity of the packaged new product to display and "sell" it in the simulated store. We call the first approach a Concept Test Market (CTM) while the second is a Simulated Test Market (STM).

The interview process for a LITMUS Concept Test Market and a Simulated Test Market occurs in three stages. For the details of process flow see Exhibits 6–4 and 6–5. For both methodologies, the

Exhibit 6–4

Concept Test Market Data Collection Process

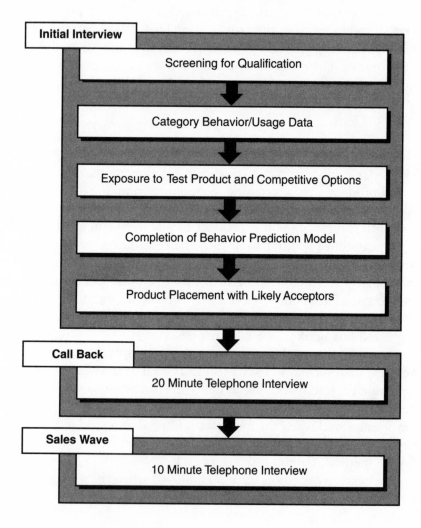

Exhibit 6–5

Simulated Test Market Data Collection Process

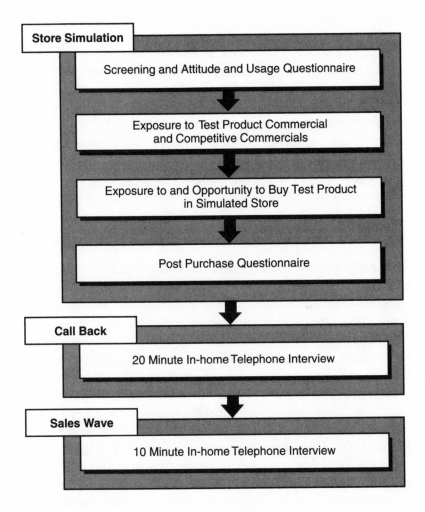

research often begins by telephone screening hundreds of prospective respondents using random digit dialing in several geographically dispersed locations. The locations are selected so that they reflect national product category and brand usage patterns.

The sample size used in a simulated test market study varies by research methodology and the number of cells to be tested. A true simulation where people have the opportunity to buy the test product requires a larger sample size than a concept-based simulation. Also, if a marketer is testing only one price point or advertising approach, that's one cell, but if the marketer is testing multiple price points or different advertising approaches, more cells need to be added.

Single cell concept test markets usually have a 300 respondent sample size. Multiple cell concept test markets require 200 to 300 respondents per cell. Single cell simulated test markets often have sample sizes ranging from 400 to 600 consumers. Multiple cell simulated test markets generally have sample sizes of 250 to 300 respondents per cell. When a model employs a factorial design, however, to test different prices, advertising, levels of competitive response, or other issues, the sample size is smaller for each cell since the cells can be combined.

The Concept Test Market Purchase Simulation

The initial interview for a concept test market study is a one-on-one interview. The researchers either pre-recruit using a telephone screen or recruit qualified consumers using mall intercepts for the initial interview. The sample definition determines consumer qualifications. For example, if a client is testing a cat food, the sample definition will probably include cat ownership and a three-month cat food purchase history. Furthermore, consumers must satisfy the appropriate demographic profile and security, which means they do not work for a competitive company or for a market research company.

The initial one-on-one interview is approximately twenty-five minutes long. This interview screens the consumers again to confirm their qualifications and it obtains background information concerning consumer attitudes and practices in the category.

For example, the interviewers establish for each respondent the number of units the consumer has bought in the test product's category in the past "x" weeks or months (depending on the category's purchase cycle) and each brand's share. This background information identifies heavy, medium, and light purchasers. It also identifies current brand buying among purchasers and non-purchasers of the new (test) product.

In the Yankelovich system, respondents also rate a short list of category attributes and benefits in terms of desirability for the Critical Attributes Analysis™ that we discuss in Chapter 7. After the interviewer collects this background information, he or she exposes the respondent to the concept in a competitive context. Yankelovich researchers always show the concept with a price and accompany it with a competitive array of the key entrants priced appropriately for the market. We like this approach because it mirrors the real world.

Following exposure to the test concept, respondents evaluate it on one or another purchase probability scale. For a LITMUS forecast, Yankelovich Partners employs a behavior prediction model. Exhibit 6–6 shows one of the model's components.

The researchers use a concept board and a competitive board as stimuli. The test product is positioned near the middle of the competitive board, with category leaders all priced according to the market. The presence of a competitive set is, in our view, key to simulating the real-world purchasing environment, although in the very successful BASES approach no competitive stimuli are shown at all.

After respondents have been exposed to the concept, they rate the critical attributes of the test product and its key competitors. Further, the interviewer establishes an anticipated purchase cycle for the test product and collects attitudinal, behavioral, and demographic information that can be used to profile people who are likely to try the product and those who probably will not try it.

Exhibit 6–6

One Example of a Cognitive Component of the Behavior Prediction Model

How helpful do you think this new (test product) would be in terms of solving any problems you may currently experience with regard to the brand you currently use?

1	2	3	4	5	6	7
Not At All Helpful At Solving Problems	Not Very Helpful	Only Slightly Helpful	Might or Might Not Be Helpful	Somewhat Helpful	Very Helpful	Extremely Helpful At Solving Problems

The researchers then place the product with respondents who express a purchase likelihood of 70 percent or more. If the test product is a line of items that vary by size, flavor, or form, the researchers give a respondent the one or two varieties that she says she would buy first. When a client wants to build the user base for diagnostic purposes, the researchers give additional products to people who rejected the concept.

After a reasonable time period (an interval that matches the product usage pattern), researchers contact respondents who have the product to gauge their reaction and likely repeat purchase. Most firms measure repeat purchase with a simple four- or five-point purchase probability scale. To avoid biasing the research, interviewers do not mention the callback interview during the initial meeting.

The Simulated Test Marketing Store Simulation

The initial interview for a simulated test market incorporates a self-administered questionnaire. Interviewers recruit qualified consumers by telephone; groups of twenty to twenty-five meet at a central facility. As in the concept test market, the sample definition describes the consumer qualifications, and the interviewers screen prospective buyers to satisfy the appropriate demographic profile and security requirements (no competitors, ad agency, or research company employees).

When consumers arrive at the central location, they complete a screening questionnaire. Although the interviewers questioned the respondents during the initial telephone call, the researchers administer an additional screen as a check on the respondents' qualifications. To ensure the sample's quality, the field personnel verify qualifications before the interview process continues.

After confirming respondent qualifications, the interviewer administers a background questionnaire. Similar to a concept test market study, this form collects background information concerning the prospect's attitudes and practices in the product category including category purchasing volume, brand purchasing behavior, and attribute desirability.

Following the background questionnaire, the interviewers expose respondents to the test product through an advertisement in a competitive environment, typically a thirty-second commercial, which in the case of a LITMUS study is inserted into a half-hour television program. For product categories that rely heavily on print or radio advertising, the research uses those vehicles. Although most product categories use more than one medium, the simulated test market research generates awareness of the new product (or re-staged brand) by way of the category's primary advertising vehicle.

When the study uses a television commercial, respondents watch a thirty-minute television program, usually a highly rated situation comedy in a theater-like setting. Four normal commercial breaks appear within the program. The third commercial break includes the test ad with "clutter" ads from unrelated categories, reproducing as closely as possible the real-world situation. The three other commercial breaks contain spots for the most heavily advertised competitors and clutter ads. The test commercial may be finished or animatic. If the study must use an animatic spot, at least one of the competitive or clutter ads is also an animatic.

To test products that rely heavily on print advertising, the research takes the portfolio approach. This is a collection of eight to ten print ads, with the test ad three-quarters into the portfolio. The researchers do not require the ads to be "tipped in" to a magazine. Typically, however, the ads are in finished form. When a product category relies heavily on radio for its advertising, respondents listen to a radio program with a commercial break with the test product ad three-quarters into the break.

The interviewers give respondents an additional questionnaire after they see the television or print advertisements or listen to the radio spot. This questionnaire generates diagnostic information concerning advertising recall and communications: What did the test advertising communicate and how persuasive was the message?

After completing this questionnaire, respondents go into the simulated store. What happens next varies somewhat depending upon the simulated test market service. In the case of LITMUS, they are brought into the store in groups of four or five where interviewers give them an order form. To simulate the local market, the competitive brands on the shelf represent 60 percent to 80 percent of category volume. The researchers have priced all test category products appropriately for the local market. The prices on the shelves reflect the products' average, everyday retail prices.

The researchers always position the test brand near the center of the eye-level shelf, which is typically the second from the top of four shelves. The researchers usually allocate test and competitive brands one shelf facing, with dominant market brands receiving two or three facings as a maximum. And they usually stock products three deep within the test category.

To establish ambiance, the researchers include surrounding products not in the test category. Respondents, however, may not buy them. These products consist of those items that typically appear near the test category. For example, if the test category is shampoo, conditioners and styling gels surround it.

To ensure awareness of the test product, the LITMUS interviewer leads respondents to the simulated store's test category section and informs them that they may buy any of the products with their own money. The interviewers further advise them to behave as they would in a real store. Often respondents pick up the merchandise and read the labels. Some respondents smell the products.

The researchers stimulate purchasing in the simulated environment through a discount that applies to all test category products—typically 30 percent. Although the shelf prices are average, everyday retail, the order form lists both the retail price and the discounted price for each test category product. When the respondents complete their shopping, they either answer a post-purchase questionnaire or take part in a focus group discussion.

The traditional ASSESSOR and DESIGNOR laboratory experiments are different from LITMUS in that consumers do not use their own money but rather are given full-price "vouchers" to buy any product they wish in the store. Although there are some other differences between the various methodologies for doing simulated test marketing research, by and large the approaches are far more similar than different.

Many firms, for example, use focus group discussions following the visit to the laboratory store for diagnostic purposes. Though they are not essential to the research, they sometimes produce interesting qualitative insights. Yankelovich conducts two focus groups for each cell in each test city. Nine respondents who represent a mix of key segments make up each: three people who bought the test product, three people who bought a competitive product, and three people who did not buy either.

The respondents who answer the post-purchase questionnaire rate the critical attributes of the test product and key competitors. The researchers collect the brand share of requirements from the respondents with one significant difference: the test brand is included in the brand list. Further, this questionnaire produces an anticipated purchase cycle for the test product. Finally, the study collects demographic information that the researchers can use to profile purchasers and non-purchasers.

After respondents complete their focus group discussion or post-purchase questionnaire, they return home with the products they bought. Interviewers call test product buyers for a post-usage diagnosis. To avoid biasing the results, the interviewers do not inform people that they will be called.

The Callback Interview

All simulated test marketing services recontact consumers who "purchased" in the laboratory store using a similar methodology. Indeed, the methodology is also similar for the callback phase of a concept test market study and a simulated test market study. Category purchase cycle determines the callback timing to ensure that consumers have time to use the product. For example, a new cigarette callback will be three to five days after the initial interview. A new laundry detergent callback will be three to four weeks after the initial interview. On average, consumers will have used at least one-half of the test product when the interviewers call back.

The interviewers attempt callbacks for every person who bought the test product (a simulated test market study) and for every person who received the test product (a concept test market study). The researchers expect an 80 percent re-contact rate. The callback interview is a twenty-minute telephone conversation during which the interviewer obtains repeat purchase, purchase cycle, and diagnostic information about the test product.

During this conversation, the interview also elicits information concerning the amount of the product used, family/household member usage, occasions for use, and open-ended likes/dislikes. After the usage questions, the interviewer records re-purchase intent on a purchase probability scale and anticipated purchase volume. With these figures, the model estimates purchase volume.

For the Yankelovich Critical Attributes Analysis™, respondents rate the same list of category attributes and benefits at the background stage during the initial interview and after the concept exposure stage. The survey thus gathers information about the product's performance versus the consumer's expectations.

At the conclusion of the callback interview, Yankelovich alone offers the product to the respondent at the regular retail price and asks if he or she would be interested in buying it again. If the study design incorporates an extended use phase, the interviewer takes actual orders and the manufacturer delivers product. To avoid biasing research results, the interviewer will not mention an additional (or "sales wave") interview during this initial callback.

The Sales Wave Interview

To differentiate between the initial callback and further interviews, researchers often use the term "sales wave" to identify those additional interviewing events. Similar to the initial callback, interviewers conduct the sales wave interview using the same methodology for a concept test market study and a simulated test market study. The sales wave timing is identical to the callback period; it matches the product purchase cycle. The sales wave is a ten-minute telephone interview with few diagnostic questions. The key data that the sales wave interviews produce are purchase quantity and repeat purchase probability. The interviewer asks the same purchase quantity and repeat purchase questions she asked during the callback interview.

Researchers conduct sales waves to assess long-term loyalty and purchase volume; sales wave interviews are necessary to determine changes in these market response variables over time. Researchers use sales waves to assess potential "wear-out," declining interest in or usage of the product (or both), and to ascertain "wear-in," the consumer's increased commitment to the brand in terms of loyalty or purchase volume. Research has learned that sales waves are required in all tests involving food, breakthrough products, and unique products that may have a different usage pattern from the category at large. Researchers employ multiple sales waves for products that indicate uncertain consumer loyalty and usage over time.

Again, just as at the end of the initial callback, the interviewer offers the product at the regular retail price. If the study incorporates an additional extended use phase, the interviewer takes orders and, again, the manufacturer delivers the product.

Measuring Trial in a Laboratory Simulation

The two methodologies we have just described—the concept test market and the simulated test market—measure buying behavior in a laboratory environment. All firms conducting simulated test marketing research employ proprietary adjustments to convert what people say they will do (in the case of the concept test market) or actually do with their own money or full-face coupons (in the case of a simulated test market) into estimates of real-world trial. The technical name for this form of trial is the "awareness-to-trial conversion." That is, the proportion of people who will buy the product at least once under conditions of 100 percent awareness and 100 percent distribution.

BASES, for example, has weights for their five-point purchase probability scale that, according to company literature, vary by product category and that are used to make the conversion from the self-report into actual behavior. The Yankelovich concept test market approach is more complicated.

Yankelovich employs the Behavior Prediction Model at the concept stage that we briefly discussed in the previous section. The Behavior Prediction Model includes the following dozen measures that cover affective as well as cognitive reactions to the test product:

1. Visceral reaction (first impression): "What is your first impression of the idea for this product?"
2. Uniqueness: "How would you rate this product in terms of its uniqueness—that is, its similarity to or difference from other items on the market?"
3. Superiority: "How does this product compare to other products that currently exist?"
4. Problem solving: "How helpful do you think this product would be in solving any problems you may currently experience with regard to these types of products?"
5. Personal relevance: "Based on what you have just seen and read about this product, what types of people do you think would like this new product?"

6. Use occasions: "Can you think of specific use occasions you might have for this product?"
7. Value for the money: "What do you think of the value of this product in terms of value for the money?"
8. Absolute price: "What is your opinion of the price of this product?"
9. Likes/dislikes: "Which of the following best describes the degree to which you like or dislike anything about this product?"
10. Clarity: "Which of the following describes the degree to which you find anything about this product confusing?"
11. Credibility: "Is there anything about this product that you find hard to believe?"
12. Overall rating: "*Overall* how would you rate this product?"

The researchers measure each factor on a seven-point scale that couples each point with a verbal description (see Exhibit 6–6).

Finally, the researchers ask consumers to rate the concept for purchase probability using an eleven-point scale, created 30 years ago by Dr. Thomas Juster, then of the Department of Commerce. The scale couples word meanings with probability estimates to enhance serious thinking on the respondents' part. Researchers have discovered through extensive experimentation that it predicts real-world behavior more effectively than the alternatives, especially for mixed and high involvement decisions. Exhibit 6–7 illustrates this scale.

Like all self-reported measures of consumer buying, this eleven-point scale overstates the actual purchasing that takes place. Much of this overstatement comes about because the research environment assumes 100 percent "awareness" and "distribution," something a company never realizes in the real world. Not all prospective consumers will be aware of the product and not all of those aware of it are able to buy it.

Even if we take the 100 percent awareness and distribution fallacy into account, however, people are more likely to say they will "buy" than in fact do buy. This is true in all product categories we have investigated. We have closely examined the relationship between people's reports on the eleven-point scale and awareness-to-trial among people who were aware of the product and for whom product was available to be purchased for numerous consumer

Exhibit 6–7

A Validated Purchase Probability Scale

10.	Certain Will Purchase	99 Chances in 100
9.	Almost Certain Will Purchase	90 Chances in 100
8.	Very Probably Will Purchase	80 Chances in 100
7.	Probably Will Purchase	70 Chances in 100
6.	Good Possibility Will Purchase	60 Chances in 100
5.	Fairly Good Possibility Will Purchase	50 Chances in 100
4.	Fair Possibility Will Purchase	40 Chances in 100
3.	Some Possibility Will Purchase	30 Chances in 100
2.	Slight Possibility Will Purchase	20 Chances in 100
1.	Very Slight Possibility Will Purchase	10 Chances in 100
0.	No Chance Will Purchase	0 Chances in 100

packaged goods. We have also looked at this relationship in durable goods and financial service cases, including a hand-held microcomputer; a color television set; a charge card fee increase; long-lasting light bulbs; new car dealer visits; overnight messenger services; a new premium charge card; personal computers for the home market; and a new clock radio.

The higher the level of self-reported behavior probability, the greater the ratio of reported purchases to probability. Yankelovich's experience indicates that usually no more than 80 percent of the people who assert they will buy, do buy. This figure declines monotonically but not linearly as self-reported purchase probability declines, but the ratio is not constant. Yankelovich therefore applies different weights to account for respondent overstatements. Depending on the product category and the situation, virtually none of the people at the low end of the scale—from "Some possibility will purchase" on down—will buy the product or service. Exhibit 6–8 illustrates this relationship between actual and self-reported probability.

Exhibit 6–8

**Relationship Between Self-Reported
and Actual Behavior Probability**

The lower the "Self-Reported" intent, the less we believe it.

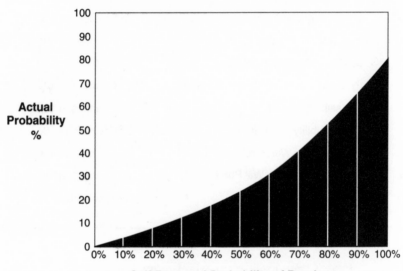

Conventional wisdom says that purchase involvement is a function of the product or service; the more expensive, complex, or unfamiliar, the more time and deliberation the consumer gives the purchase. An automobile, by this view, is a high involvement decision product; toothpaste is low. In fact, purchase involvement is not a function of the product, but of the consumer. Some toothpaste purchasers who score high in compulsive neuroses will spend more time in front of a supermarket display deciding between brands, sizes, and packages than some car buyers do in choosing a new car. We once found that the product that provoked the highest consumer involvement was bathroom wallpaper—not an expensive, complex, or unfamiliar product.

While chairman of the Yankelovich organization, Clancy developed three sets of weights to adjust the scale for low, moderate, and high involvement purchases. Low involvement purchases reflect the greatest overstatement; they are typically priced under $10. Consumers spend the least time considering their purchase. They are low risk, routine, or impulse purchases. Further, the product alternatives offer minimal differences.

Moderate involvement purchases, which show moderate overstatement, are often priced between $10 and $99. The consumer spends a modest amount of time processing information during purchase consideration. Moderate involvement purchases include such things as inexpensive services or durables and over-the-counter drugs.

High involvement purchases, which experience the least overstatement, are usually priced over $99 and/or involve a high level of personal or physical risk (e.g., a permanent hair color). The consumer spends the most time learning about the product category, evaluating the different brand evaluations, and forming his or her attitude about the item during the purchasing process. The consumer sees these products more closely tied to one's identity and to peer group influence than are moderate or low involvement purchases. Greater differences exist among product alternatives. High involvement purchases include more expensive consumer services and durables.

Adjusted scores on the eleven-point purchase probability scale are then combined with the twelve affective and cognitive measures described earlier into a six-factor regression equation that forecasts trial, given awareness and distribution. The components of the model are shown in Exhibit 6–9.

The model adjusts for responses that are inconsistent, such as the respondent who claims a 90 percent purchase probability but indicates that the product is not appropriate, will not be helpful, and will not have many uses.

Combining the eleven-point purchase probability scale with the affective and cognitive dimensions reduces the discrepancies between the prediction and real-world performance. Yankelovich has reported that the percentage forecasting error has declined from 21 percent to an average of 14 percent by using the full behavior prediction battery.

The conversion of laboratory behavior into estimates of real-world trial is a different process than a full simulated test market (as opposed to a concept test market we have just been discussing). The DESIGNOR model, as an illustration, employs an algorithm which

Exhibit 6–9

A Behavior Prediction Battery

Affective Measures	Cognitive Measures	Behavioral Measure
• First Impression	• Price	• 11-Point Purchase Probability Scale
• For People Like Me	• Value	
• For Occasions I Experience	• Clarity	
• Likeability	• Believability	
• Overall Impression	• Uniqueness	
• Helpful at Solving Problems	• Superiority	

[b1(Factor 1) + b2(Factor 2) + b3(Factor 3) ... + b13 (11 Point Scale)] = Forecasted Behavior

marries perceptual/preference information with laboratory "purchase" data (as generated by the "voucher" experiment).

In contrast, at the simulated test marketing stage Yankelovich relies exclusively on the proportion of people who buy the test brand. This percentage—adjusted by norms collected over a twenty-five year period—enables the Yankelovich organization to estimate what people will do in the real world based on what they do in the laboratory setting.

Measuring Trial due to Sampling

If sampling takes a large proportion of the marketing budget, the research tests its impact on trial. The LITMUS system has tested plans that incorporate direct mail, trial size with coupons, free in-store sampling, and taste sampling. Since the system exposes all respondents to advertising or to a concept board, when the research includes sampling the trial factor measured is the awareness-to-trial due to both advertising and sampling.

When the company uses direct mail sampling, it sends samples to a list of potentially qualified consumers. Since the recruitment success rate is approximately one respondent for three contacts, the company must mail samples to at least three times as many prospects as the research requires. The researchers then recruit consumers who have received the samples to take part in the research. To avoid bias, the researchers do not tell these people that the sample they received in the mail is the test product. The percentage of respondents who buy the test product in the simulated store reflects the awareness-to-trial figure that the researchers can attribute to direct mail sampling and advertising.

The researchers have tested trial size samples with "Act Now!" coupons in a simulated store by duplicating the promotion as it would be in the real world with a trial size display. The percentage of consumers who buy in the simulated store denotes the awareness-to-trial figure that the researchers can attribute to advertising and sampling with an Act Now! coupon.

The researchers test free in-store sampling by handing samples to respondents as they enter the simulated store. The percentage who buy in the simulated store signifies the awareness-to-trial figure attributable to advertising and sampling.

The researchers conduct food product taste sampling in both simulated and concept test market methodologies. The researchers offer taste samples in the simulated store (a simulated test market study) or during the initial interview (a concept test market). The percentage of respondents who buy the product in the simulated store indicates the awareness-to-trial figure attributable to advertising and sampling. The researchers use the Behavior Prediction Model to forecast the awareness-to-trial figure attributable to advertising and sampling in a concept test market study.

Measuring Repeat Purchase Probability

Most simulated test marketing services obtain the first repeat purchase probability estimate through the initial callback interview after the respondent has had the opportunity to use the test product. Each system produces a purchase figure that is an "ever" repeat probability. That is, it forecasts the probability that a person who tries the test product will ever buy it again.

The first repeat purchase probability is a function of a four- or a five-point scale question. LITMUS system researchers forecast first repeat purchase probability in a competitive context. Interviewers ask the four-point repeat purchase intent question using the test product's retail price. The interviewer also reminds the respondent of the competitive products' retail prices.

Besides the first repeat purchase probability, the system also provides a Year One repeat figure. The Year One repeat is the percentage of people who try the product and who buy it one or more times during the launch year. This figure is less than or equal to the repeat figure forecast because it depends on the trial build, all commodities volume distribution, and the purchase cycle. The Year One repeat figure will be less than the first repeat purchase probability figure because people who buy the product for the first time during Year One's last purchase cycle will not have the opportunity to buy again during the launch year.

For example, assume the research indicates a food product that has a first repeat purchase probability forecast of 55 percent; it has a purchase cycle of one unit every four months; and it has a slow trial build. Such a combination of first repeat purchase probability, purchase cycle, and trial build may yield a Year One repeat of 20 percent. In this case, only 20 percent of the people who try the product have an opportunity to buy it again during the first year. However, 55 percent of all people who try it will eventually repurchase the product—assuming the manufacturer maintains distribution.

The Purchase Cycle

The product's purchase cycle reflects the number of occasions the new or re-staged product's franchise will buy it during the course of, say, the first year. The franchise is that consumer segment that the research anticipates to be the product's loyal consumers. Thus, the researchers estimate the purchase cycle based on the franchise's responses to the callback and sales wave interview questions about the anticipated purchase volume and the anticipated share of requirements.

For product categories with a known distribution of heavy and light purchasers, sophisticated STM systems include the option of using a purchase interval distribution rather than using an average purchase cycle. For example, if the simulated test market research indicates that the franchise for a new food product will buy four units a year on average, the model will use a purchase cycle of one unit every three months. If the marketing manager provides additional research, however, indicating that half of the franchise buys two units a year and half buys six units a year (averaging to four units a year), a system such as LITMUS will use the full distribution of repeat purchases, instead of the average, for forecasting purposes.

Share of Requirements

Most simulated test market systems today evaluate purchase volume of the test product based on its anticipated share of requirements. The interviewer determines the test product's share of requirements in two ways during the callback and sales wave interviews.

First, the survey determines the number of category units the respondent plans to buy in the next "x" weeks or months (depending on the category's purchase cycle) and the number of test brand units the respondent will buy in the next "x" weeks or months (again, depending on the category's purchase cycle). This generates a share of requirements in a non-competitive context.

Second, the survey generates figures that show in a competitive context for each respondent how much each brand—including the test brand—accounts for the consumer's product category requirements. The average of these two share of requirement figures generates the purchase volume figure for the test product.

Management Implications

The purpose of this chapter was to describe the three different types of inputs that drive any simulated test market volume forecast. The first input is intelligence about the product category itself; the second is detailed information on a month-by-month basis about the marketing plans designed to support the new brand; the third is market response to the new entry as measured by the simulated test market laboratory experiment.

Although the specific requirements of different STM consulting services vary to some degree, the similarities between them are striking. Marketers familiar with one service generally find it easy to understand another. Researchers who have worked for one STM consulting firm have generally found it easy to make the transition to another.

Marketers and researchers need to remember an important caveat in simulated test marketing research every time they conduct an STM: the three types of input are critical in determining the outcome. Marketers who provide flawed category data or of hastily organized marketing plans or questionable laboratory experiments run a serious risk of a bad forecast. Given the increasing importance placed on an STM forecast by new product marketers, its high visibility, and the amount of money at risk in a new product introduction, the potential problem here is very serious.

Perhaps the most common problem in simulated test marketing study is a marketing plan that promises too much. This is the undoing of many new products as revealed in the autopsies we discuss in Chapter 13. Managers overpromise what they can actually deliver and the automated forecasting routines of an STM model carry out the plans, which may bear little relationship to what is actually deployed in the real world. The result can be a forecast significantly higher than anything the company ever achieves. When this happens, marketing managers sometimes blame the model; they should blame themselves.

7

How Simulated Test Marketing Can Improve a Marketing Plan

Today, many major packaged goods marketers—and all of the sophisticated ones—employ simulated test marketing to forecast the performance of a new product introduction prior to a real-world introduction. With everyone using this new technology, a volume forecasting capability offers no particular competitive advantage to any one firm. As a result, new product failure rates continue to climb. As we discussed in Chapter 1, the failure rate for new packaged goods is currently 91 percent, an increase of about ten points in just a decade. New services, including financial products, television programs, and Hollywood productions, fail about 80 percent of the time, while fast food products experience a death rate of approximately 99 percent.

Typically, marketing managers test too few plans before introducing a new (or re-positioned) product into the real world. As we noted in Chapter 2, most do not even realize how many plans they could test. Simulated test marketing research can go beyond volume forecasting to provide managers with the tools they need to diagnose a new product's targeting, positioning, and pricing—indeed, the entire marketing plan. Simulated test marketing *can actually improve a marketing plan.* This chapter shows how and discusses such issues as line item distribution and cannibalization, issues that a simple volume forecast does not address.

143

How an STM Model Offers Targeting Guidance

When introducing a new product, a line extension, or re-staged product, company executives speculate about who is most likely to try and to continue to buy the product. Identifying the group most likely to try and to continue buying yields the product's target group. The marketing manager can spend the marketing budget more efficiently by scheduling the media and the promotion that reaches the target group. Moreover, the advertising agency can improve the creative concept and copy's effectiveness when it is tailored especially for the target market.

Simulated test market research results can provide answers to targeting questions. The system compares the trial rate by different demographic, user, and geographic groups to determine if differences in trial appeal exist. A profile of buyers and non-buyers further defines the most likely prospects to try the product. Besides generating a profile of the prospects most likely to try the item, the simulated test market research also paints a profile of those consumers who are loyal to the test product or service.

To show how a marketer can use trial rates for targeting, consider the example of a new, moderately priced wine cooler, Cooler-Lite. Exhibit 7–1 shows the strong appeal of this new product among women—a 43.7 percent trial probability—compared to the appeal among men—a 15.2 percent trial probability. Moreover, the concept performs best among younger, downscale consumers, a very different target than the marketer intended. This suggests either that the concept or advertising copy or both need to be "fixed" to better position the new entry or the marketer might re-evaluate the target against for which Cooler-Lite was designed.

A problem with Cooler-Lite was clearly evident when simulated test market research was called upon to show the appeal of the concept among different types of users. This research discovered that the new entry had its greatest appeal among very light users who would buy the product primarily for parties rather than for themselves. This disappointing discovery contributed to the low projected usage level for the new brand and anticipated marketplace failure.

These diagnostics show the marketing manager that a potential exists for additional volume if the company can increase trial appeal among heavier category purchasers. Conversely, the company

Exhibit 7–1

Awareness-to-Trial of Cooler-Lite by Selected Demographic Groups

Total	**29.9%**
Gender	
Female	43.7%
Male	15.2%
Age	
18-34	32.5%
35-44	33.5%
45-54	27.7%
55 or Older	26.9%
Marital Status	
Married	33.1%
Not Married	23.9%
Education	
College Graduate	24.1%
Not College Graduate	32.5%
Total Household Income	
Under $25,000	37.4%
$25,000-$34,999	30.0%
$35,000-$49,999	26.7%
$50,000 or over	26.6%
Presence of Children	
Have Children Under 18	30.8%
No Children Under 18 at Home	28.2%

could position Cooler-Lite as the special party beverage by taking advantage of its higher trial among those consumers who buy it especially for parties. This is a classic marketing problem: the manager must choose between dominating one segment or broadening appeal among several segments. Often, by diluting the impact in each segment, a company's attempt to expand fails on both fronts.

Exhibit 7–2

Awareness-to-Trial of Cooler-Lite by User Group

Total	**29.9%**
Times Per Month Purchase Spirits, Wine or Beer	
Less than One	39.2%
One to Less than Two	27.8%
Two to Less than Two	27.0%
Three to Less than Four	28.0%
Four or More	23.0%
Purchase Spirits	
For Parties Only	35.1%
For Parties and Personal Use	24.4%

Additional market research can help the marketing manager to determine the best alternative.

Trial rates may differ by geographic region as a result of differences in the category development index (CDI) or the brand development indices (BDI). In the Cooler-Lite example, the simulated test market research indicates that trial is significantly higher in the West (Exhibit 7–3).

Exhibit 7–3

Awareness-to-Trial of Cooler-Lite by Geographic Region

Total	**29.9%**
Region	
East	25.7%
Midwest	26.0%
West	38.0%

How an STM Model Profiles the Purchasers and the Franchise

Simulated test marketing research can also provide a profile of the test product's purchasers and the loyal repeaters, often called "the franchise." To illustrate the type of consumer profile data available, here are the purchaser and franchise profiles generated by the simulated test market for a new premium shampoo, Fresh 'n Clean.

Although the company positioned Fresh 'n Clean as appropriate for men and women, the profile of purchasers and non-purchasers indicates that there were significantly more female purchasers and significantly fewer male purchasers. Purchasers of Fresh 'n Clean also tended to be married, professional, and college educated with higher income levels (Exhibit 7–4).

Exhibit 7–4

**Demographic Profile of
Fresh 'n Clean Purchasers vs. Non-Purchasers**

	Purchasers (328) %	Non-Purchasers (769) %
Gender		
Female	72	52
Male	28	48
Marital Status		
% Married	82	62
Occupation of Household Head		
Professional	55	37
Technical/Sales	9	11
Adminstrative/Clerical	16	14
Other White Collar	6	6
Craftsman/Skilled Laborers	5	22
Other Blue Collar	1	2
Education		
College Graduate	43	25

A comparison of brands purchased in the past twelve months by purchasers and non-purchasers indicated that purchasers were more likely to purchase brands A, B, C, D, F and G than non-purchasers (Exhibit 7–5). Since the company was positioning Fresh 'n Clean as a premium product and brands A, B, C, D, F and G were also positioned as premium brands, these results are not surprising.

A profile of the ultimate franchise, the loyal repeaters, provides the marketing manager with additional targeting guidance. To segment the franchise in the simulated test market research, the researchers define the franchise as those who would definitely or would probably repurchase Fresh 'n Clean. Consistent with the purchaser profile, members of the franchise are more likely to be married and college educated (Exhibit 7–6). Examining the brands consumers bought in the past year indicates only one brand that loyal repeaters buy significantly more often than those who are not

Exhibit 7–5

**Brand Profile of
Fresh 'n Clean Purchasers vs. Non-Purchasers**

Bought in Past Year	Purchasers (328) %	Non-Purchasers (769) %
A	83	67
B	77	59
C	44	20
D	34	16
E	29	29
F	33	11
G	29	12
H	15	12
I	8	8

Exhibit 7–6

**Demographic Profile of
Repeat Buyers (i.e., The Franchise)**

	Definitely/Probably (211) %	All Others (60) %
Marital Status		
Married	77	56
Not Married	23	44
Employment		
Full-time	54	47
Part-time	21	27
Not Employed	25	26
Education		
High School	–	3
High School Graduate	14 ⟩ 63	33 ⟩ 78
Some College	49	42
College Graduate	27 ⟩ 37	14 ⟩ 22
Post-Graduate Work	10	8

franchise members. These consumers are more likely to have bought Brand A in the past twelve months (Exhibit 7–7).

Since members of the loyal franchise also buy Brand A, the marketing manager can analyze Brand A's attributes to understand the type of product these people typically buy. Moreover, since Brand A will compete strongly with Fresh 'n Clean, the marketing manager will gather all available marketing information about Brand A in an attempt to obtain a competitive advantage.

How an STM Model Offers Positioning Guidance

The simulated test market research provides targeting guidance by identifying the test product or service's buyers and non-buyers. Many questions and hypotheses remain, however, regarding why consumers

Exhibit 7–7

Profile of Fresh 'n Clean Brands Purchased in Past 12 Months

Bought in Past Year	Definitely/Probably (211) %	All Others (60) %
A	48	27
B	27	28
C	6	7
D	4	4
E	1	3
F	5	14
G	2	3
H	4	3
I	–	2

buy the new product and which product attributes and benefits the marketer should stress. For example, should the marketer assert:

"Newbrand is a sexy, erotically charged product," or:

"Newbrand is convenient to use," or:

"Newbrand smells fresh," or something else entirely?

Further, marketing managers want to know *why* consumers reject the test product or service and what problems the product must overcome to attract those consumers who rejected it. For example:

"Is Newbrand a poor value?"

"Is Newbrand inconvenient to use?"

"Does Newbrand satisfy the consumer's expectations?"

One approach to answering these questions is the Critical Attributes Analysis™ developed by the Yankelovich organization and described in *The Marketing Revolution*.

Critical Attributes Analysis™ examines both attitudinal and behavioral attributes ratings. By combining attitudinal and behavioral measures, the analysis enables the marketing manager to identify those attributes and benefits that most highly motivate a consumer's purchasing decision. It provides insights regarding factors contributing to or inhibiting trial interest.

Critical Attributes Analysis™ requires the following measurement sequence:

1. Category desirability ratings. How desirable consumers rate ten to twenty different product attributes and benefits in terms of self-reported desirability.
2. Exposure to the new or re-staged product or service.
3. Market response to the new brand (trial and repeat).
4. Brand ratings for the new and established products on the same set of attributes and benefits and an overall preference measure, often a ten-point constant sum scale.
5. Motivating power calculations (a combination of self-reported desirability and leverage).
6. Post-purchase brand rating and purchasing analysis.

Before the researchers expose respondents to the test product's advertising and the simulated store, they ask them to evaluate a list of product characteristics in terms of desirability. These characteristics include tangible attributes such as "easy to use" and "relatively inexpensive." In addition, they contain intangible benefits such as "make me feel very sexy," or "I feel I'm doing the most for my skin."

The research employs a five-point scale ranking from "absolutely essential" to "not at all desirable." Here is the specific wording and format for the desirability question:

Listed below are some statements that many people use to describe what they look for in [*a product or service in the test category*]. Please tell us how desirable each one is to you, using the scale below. If no one answer captures your feelings completely, just give us the answer that comes closest. (CIRCLE ONLY ONE FOR EACH STATEMENT)

5 = Absolutely essential
4 = Very desirable
3 = Somewhat desirable
2 = Slightly desirable
1 = Not all desirable

Once the researchers have interviewed respondents to learn their background habits and practices—an interview that includes the desirability question—they expose respondents to an advertisement or a concept, depending on the stage of development. This exposure includes competitive and clutter ads or competitive concepts to simulate the marketplace environment. When a product is available, the researchers show the actual item and competitive products in a simulated store.

Following exposure to the test stimulus, the researchers administer a post-exposure evaluation questionnaire. This portion of the interview contains the brand ratings question. Here the researchers ask respondents to evaluate the test brand and selected competitors according to the same set of attributes and benefits used in the desirability question. The researchers use the answers to this question

Exhibit 7–8

Example of a Leverage Analysis

Respondent: #007
Attribute: **A Wine for Romantic Occasions**

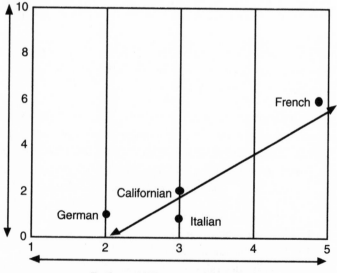

in conjunction with a behavioral intention question to conduct an individual respondent leverage analysis.

Leverage analysis correlates, on an individual respondent basis, future purchase behavior with the degree to which the respondent perceives brands to contain a specific attribute or benefit. In other words, if a person sees a product to have a valuable benefit it is more likely the person will buy the product in the future. The leverage analysis supplements what consumers say they want (that is, "desire") with what appears to drive their purchasing behavior.

For example, in an analysis of different wines, one respondent said that "romance" is only slightly desirable, but leverage analysis revealed a strong positive relationship with a correlation of 0.9 (Exhibit 7–8). While the respondent said romance was unimportant, she rated French wine very high on that attribute, and she bought more French wine than any other type.

Here is the specific wording and format of the brand rating question used in the leverage analysis:

Now here are some statements that may be used to describe [*products or services in the test category*]. Please tell us how you would rate each of the [*product or service brands*] listed on each statement, whether you have used these brands or not, using the scale below. (RECORD ONE RATING FOR EACH BRAND BEFORE CONTINUING TO THE NEXT STATEMENT)

5 = Describes completely
4 = Describes very well
3 = Describes somewhat
2 = Describes slightly
1 = Does not describe at all

The research includes a behavioral intention question relating to the brands the respondent rated previously in the post-purchase portion of the interview, such as:

Now assume that only the following brands are available in stores where you shop,

Brand A (test brand)
Brand B
Brand C
Brand D

Thinking about your next ten purchases of [*products or services in the test category*], how would you allocate those ten purchases among these brands? (THE TOTAL MUST EQUAL TEN. WRITE IN NUMBER ON THE LINE NEXT TO APPROPRIATE TYPE SPECIFIED. IF NONE, ENTER 0. NO RANGES PLEASE.)

Brand A [*Test brand*] _____
Brand B   _____
Brand C   _____
Brand D   _____
Total = 10

We have observed that there is usually a significant difference be-tween the desirability and leverage ratings (Exhibit 7–9). That is, a difference exists between what consumers say they want and what they indeed buy. Yankelovich reconciles these differences with a proprietary submodel that weights the two components—self-re-

Exhibit 7–9

**The Relationship Between
Desirability Ratings and Leverage Coefficients**

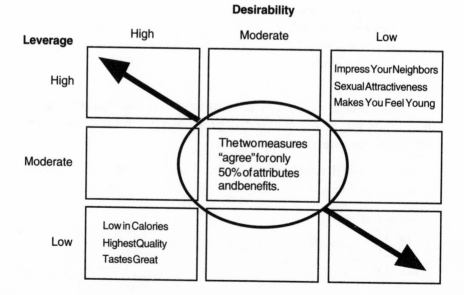

Exhibit 7–10

Two Components of Motivating Power

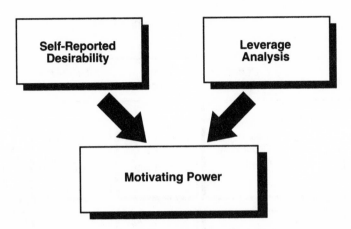

ported desirability and leverage—at the individual respondent level in order to create a new measure labeled "motivating power."

Assume that a study includes twenty attributes and benefits and 600 respondents were interviewed. For every respondent there are twenty A/B ratings and twenty correlation/leverage calculations. In total, that's 20 times 2 times 600 separate computations, or 24,000 individual level calculations that are combined into twenty different motivating-power scores, one for each of the attributes and benefits.

Yankelovich then examines motivating power among the total sample, as well as for purchasers of the test product or service, and for people who did not buy the product. This enables the marketing manager to understand the elements that influence consumer purchasing behavior in a given product category as well as to assess similarities and differences between buyers and non-buyers. Further, the system contrasts the test product's motivating power with its competition's (Exhibit 7–11).

To illustrate the usefulness of the motivating power score, Exhibit 7–12 shows the results among purchasers of a Critical Attributes Analysis™ for a new, environmentally safe disposable garbage bag, EnviroBag. The research found that, for the total sample, the category's highly motivating characteristics were "value," "price,"

Exhibit 7–11

Blueprint for Action

Client versus Competition

Motivating Power		Client Superior	Parity — Both Excel	Parity — Neither Excels	Client Inferior
	High	Immediate Positioning Opportunity: • Enhance	Price of Entry • Maintain	Potential Opportunity for Someone • New Product?	Key Weakness • Fix if Possible
	Low	Potential Positioning Opportunity • Increase Salience?	Over Investment • Cut Costs	No Action	No Action

"strength," "leakproof," "dependable," and "not ripping." The category characteristics low in motivating power were "well-known brand," "drawstring," and "handle can tie."

When we look at the motivating power of these characteristics among people who do not buy EnviroBag, we immediately see an important difference. EnviroBag buyers rate "re-cyclable" as a highly motivating attribute while people who did not buy EnviroBag rate it as having a low motivating power. Further, buyers rate "environmentally safe" and "degradable" as high in motivating power while non-purchasers rate these factors as moderately motivating. It is not surprising that, in this case, buyers and non-buyers of this environmentally positioned product have very different attitudes toward environmental issues as they relate to disposable garbage bags.

Although comparing motivating power by purchasing group is useful in assessing the new product or service's positioning, comparing brand ratings by attributes and benefits explicitly shows the

Exhibit 7–12

Critical Attributes Analysis
EnviroBag versus "Brand B"

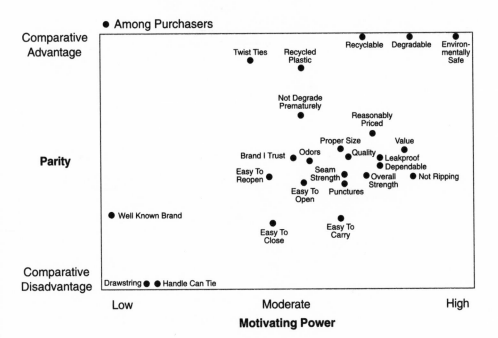

product's strengths and weaknesses in the competitive environment (Exhibit 7–13).

For a new product or service to generate trial, prospects must view it as having a comparative advantage over the competitive products for at least some of the highly motivating characteristics. Those attributes and benefits that consumers consider the product to have a comparative advantage represent an immediate positioning opportunity. The highly motivating characteristics the consumers consider test product to be at parity compared to other brands represent the category's price of entry. Parity, however, is not enough to generate trial in the highly competitive marketplace. A company must combine parity with a comparative advantage for at least some highly motivating characteristics. When consumers believe that a new product is at a comparative advantage for highly motivating factors, the positioning should reflect it.

Exhibit 7–13

Critical Attributes Analysis
EnviroBag versus "Brand B"

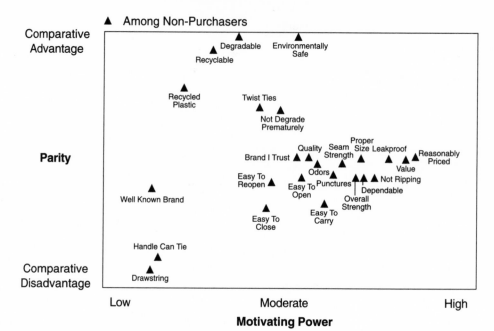

▲ Among Non-Purchasers

Comparing brand ratings between the new product, EnviroBag, and an existing product, Brand B, shows that among purchasers, EnviroBag is at a comparative advantage for its pricing and environmental characteristics. However, consumers rate it at parity or at a comparative disadvantage for the remaining highly motivating factors.

Non-purchasers rated EnviroBag at parity with Brand B for all motivating attributes. Although they rated EnviroBag at parity for their highly motivating characteristics, that provides no incentive to switch their buying from Brand B to EnviroBag. To foster trial, EnviroBag needs a positioning that generates a comparative advantage for more of the highly motivating characteristics.

An alternative to the Yankelovich approach is a positioning model called PERCEPTOR that Novaction has employed successfully as part of its DESIGNOR simulated test marketing service in the United States and internationally. PERCEPTOR is a very powerful tool

Exhibit 7–14

Perceptor Diagnostic Analysis

Preference vs. Positioning Response

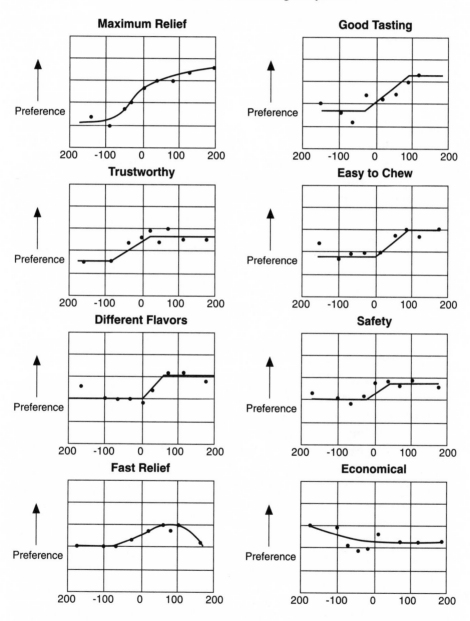

that examines the relationship between consumer perceptions of a new brand and their preferences. Sometimes the relationship is positive, or negative, or even curvilinear. Sometimes there is no relationship at all as indicated in Exhibit 7–14, which is based on a recent application of this model.

How an STM Model Can Test a Line of Items

Often, a marketer will want to use simulated test market research to evaluate a new or re-staged line of items that differ in flavor, size, form (liquid versus powder, for example), or some combination of these. Since retail shelf space is limited, few companies are able to distribute all items in a line. Retailers choose the varieties they believe will be the most popular, but a supplier can influence that choice with convincing research.

Simulated test marketing research systems have two procedures to deal with this issue that use the all commodity volume (ACV) distribution for a line of items. One procedure assumes that the company will accomplish full distribution and that consumers will find any items in the line they want. In this case, the system bases the volume forecast on the "any item" ACV distribution for the line. In other words, the any item ACV distribution represents the probability that the consumer can find any item.

When the marketer assumes that the consumer will *not* be able to find the exact item he or she prefers, an STM can employ a second procedure. This accounts for the divergence of line and item ACV distribution in generating a volume forecast; the customer's probability of finding a particular item is lower than her finding any item in the line. To model the line item's impact on the forecast, a smart STM can account for actual expected distribution and for consumer preference for specific items and generate three separate forecasts with maximum, minimum, and moderate ACV distribution levels.

The first forecast is a *maximum* distribution forecast using the "any item" of the entire line's ACV distribution. This forecast assumes that the consumer will find the item he or she wants. (This is the same forecast that the first procedure produces.)

The second forecast is a *minimum* distribution forecast based on the extremely conservative assumption that no consumer will buy an item other than the size, flavor, or form he or she prefers. The model calculates a minimum distribution by weighting the anticipated ACV distribution by the item purchase share on an item-by-item basis.

Finally, a smart system can turn out a *moderate* distribution forecast based on the average number of acceptable brand choices among loyal buyers. The research determines the average number of acceptable choices through a constant sum question that interviewers ask the loyal buyers; essentially, how many acceptable brand choices does the line contain? The system assumes a linear relationship between effective distribution and the average number of brand choices.

Exhibit 7–15 indicates that if a marketer is unable to achieve full distribution of a five-item line—not every consumer can find the exact item he or she wants—the failure affects Year One sales significantly. The forecast based on "any item," or maximum distribution, is 8 percent higher than the moderate distribution forecast. In

Exhibit 7–15

STM Forecast for a New Line

	Minimum Distribution	Moderate Distribution	Full Distribution
Effective Distribution			
Month 1	67%	73%	80%
Month 2-12	72%	78%	85%
Awareness			
Range - Year 1	21-27%	22-29%	23-31%
Average	25%	27%	29%
Penetration			
% Ever Tried at End of Year 1	15.6%	16.8%	18.1%
Volume			
(MMs of Cases)	3.78	4.07	4.38
(MMs of Units)	45.36	48.90	52.62

this case consumers indicated that the average number of acceptable choices among the five items was 2.8.

The most conservative assumption—that consumers will buy only the one item they prefer—results in a forecast 16 percent lower than the one based on the maximum distribution.

How Sensitivity Analysis Can Improve a Plan

Since marketing managers tend to test few marketing plans, simulated test market researchers have developed sensitivity analysis methods to diagnose a plan's various elements. One of the most widely used of these methods was developed by Kevin Clancy and Lisa Carter of the Yankelovich organization working with Professor Joseph Blackburn of Vanderbilt University more than a decade ago.

Sensitivity analysis allows marketing management to explore the effect each element in the marketing plan has on sales, on profits, or on both. It automatically derives additional forecasts for each component in the marketing mix by increasing and decreasing the component's value by 10, 20, 30, 40, and 50 percent (or more) while holding all other plan elements constant. This type of analysis provides managers with insights into the relative cost-effectiveness of every component in the marketing mix. Sensitivity analysis will examine the relative cost-effectiveness of the marketing plan's various components.

Exhibit 7–16 illustrates the type of information the system provides to show what would happen to sales if the marketer increased and decreased spending on each marketing ingredient.

This sensitivity analysis example illustrates a $13.9 million marketing plan. The company has allocated 46 percent of the marketing dollars to coupons and 54 percent to advertising. The analysis shows that it is inefficient to allocate such a large proportion of the budget to coupons; such spending has reached the point of diminishing returns. If the company reduces the coupon budget by $1,285,000 (a 20 percent reduction, which the model forecasts will reduce sales by 292,000 units) and spends $1,097,000 more on thirty-second daytime television advertising (a 50 percent increase, which the model forecasts will increase sales by 672,000 units), the net sales increase is 380,000 units with a cost saving of $188,000.

Similarly, if the company shifts $74,000 out of prime time fif-

Exhibit 7–16

Example of a Sensitivity Analysis for Selected Marketing Components

	% Change in Marketing Plan Element									
	-50%	**-40%**	**-30%**	**-20%**	**-10%**	**+10%**	**+20%**	**+30%**	**+40%**	**+50%**
Prime 15 Second ($738.6M)										
Change in Sales (000s of Units)	-115	-97	-71	-44	-27	+27	+44	+71	+88	+115
Cost (000s of $)	-369	-295	-222	-148	-74	+74	+148	+222	+295	+369
Prime 30 Second ($4,351.6M)										
Change in Sales (000s of Units)	-920	-725	-531	-345	-168	+168	+327	+476	+628	+779
Cost (000s of $)	-2,176	-1,741	-1,305	-870	-435	+435	+870	+1,305	+1,741	2,176
Day 15 Second ($187.5M)										
Change in Sales (000s of Units)	-52	-44	-35	-27	-9	97	+27	+35	+44	+53
Cost (000s of $)	-94	-75	-56	-38	-19	+19	+38	+56	+75	+94
Day 30 Second ($2,193.2M)										
Change in Sales (000s of Units)	-779	-610	-451	-301	-150	+142	+284	+416	+549	+672
Cost (000s of $)	-1,079	-877	-658	-439	-219	+219	+439	+658	+877	+1,097
Couponing ($6,426M)										
Change in Sales (000s of Units)	-725	-584	-434	-292	-142	+142	+292	+434	+575	+717
Cost (000s of $)	-3,213	-2,570	-1,928	-1,285	-643	+643	+1,285	+1,928	+2,570	+3,213

teen-second television spots (a 10 percent reduction that will reduce sales by 27,000 units) and adds $75,000 to the daytime fifteen-second spot budget (a 40 percent increase that will increase sales by 44,000 units), the $1,000 cost increase results in a 17,000 unit sales increase.

The system uses the sensitivity analysis information to construct a marginal cost relationship for each marketing plan element. The marginal cost represents the incremental dollars a company needs to generate one additional unit of sales while holding all other spending constant. The lower the marginal cost, the more efficient the media, couponing, or sampling.

Using Exhibit 7–16, the marginal cost is the change in cost divided by the change in sales. The marginal cost varies as sales vary. The average marginal cost for all expenditure levels, therefore, shows the relative efficiency of each vehicle as shown in Exhibit 7–17.

As the sensitivity analysis showed earlier, coupons are the least efficient vehicles in this $13.9 million plan because they have the highest marginal cost. In this example, if the marketer adds additional coupons to the plan, an incremental unit will cost $4.45 in coupons; by contrast, an incremental unit will cost only $1.51 in incremental daytime thirty-second commercial expenditures.

Sensitivity analysis clearly shows the marketing manager that, for this product and spending level, the promotion plan is less efficient than every element of the advertising plan. Since the system can test more than one marketing plan, it is likely that the marketing manager will test additional plans that incorporate the efficiencies the sensitivity analysis reveals, thereby improving the final plan's potency.

It is surprising to us that more simulated test marketing researchers do not employ sensitivity testing technology. At professional meetings where we have presented this approach we've been

Exhibit 7–17

Marginal Cost of Marketing Elements
Based on a $13,900,000 Marketing Plan

Marketing Vehicle		Average Marketing Cost
Coupons		$4.45
Prime Time:	:15 Commercial	$3.13
Prime Time:	:30 Commercial	$2.59
Daytime:	:15 Commercial	$1.72
Daytime:	:30 Commercial	$1.51

asked, "How is it possible that you can do this kind of analysis?" Or told, "Sensitivity analysis takes STMs well beyond their capabilities!" To the cynics and critics, sensitivity researchers answer, "Nonsense!"

How is it, we ask, that every STM firm in the industry is pleased to tell clients that they can accurately, validly forecast new product sales if the advertiser changes media weight, promotional plans, or other components in the marketing mix, and not have a model that incorporates the effects of these changes on marketplace response? If the model exists, then it can be programmed to do sensitivity analyses. After all, a sensitivity analysis only represents the coupling of a valid STM model with some automated intelligence programming to produce the type of output shown in Exhibit 7–16. Any marketer or service that can't provide a detailed sensitivity analysis doesn't have a sophisticated model of the marketing process in the first place.

How an STM Model Can Analyze Volume Sources and Cannibalization

After learning a new product's projected volume, marketing managers usually want to know the volume's source. Volume source is important because managers want to know their competitors' identities. Moreover, they want to know if the volume represents sales the new product will take from the company's existing brands. In short, they want to know how much a new product cannibalizes their own brands.

A simulated test market research system computes a new or re-staged product's volume sources by analyzing and comparing the share of requirements among the product's target market (or franchise) at two stages of the simulated test market research: before prospects see the advertising or the product and after customers use the product. The shift in the share of requirements provides guidance with respect to the contribution of various brands to the new or re-staged product's sales volume. In other words, if the leading brand had a 75 percent share of market before the company introduces a new brand, and if the leader's share falls to 72 percent after the introduction, the 3 percent loss is considered the new brand's effect.

When the new or re-staged product is a line extension or competes with the company's other products, the system estimates the impact on existing or parent brands. To increase the measurement validity (because it can be difficult to gauge cannibalization) the model employs a multi-phase approach. The STM system can take as many as four separate actions to capture cannibalization's impact:

1. Share disaggregation.
2. Disproportionate draw.
3. Constant sum.
4. Test cell versus control cell comparison.

The Yankelovich LITMUS system, for example, finds the mean of the four approaches to estimate the new product's cannibalizing impact on the parent brands. In the case of LITMUS, researchers have been able to validate the system's ability to estimate cannibalization in twenty-nine cases. Looking at the impact of a new or re-staged product on a current brand's sales, the forecast was within 10 percent of the actual impact in twenty-six of the cases.

To illustrate the four convergent methodologies which the system uses to forecast cannibalization take a hypothetical example. Assume a 38 percent current parent brand share, a past three-month penetration for the parent brand of 44 percent, and an STM model projected 2.6 percent share for the new entry.

Share Disaggregation

The share disaggregation approach parallels the approach the system employs to forecast the sales of any new or re-staged brand or line extension. Instead of coupling the market response data for the entire sample with the marketing plan, however, this approach couples the market response data obtained from the current brand buyers with category data for this group (in terms of size and volume) and to the marketing plan; with this data the model forecasts this group's share of the new brand's sales. The system follows the same procedure for those outside the current franchise (Exhibit 7–18).

To disaggregate the new entry's forecast share, researchers re-weight the forecasts for the current franchise and non-buyers of the current brands by the actual penetration of brand buyers and non-buyers in the market. In this case, brand buyers represent 44 per-

Exhibit 7–18

Share Disaggregation Approach

Model Inputs	Current Parent Brand		
	Purchases	Non-Purchases	Total
Trial	35%	28%	33%
Repeat	30%	34%	31%
Usage (Units/Yr.)	87.6	72.7	83.3

cent of the market and non-buyers 56 percent. This re-weighted forecast is then employed to allocate the anticipated share between the parent brand's current buyers and non-buyers.

In the example, although the model forecasts the new entry achieving a 2.6 percent share of market, 52 percent of the volume will come from current brand users, or a cannibalizing share of 1.35 percent. The remaining 1.25 percent share will come from people who do not now buy the parent brand. Thus, based on the share disaggregation approach, the incremental share achieved by the brand is only 1.25 percent.

Disproportionate Draw

To calculate the (dis)proportionate "draw" from the existing brand's franchise, researchers develop a buyer and repeat purchaser profile in terms of past brand and category behavior. They then contrast that against the total sample. Profiling people who first try the product and the people who subsequently repeat their purchases by past three-month purchasing (Exhibit 7–19) reveals that people who buy the product for the first time (members of the new entry franchise) are no more likely to be users of currently available parent brands than non-franchise members. Therefore, we can expect a proportionate draw from the franchise.

Since we expect a proportionate draw and since the current share of parent brand products is 38 percent, this methodology

Exhibit 7–19

Disproportionate Draw Approach

		New Entry	
	Total Sample	Purchasers	Franchise
Purchased Any Parent Brand (Past 3 Months)	63%	69%	63%

suggests that 38 percent of the new entry's sales, or 1 share point, will be taken from the parent brand(s). The other 62 percent, or 1.6 share points, will be incremental to the parent brand's sales.

Current and Future Purchases Measured by a Constant Sum Scale

The constant sum approach examines pre/post shifts in brand purchasing. The researchers obtain the information concerning brand shifting by a constant sum approach at three interviewing points: pre-product exposure, post-product exposure, and post usage (Exhibit 7–20).

The constant sum share of purchases reveals that the share of the brand family including the new entry increases by 3.4 percent due to the new entry's introduction. Increasing the brand family's actu-

Exhibit 7–20

Constant Sum Approach

	Pre-New Entry	Post-New Entry	Share Point Increase	% Increase
Parent Brands (Based on Constant Sum)	40.8%	42.2%	+2.4%	+3.4%

al current share, 38 percent, by the increase of 3.4 percent means that the company's *overall* market share will grow to 39.3 percent. The model attributes an incremental 1.3 share points to the new entry. Since the projected share for the new entry is 2.6 percent, the new entry will take 1.3 share points from the existing brand and generate an incremental 1.3 share points.

Control Cell

The researchers often incorporate a control cell into the study design when they are testing a line extension or a re-staging, or when the company must know the new entry's impact on existing brands to decide whether to introduce the product or not. They use the control cell to observe the current brand's performance in a simulated store setting. It generates a measure of the incremental trial, repeat purchase, purchase cycle, and ultimately sales over those the current brand enjoys (Exhibit 7–21).

In this case, when we compare the control and test cell's share of requirements the forecast indicates that the parent share will increase by 2.8 percent from 88 percent to 90.5 percent. Applying this increase to the current parent 38 percent share yields a new share of 39.1 percent—a gain of 1.1 share points and a loss of 1.5 share points for existing brands.

Exhibit 7–21

The Control Cell Approach

	Across All Parent Brands	
	Control	Test
Lab "Trial" (Penetration) of Any Parent Brand	9%	19%
Lab "Trial" Units per Transaction	13.8	10.8
Repeat	67%	55%
Total Parent Brands' Share of Category Requirements	88%	90%

Convergence

The results of the four separate methodologies for cannibalization fall within one half of a share point of one another (Exhibit 7–22).

The incremental share points resulting from the launch range from 1.1 to 1.6 share points. Averaging the four approaches indicates the company will enjoy approximately 1.3 incremental market share points by launching the new entry.

How an STM Model Can Provide Pricing Guidance

In the past, marketers have given minimal attention to the role of pricing in developing marketing strategy. The marketing drama's starring roles went to product development and advertising. Of course, marketers have paid lip service to the four Ps—product, price, place, and promotion. But in practice, most companies have used pricing only tactically, to support promotional strategies, or to launch new products.

Studies revealed that in the 1950s almost all major American companies treated pricing as a purely financial decision.[1] In the 1960s, less than half the marketing executives responding to a survey cited pricing as an important marketing responsibility. In the 1970s, attitudes began to change as de-regulation and international competi-

Exhibit 7–22

Comparison of the Four Approaches

	New Entry Unit Share	–	Net Parent Unit Share Cannibalization	=	Incremental Parent Unit Share Points
Share Desegregation	2.6	–	1.35	=	1.25
Disproportionate Draw	2.6	–	1.0	=	1.6
Constant Sum	2.6	–	1.3	=	1.3
Control Cell	2.6	–	1.5	=	1.1

tion lead to pricing that threatened the positions of many established companies. Even then, however, most executives thought of pricing in terms of defensive tactics—not active strategies.

By the 1980s, marketing executives began to recognize the potential and significance of pricing as a marketing function. In two consecutive studies by Fleming Associates during the 1980s, top American marketing executives cited pricing as the most critical issue currently confronting them.

Simulated test market research companies have employed STM technology to provide marketing managers with the answer to the marketing question of the 1990s: "What is the optimal price?" The manager can base an optimal pricing decision on either attitudinal or behavioral data.

When concept test market research employs the full profile trade-off analysis—in a LITMUS study, the Product Feature Optimizer—attitudinal data determines the optimal price. For a more complete discussion of this approach see Chapter 6 in *The Marketing Revolution*. When the simulated test market research uses either multiple cells or multiple cells with trade-off analysis, behavioral data provides the optimal price.

Testing the Effect of Price at the Concept Stage

Here is how trade-off analysis was used to find the optimal price-feature combination for a new financial service. A major American brokerage firm was interested in launching a new service that would permit customers to deal with the firm through their personal computers. Although management felt that brokerage customers would pay a fee to have computer access to their accounts, the company was not sure what features the service should have or how to price it. The firm's basic problem was to identify the optimal combination of features and price. The more features the system included, the more it would cost to set up and maintain. Thus, management wanted to include only those that customers were willing to buy.

To undertake the trade-off analysis, the research company randomly selected 500 prospective users from a master list of all the brokerage firm's customers with relatively large current account balances. Researchers conducted interviews that averaged approximately forty-five minutes in each customer's home. During the appointment, interviewers showed respondents eighteen different combinations of possible features and prices. These eighteen combinations represented a carefully selected mix of six different factors: hours of operation, the types of information that the customer could request, the ability to move funds between accounts, the ability to place orders, access to a personal credit line, and the service's monthly charge.

Respondents rated each configuration, then later in the interview rated the individual factors and levels using simple purchase intent rankings. The system then used these data to develop a "micro model" of the potential market, which enabled the research firm to estimate the number of consumers who, once they became aware of the service, would sign up for each of the more than 500,000 possible feature combinations. The trade-off analysis showed that price was a critical determinant of interest for this new home banking service. Averaging across the different combinations of features, Exhibit 7–23 shows the impact of price on the predicted aware-

Exhibit 7–23

How Price Affects Trial

Monthly Service Charge ($)	Predicted % of Customers Who Would Sign Up (Assuming Awareness and Opportunity)
$ 5*	49%
10	37%
15*	23%
20	15%
25*	9%
30	4%

* These three levels were included in the tradeoff experiment. The other levels were estimated using Monadic Ratings.

ness-to-trial (the example assumes 100 percent awareness and an opportunity to buy the service).

Given the importance of price, company management wanted to ensure that the service included only those features that justified their value to potential users. Consequently, management paid particular attention to the utilities attached to various attributes. Exhibit 7–24 shows the utilities associated with hours of operation and with price.

These showed that customers would find a service that was available twelve hours a day and cost $15 slightly more attractive than one that was available only eight hours a day but cost only $5. Further, the smaller utility increases for twenty-four hour and everyday services indicate that customers would be unwilling to pay an additional $10 for those features.

Using a proprietary procedure, the research firm estimated utilities for more features and price levels than the trade-off questionnaire actually included. Thus, the system forecasts the gain (or loss) in sales at any price change that accompanied a change in features. By evaluating the sales gains and losses associated with various combinations of features, the brokerage management was able to select an optimal combination of price and features.

Exhibit 7–24

How Hours and Price Affect Utilities

	Utility	Monthly Service Charge ($)	Utility
Hours of Operation			
8 Hours, Weekdays (9am - 5pm, Mon-Fri.)	-67	$5	+48
12 Hours, Weekdays (8am - 8pm, Mon-Fri.)	-6	$15	-15
24 Hours, Weekdays	+24	$25	-33
24 Hours, Everyday	+37		

Testing Price at the Simulated Test Marketing Stage

When a company has chosen a product's features and pricing is the remaining issue, STM researchers can design a study to observe the effect of price on product trial and repeat purchase in the laboratory environment. Such research uses multiple cells to test alternative prices and, coupled with trade-off analysis, to estimate the optimal price. One case used multiple cells to test two to four different prices, as Exhibit 7–25 shows, for a small home appliance. The model can use multiple cells coupled with trade-off analysis to test three to ten prices. Exhibit 7–26 depicts the results of such an analysis for a microwave entree.

How an STM Model Measures Product or Service Performance

The callback questionnaire the researchers administer during the in-home use phase of the simulated test market research includes

Exhibit 7–25

Pricing: Durable Application

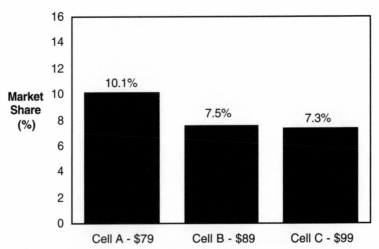

Exhibit 7–26

Pricing: Packaged Goods Application with Trade-Off Added

Product: **Microwave Entree**
Budget: **$8MM**

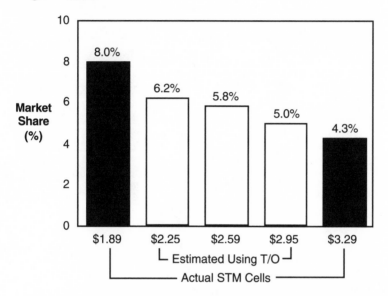

an additional rating of the test product on the attributes that consumers rated during the pre-usage phase. Comparing the ratings before and after use allows the model to assess the product's or service's fulfillment against the consumer's expectations that the advertising created.

Comparing attribute ratings shows a significant change in the ratings of ten attributes after consumers have used the product (Exhibit 7–27). EnviroBag performed better than expected for five attributes: "leakproof," "quality," "odors," "recycled plastic," and "brand I can trust." The product did not perform as expected for two other attributes: "easy to close," and "easy to re-open." The remaining attributes performed as expected. This information tells the marketing manager that, to compete successfully over the long run, the company must improve on the characteristics that did not perform as well as expected and to stress those that performed better than expected.

Exhibit 7–27

**Pre/Post Usage Ratings of
EnviroBag on Ten Selected Characteristics**

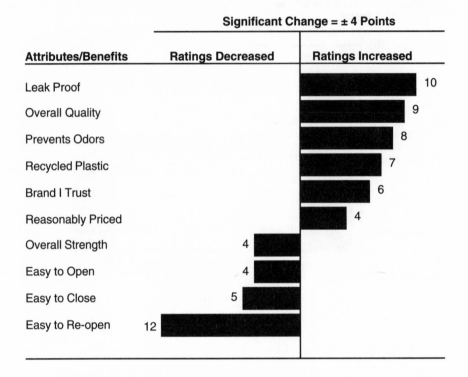

Management Implications

The purpose of this chapter was to explore and describe a variety of tools and approaches that simulated test marketing researchers are using to go well beyond the volume forecasting capabilities of current STM models. Today, as we have said repeatedly, most new products and services introduced in the real world are failures and, not surprisingly, most STMs forecast failure. What managers need to know is not simply how the new product can be expected to perform but what needs to be done to make it a success.

Targeting, positioning, advertising, line extensions, cannibalization, pricing, and product/service quality are among the issues that can be researched and analyzed in a simulated test marketing experiment to build better marketing plans. Indeed, as we have argued elsewhere, in this age of marketing failure when 80 to 99 percent of new products and services, packaged goods and durables, consumer and industrial, are forecast to be failures, technology that builds better plans has become an imperative.

The better simulated test marketing services today can tell you not just how you will do (i.e., how the new or re-staged product will perform), but what to do (i.e., what changes need to be made) to ensure a successful introduction.

III

Theory and Research Using Simulated Test Marketing

8

Forecasting Awareness
for New and Established
Products and Services*

During the last decade, marketing managers have increasingly relied on consumer awareness measures as important indicators of
whether a marketing program for a new or established product or
service will succeed or fail. Managers often design marketing campaigns—especially advertising campaigns—to increase a brand's
awareness in the minds of the target market's consumers. Awareness
measures as indicators of communication effectiveness are popular
because consumers must be aware of a product before they will buy
it.[1] Managers, therefore, often operate under the assumption that
sales and market share gains will follow awareness increases.[2] In addition, managers rely on awareness measures because they provide a
convenient and inexpensive way to track market performance in situations where it is more difficult or more costly to obtain other measures, such as changes in buying intentions or in actual behavior.[3]

One can readily see the convenience and cost savings in using
awareness as a measure of communication effectiveness in campaigns for established products, which tend to resist immediate
changes in other attitudinal and behavioral criteria. In such in-

---

*This chapter is based on Blackburn, Joseph D., Kevin J. Clancy, and R. Dale Wilson,
"Forecasting Awareness of New Products and Penetration of New Campaigns for Established Products: Applications of Litmus II," Boston University School of Management Working Paper, 1990 and Blackburn and Clancy "Notes on Forecasting New
Product Awareness" Management Science, Vol. 23, No. 3, 1984.

stances, the company may be hesitant to measure the small changes a campaign produces—such as a 0.3 percentage point market share shift or a 4 percent change in the proportion of consumers who include the test brand in their evoked set—because the research methodology would require a large and expensive sample. Rather, the company can use awareness measures as an inexpensive "leading indicator" of campaign success.

While awareness information is important for established products, it is perhaps even more important for new products. This is so because companies apply awareness measures widely in forecasting, tracking, and diagnosing results before, during, and after test marketing. In most simulated test market methodologies, estimated awareness shows a linear effect on the eventual market share forecast; as awareness rises, so does share. New product marketing managers, moreover, invariably include awareness measures in research studies designed to track campaign performance. The common label this research carries is "awareness, trial, and usage studies," or simply "ATU studies."

Finally, new product managers routinely diagnose campaign outcomes, seeking ways to improve them and investigating factors held critical to brand success. The brand awareness level is one of the critical factors. In the vast majority of cases, managers seek opportunities to improve campaign performance by effecting and maintaining higher awareness levels.

Because awareness is so important in evaluating marketing and communication program effectiveness, it is crucial to understand what determines awareness, the most useful measures of awareness, and how simulated test market research can predict the level of awareness that will be achieved for the new product. Blackburn, Clancy, and Wilson have used the LITMUS awareness subsystem in empirical research to investigate all of these issues. The results of this research are the basis of this chapter.

How to Measure Awareness

The recent literature on brand and campaign awareness measurement indicates that contemporary research commonly applies a variety of specific measures. Our experience suggests that two consumer awareness measures are most appropriate; the choice of measure depends on the marketing situation. For new products and services, we have found total brand awareness to be an appropriate criterion. For new campaigns for established products and services, we have found tracer element penetration (also known as campaign awareness) to be the appropriate measure.

Exhibit 8–1 shows a number of different awareness measures in widespread use and illustrates their operational definitions (in this

Exhibit 8–1

Alternative Measures of Awareness

Awareness Measure	Operational Definition for Soft Drinks
First Brand	"When you think of soft drinks, what is the first brand which comes to mind?"
Unaided Advertising	"Which brands of soft drinks have you seen or heard advertised during the past 90 days?"
Aided Advertising	"Have you seen or heard any advertising for Pepsi during the past 90 days?"
Partially Aided Tracer Penetration	"Which brand of soft drink ... ?" - advertises 'The choice of a new generation' (Slogan example) - advertises 'One hundred percent caffeine free' (Message example) - uses Bill Cosby to advertise their product (Spokesperson or dominant visual example)
Fully Aided Tracer Penetration	"Have you seen or heard any advertising for Pepsi during the past 90 days which uses the slogan 'The choice of a new generation'?"
Unaided Brand	"What are all the different brands of soft drinks you can think of?"
Aided Brand	"I'm going to read you a list of soft drink brands. For each one I name, please tell me if you've ever heard of it."
Total Brand	Unaided and aided brand awareness

case, soft drinks), that is, how the questions are asked in a research study. As the figure's last line indicates, total brand awareness is a combination of unaided and aided brand awareness.

There are two separate measures of tracer penetration: partially aided tracer penetration and fully aided tracer penetration, both measured by helping the consumer's recall with partial or complete cues. Tracer penetration refers to consumer playback of some as-

Exhibit 8–2

**Features of Awareness Measures for New Campaigns
for Established Products and Services**

Awareness Measure	Typical Level	Comments
First Brand	Very close to market share	Behaves much like market share; resists change; insensitive to changes in the marketing mix
Unaided Advertising	Approximately two times the brand's share of voice	Behave like attitudinal measures; closely correlated with evoked set measures for the product category
Unaided Brand	Approximately two to three times market share	
Partially Aided Tracer Penetration	Approximately one to two times the brand's share of voice	Behave like new product brand awareness measures, but the first measurement tends to be difficult to predict. After the "advertising impact" or the new campaign is observed, tracer penetration measures are easier to predict.
Fully Aided Tracer Penetration	Approximately two to three times the brand's share of voice	
Aided Advertising	Approximately two to four times the brand's share of voice	Changes only with major changes in various aspects of the advertising program
Total (Unaided and Aided)	Extremely high, often in the 80-95% range	Changes only with massive changes in the marketing mix

pect of the advertising unique to the particular campaign. The tracer—or signaling—element is something unique to a particular advertising campaign. This may be a message, a slogan, a dominant visual, a spokesperson, or even a musical score.

Our experience with new product introductions suggests that total brand awareness strongly correlates to consumer trial purchase, is quite sensitive to changes in various marketing mix elements, and, happily, can be forecast accurately with a sophisticated model of the awareness-generating process.

For new campaigns for established products and services, however, total brand awareness is inappropriate because it tends to be relatively stable over time and is not very sensitive to marketing mix changes. We have likened it to trying to move a ping pong ball in a jar of peanut butter. Since marketing program changes tend not to alter this relatively immutable measure of awareness, it is a relatively poor predictor of changes in future consumer behavior for established products.

Tracer element penetration, on the other hand, is an appealing measure of awareness for established products because it is more sensitive to marketing mix changes, and, for strong, successful campaigns it correlates positively with purchase behavior. Exhibit 8–2 shows how the various awareness measures behave with new and established products and services.

The Results of Calibrating Forecasts with Actual Data

To examine and improve simulated test marketing research's ability to forecast new product introduction awareness, Blackburn, Clancy, and Wilson analyzed the awareness forecasts for twenty-one products and four services. They compared awareness forecasts made at the STM stage with the awareness levels the products and services achieved in the marketplace following their introduction (Exhibit 8–3).

To generate the "original forecast" figures, data from the marketing plan as well as marketing and consumer research studies were used as input in the LITMUS awareness submodel. This resulted in twenty-five different awareness forecasts over a twelve-month period.

For each product or service introduction, Exhibit 8–3 contrasts the projected awareness with the actual awareness achieved at the

Exhibit 8–3

Awareness Forecasts for New Product/Service Campaigns

	Actual Year-end Awareness	Original Forecast			Forecast After Calibration		
		Forecasted Awareness	Difference	Percent Error[a]	Forecasted Awareness	Difference	Percent Error[a]
Products:							
1	35	39	-4	11.4%	37	-2	5.7%
2	57	66	-9	15.8	65	-8	14.0
3	70	72	-2	2.9	70	0	0.0
4	76	83	-7	9.2	79	-3	3.9
5	79	72	7	8.9	76	3	3.8
6	32	34	-2	6.3	34	-2	6.3
7	45	48	-3	6.7	48	-3	6.7
8	70	62	8	11.4	70	0	0.0
9	32	30	2	6.3	36	-4	12.5
10	18	12	6	33.3	15	3	16.7
11	30	24	6	20.0	26	4	13.3
12	43	45	-2	4.7	43	0	0.0
13	54	51	3	5.6	52	2	3.7
14	57	52	5	8.8	54	3	5.3
15	65	57	8	12.3	57	8	12.3
16	57	63	-6	10.5	58	-1	1.8
17	49	49	0	0.0	49	0	0.0
18	53	48	5	9.4	51	2	3.8
19	54	47	7	13.0	48	6	11.1
20	56	58	-2	3.6	57	-1	1.8
21	37	51	-14	37.8	35	2	5.4
Services:							
1	28	22	6	21.4	25	3	10.7
2	12	16	-4	33.3	17	-5	41.7
3	45	41	4	8.9	42	3	6.7
4	30	37	-7	23.3	32	-2	6.7
Overall Mean[b]	47.36 (17.66)[c]	47.16 (17.88)	5.16 (3.00)	12.19 (10.05)	47.04 (17.46)	2.80 (2.18)	7.76 (8.56)
Products Mean[b]	50.90 (16.26)	50.62 (16.85)	5.14 (3.23)	11.33 (9.25)	50.48 (16.47)	2.71 (2.33)	6.10 (5.19)
Services Mean[b]	28.75 (13.50)	29.00 (11.92)	5.25 (1.50)	21.73 (10.02)	29.00 (10.61)	3.25 (1.26)	16.45 (16.94)

[a]Percent errors are calculated as: |(actual awareness - forecasted awareness)|/actual awareness.
[b]Absolute values are used in calculating the means.
[c]Standard deviations are given in parentheses for each mean.

end of the twelve-month period. Actual awareness was measured using standard, unaided and aided awareness questions combined into a measure of total awareness among large representative samples of the target market.

One would expect some errors in these forecasts. These result from—among other reasons—the differences between the marketing plan used in the simulated test market forecast and the plan the company actually implemented. Another major reason why forecasts and reality differ is because of competitive effects. Marketers today are increasingly savvy and sometimes attempt to poison a competitor's test market results. In addition, due to sampling error, a three- to six-point variation at the 0.10 level of statistical significance occurs in the actual awareness measurement.

Following the launch of a new product or new campaign, tracking study data may be used to help calibrate the model and improve forecasts of awareness, trial, and purchase. Sometimes the research company doing the STM undertakes these tracking studies; often, however, the marketer hires an independent research company to collect the awareness data.

Exhibit 8–3 shows the level of accuracy achieved in the total brand awareness forecasts for each case and for the totals. For products and services combined, the mean error is only 5.16 points with a standard deviation of 3.00 points. Calibration reduces the error to 2.80 points with a standard deviation of 2.18 points. The overall percentage error for all twenty-five cases is 12.19 percent (with a standard deviation of 10.05) before launch; this drops to 7.76 percent (with a standard deviation of 8.56) using awareness, trial, and usage data to calibrate the model.

The figures in Exhibit 8–3 indicate that, although the original forecast experiences a 12.19 percent error with a 5.16-point mean difference, calibrating the model with awareness, trial, and usage data results in a more accurate forecast of total brand awareness. For all twenty-five introductions, after calibrating the model with ATU data, the forecasting error, as measured by the mean absolute difference, tumbles 46 percent—from 12.19 percent to 7.76 percent. However, in six of the twenty-five cases (products number 6, 7, 9, 15, 17, and service number 2), the original forecast was as good as or better than the post-calibration forecasts.

New Campaigns for Established Products and Services and New Corporate Campaigns

For a new corporate campaign or one re-staging (re-positioning) an established product, the LITMUS awareness model forecasts and tracks tracer penetration as the awareness measure. Exhibit 8–4 shows fifteen cases in which Blackburn, Clancy, and Wilson examined the impact of calibrating awareness forecasts for eight re-staged products, four re-staged services, and three new corporate advertising programs. Exhibit 8–4 indicates the original forecast results generated before re-launch and the forecasts generated using one wave of awareness, trial, and usage data to calibrate the model.

For the fifteen cases presented in Exhibit 8–4, the overall mean percentage error was 23.75 percent for the original forecasts and 13.14 percent for the forecast after calibration. The forecasting errors for product re-stagings, 14.44 percent, are considerably smaller than the forecasting errors for service re-stagings, 47.18 percent. Further, the calibrated forecasts for product re-stagings have a smaller forecasting error, 5.76 percent, than the calibrated forecasts for service re-stagings, 27.95 percent. The accuracy for the new corporate campaigns falls between the accuracy for product and service re-stagings, a 17.37 percent error for the original forecasts and a 13.07 percent error for the calibrated forecasts.

Awareness Forecast Comparisons: New Versus Existing

When we compare the original forecasts for new products and services to those for established products and services, we see that the mean percentage error for the re-staging campaigns, 23.8 percent, is considerably higher than that for the new product and service campaigns, 13.0 percent (Exhibit 8–5). The calibrated forecasts for new products and services show the same pattern: a 13.1 mean percentage error for re-staged products versus a 7.8 mean percentage error for new products.

Moreover, even after calibration, the forecasts for re-staged products, with a 13.1 mean percentage error, are slightly less accurate than the original forecasts for new products and services, with a 13.0 mean percentage error. These results indicate that it is more

Exhibit 8–4

Awareness Forecasts for New Campaigns for Established Products and Services and for New Corporate Campaigns

	Actual Year-end Awareness	Original Forecast			Forecast After Calibration		
		Forecasted Awareness	Difference	Percent Error[a]	Forecasted Awareness	Difference	Percent Error[a]
Products:							
1	45	48	-3	6.7%	48	-3	6.7%
2	49	55	-6	12.2	47	2	4.1
3	63	54	9	14.3	58	5	7.9
4	30	38	-8	26.7	29	1	3.3
5	52	63	-11	21.2	56	-4	7.7
6	59	55	4	6.8	57	2	3.4
7	66	59	7	10.6	63	3	4.5
8	47	55	-8	17.0	51	-4	8.5
Services:							
1	22	15	7	31.8	19	3	13.6
2	12	21	-9	75.0	17	-5	41.7
3	8	3	5	62.5	4	4	50.0
4	31	37	-6	19.4	33	-2	6.5
Corporate:							
1	16	18	-2	12.5	18	-2	12.5
2	47	55	-8	17.0	42	5	10.6
3	31	24	7	22.6	36	-5	16.1
Overall Mean[b]	38.53 (18.62)[c]	40.00 (19.19)	6.67 (2.41)	23.75 (19.68)	38.53 (18.01)	3.33 (1.35)	13.14 (13.89)
Products Mean[b]	51.38 (11.53)	53.38 (7.54)	7.00 (2.62)	14.44 (6.98)	51.13 (10.44)	3.00 (1.31)	5.76 (2.16)
Services Mean[b]	18.25 (10.34)	19.00 (14.14)	6.75 (1.71)	47.18 (25.93)	18.25 (11.87)	3.50 (1.29)	27.95 (21.14)
Corporate Mean[b]	31.33 (15.50)	32.33 (19.86)	5.67 (3.21)	17.37 (5.06)	32.00 (12.49)	4.00 (1.73)	13.07 (2.79)

[a]Percent errors are calculated as: |(actual awareness - forecasted awareness)|/actual awareness.

[b]Absolute values are used in calculating the means.

[c]Standard deviations are given in parentheses for each mean.

difficult to forecast consumer awareness of new campaigns for established products than it is to forecast awareness for entirely new products and services.

Exhibit 8–5

Summary of Awareness Forecasting Experience

Type of Campaign	Number of Cases	Original Forecasts		Forecast After Calibration	
		Average Error in Awareness Forecasts	Average Percent Error	Average Error in Awareness Forecasts	Average Percent Error
New:					
Products	21	5.1 Points	11.3%	2.7 Points	6.1%
Services	4	5.3	21.7	3.3	16.5
Overall	25	5.2	13.0	2.8	7.8
Established:					
Products	8	7.0	14.4	3.0	5.8
Services	4	6.8	47.2	3.5	28.0
Corporate	3	5.7	17.4	4.0	13.1
Overall	15	6.7	23.8	3.3	13.1

The data further indicate that employing an awareness, trial, usage research study to revise the STM model forecast increases the STM's predictive validity considerably. However, the awareness calibration influences forecasting accuracy more in the case of product and service re-staging forecasts than it does for new product and service introduction forecasts. For re-staged products and services, the mean absolute difference between actual year-end awareness and projected year-end awareness due to calibration is 57.1 percent and 48.5, respectively; it is 47.1 percent and 37.7 percent for new products and services, respectively. For new corporate campaigns, the use of awareness tracking data to calibrate the figure reduces the mean absolute difference by 29.8 percent.

The figures clearly show that one wave of awareness tracking data helps produce a sharp increase in forecasting accuracy. The experience further shows that adding data from two or three waves of tracking research can yield even better forecasts. Several waves of awareness, trial, and usage research allow a much less sophisticated model to make the year-end forecasts. The model turns out these forecasts during the launch, however, rather than before the launch.

Although a 23.8 percent overall *average* campaign awareness level error for existing products, services, and new corporate campaigns is not unreasonable, it is clear that campaign awareness levels for established services are considerably more difficult to forecast than awareness for established products or established corporate campaigns. The small sample of four cases had a low 19.4 mean percentage error and a high 75.0 percentage error (with a mean between the two of 47.2 percent). After calibration, the mean percentage error fell to 28.0 percent for established services, which is still much higher than the error for established products or corporate campaigns.

A similar relationship exists for new products and services. New products had a 11.3 mean percentage compared to a 21.7 mean for new services. After calibration, the mean error fell to 16.5 percent for services and to 6.1 percent for products.

One reason it is so difficult to forecast service awareness is that service marketers use direct mail and public relations widely. Current simulated test marketing models do not fully capture these activities. For example, during the American Express Platinum Card introduction, the LITMUS system found that, due to the corporation's public relations efforts, 34 percent of the target market knew of this new service before the advertising campaign began.[4] Only a model that captures the effects of public relations—which no STM system currently does—can forecast new service campaigns well.

How Additional Variables Influence the Awareness Forecast

As Chapter 5 discussed, adding variables concerning the marketing plan improves the awareness forecast's accuracy. The same twenty-one new products that were examined to assess the impact of calibration on awareness, trial, and usage data were also used to assess the impact of adding variables for purposes of awareness modeling. Since the model made the forecasts for each product at different times, the Exhibit 8–3 forecasts are those made by the version of

LITMUS in use at that time; they correspond to the same version in Exhibit 8–6.

Six different versions of the model were used to examine the impact of adding marketing plan variables. The simplest model, represented by X_1, uses only gross rating points, an expression for initial awareness, a ceiling effect, and a forgetting effect to generate an awareness forecast. Five additional versions of the model were built by adding variables—media schedule, media impact and share of voice, advertising impact, promotion (coupons and samples),

Exhibit 8–6

**Effect of Adding Variables on
Awareness Forecasts for New Product Campaigns**

	Variables Used in LITMUS Forecasts[a]					
	(x_1) GRPs Only	(x_2) x_1 plus Media Schedule	(x_3) x_2 plus Media Impact and SOV	(x_4) x_3 plus Advertising Impact	(x_5) x4 plus Promotion	(x_6) x_5 plus Distribution and Product Category Effects
Mean Difference[b]	13.52 (12.40) [d]	9.90 (13.27)	5.62 (3.37)	4.00 (2.57)	3.24 (2.21)	2.76 (1.70)
Mean % Error[b]	28.98 (31.51)	20.00 (32.85)	12.71 (10.84)	8.99 (7.47)	7.35 (6.93)	6.20 (5.41)
Percent Reduction in Mean Error[c]	–	30.99	56.14	68.98	74.64	78.61
Correlation with Actual Year-end Awareness	.81[e]	.80[e]	.92[e]	.96[e]	.98[e]	.98[e]

[a] In addition to the variables identified in the column headings, the Litmus model also includes terms representing initial awareness, a ceiling effect, a forgetting effect, and a ghost awareness factor.

[b] Absolute values are used in calculating these means.

[c] Calculated as: (mean percent error for Model x_1 - mean percent error for any Model x_2 through x_6) /mean percent error for Model x_1.

[d] Standard deviations are given in parentheses for each mean.

[e] $p < .001$

and distribution and product category effects—to the simple model (Exhibit 8–6).

Variable set X_6 represents a very sophisticated model used to forecast awareness. Experience indicates that reordering the sequence in which the variables were added would not significantly alter the incremental effect of each on the forecast's accuracy. This is due to low level of redundancy in the predictor variables.

Exhibit 8–6 demonstrates that adding variables to the simulated test market research improves accuracy substantially. The mean differences, calculated by using the absolute difference between the actual year-end awareness and the awareness forecast for each variable set, X_1 through X_6, decreases monotonically as the awareness model includes more variables. In addition, the mean percentage error decreases from 28.98 percent for variable set X_1 to 6.20 percent for variable set X_6. (We calculate these for each product by dividing the absolute difference by the actual year-end awareness measure.) Each correlation is significant at the 0.001 level. The Pearson correlation coefficients for awareness based on X_i increases from 0.81 for X_1 alone to 0.98 for the full battery of factors expressed as X_6; they have, therefore, a strong correlation.

To determine the degree of variability among the six means in Exhibit 8–6, we ran a one-way analysis of variance (ANOVA) on the data. The result, which tests the null hypothesis that these six means are equal, yields an F-value of 2.27, where $p = 0.0519$. This suggests that at the 90 percent level of confidence the hypothesis of equality across all six means is rejected.

Paired sample t-tests for each pair of means were run to examine the differences across all six mean awareness forecasts. J. Scott Armstrong discusses this procedure in *Long-Range Forecasting: From Crystal Ball to Computer*. He suggests comparing model forecasts using t-tests that incorporate Tukey's HSD procedure to control for statistical effects of multiple comparisons.

The multiple comparison test results, summarized in Exhibit 8–7, suggest the relative contribution of adding variables to the model when we use it to forecast new product awareness. Exhibit 8–7 indicates that the mean level of actual awareness, Y, is significantly different at the 0.05 level for a two-tailed test from the mean awareness forecast for the simple model X_1 and variable X_2. However, it is not significantly different from X_3.

Exhibit 8–7

Differences Between Means for Awareness Forecasts[a]

	x_1	x_2	x_3	x_4	x_5	x_6
y	13.53[b]	9.34[b]	0.76	0.47	0.38	0.10
x_1		4.19[b]	14.29[b]	14.00[b]	13.91[b]	13.43[b]
x_2			10.10[b]	9.81[b]	9.72[b]	9.24[b]
x_3				0.29	0.38	0.86
x_4					0.09	0.57
x_5						0.48

[a] Differences between means are presented as absolute values.

[b] $p < .05$ Using Tukey's HSD method of multiple comparisons (cf. Armstrong 1985, pp. 462-7).

The mean projected awareness levels for the most simple forms of the awareness equation, using variables X_1 and X_2, are significantly different for each paired comparison. Therefore, the awareness generated using only gross rating points, or GRPs, plus the media schedule yields mean forecast awareness levels significantly different from the mean actual awareness levels and the awareness levels generated with additional marketing variables.

The mean for X_3 is significantly different from X_1 and X_2. However, the mean for X_3 is not significantly different from Y, actual awareness, or any other of the awareness forecast means. Thus, the addition of media impact and share of voice to the GRPs and the schedule significantly improves the awareness forecast.

These comparisons suggest that, on average, a sophisticated model which includes a combination of GRPs, media schedule, media impact, and share of voice provides an extremely powerful awareness forecasting tool. The incremental value of adding the variables in X_4, X_5, and X_6—advertising impact, promotion, and distribution and product category effects—is smaller than the incremental value of adding media impact and share of voice.

When we examine new products 5, 8, 15, and 21, we see clearly the results of adding marketing variables to the awareness forecasting model. They illustrate how a forecasting model is designed to incorporate relevant variables into the model's structure. These cases, which represent new cigarette brands supported with a first-year advertising budget of approximately $50 million each, are unique because they employ no television advertising.

The lack of television, combined with a budget level that most other product categories would consider quite high, causes an unusual relationship between the budget level and the exceptionally high number of gross rating points that these companies can buy in print media. As a result of these unique cigarette category factors, projected awareness of these new cigarette brands at the end of Year One using only GRPs and the media schedule, variable sets X_1 and X_2, reaches the ceiling level of predicted awareness, 95 percent. Adding media impact and share of voice, variable set X_3, greatly improves the accuracy of these forecasts.

Management Implications

The research reported in this chapter suggests that total brand awareness is a reasonable awareness measure for new products and services, while campaign penetration (based on recall of campaign tracer elements) is a more appropriate awareness measure for established products and services. The research, moreover, also reveals that a sophisticated awareness forecasting submodel can be used successfully to forecast awareness of a new product or a new campaign and that these forecasts can be generally improved by calibrating the model based on early returns from an in-market tracking survey.

One disturbing discovery is the relative difficulty in predicting awareness of new campaigns for established services. Although the number of such cases we have examined here is too small to draw firm conclusions, the fact remains that most new service campaigns are supported by sizable levels of public relations activity and direct mail. Yet no STM model in widespread use explicitly takes PR into effect and only one model, LITMUS, captures the effects of direct mail.

Finally, this research shows that the addition of media impact, share of voice, advertising impact, distribution, and other category effects significantly improves the awareness forecast relative to a forecast that includes only gross rating points and media schedule. Stated differently, a more complete model works better than a parsimonious model. Awareness forecasting methods, as a result, based on gross rating points and even media schedule will not perform as well as those which include a larger number of advertising/marketing elements. Since most STM models have become more sophisticated over time, representing the convergence of mathematical modeling and laboratory simulation that we talked about first in Chapter 3 and again in Chapter 5, brand and campaign awareness forecasting capabilities have improved and sales forecasting validity has improved as a result.

9

In Search of the Best Media
Weight and Schedule*

Two recurring questions in contemporary marketing are: "How much money should we spend on advertising?" and "What media schedule should we employ?"

Since research has proven the accuracy of simulated test marketing sales and consumer awareness forecasting models,[1] companies can apply this technology to help answer these questions. We will show how a smart simulated test marketing model can be employed to answer media expenditure and timing questions. In this chapter, which is based on the work of Blackburn, Clancy, and Wilson, we will use the LITMUS simulated test marketing model to explore the relationship between media weight/timing and consumer awareness and market share for new and established products. This relationship was examined using prototypical new product marketing plan parameters and prototypical new campaigns for established products. This chapter explains the methodology employed to evaluate media weight and timing and the research's results.

How We Set Marketing Plan Parameters

To examine the effects of differences in media expenditures and media timing patterns, all other key marketing plan parameters

*This chapter is based on Blackburn, Joseph D., Kevin J. Clancy, and R. Dale Wilson "The Effects of Media Timing and Media Weight on Market Response for New and Established Products," Boston University School of Management Working Paper, 1990.

were assigned "typical" values. We used the experience gained in applying the LITMUS model since 1982 to delineate profiles for the prototypical new product campaigns and new established product campaigns. These profiles consisted of marketing plan and market response parameters necessary to run the model.

The marketing plan parameters included all aspects of the media mix, the advertising's attention-getting power, media impact, share of voice, and all commodity volume distribution. The market response parameters included an initial level of consumer awareness and forgetting, a ceiling on awareness, the average package size the consumer buys the first time and on repeat occasions, the annual consumption rate, the awareness-to-trial rate, and the multiple repeat buying rates.

To develop eight variants for each of the base cases, the same historical experience was drawn upon to detail the "typical" new and established products. This was accomplished by systematically altering six of the key market response parameters the model manipulates as inputs:

1. The advertising's attention-getting power.
2. Media impact.
3. All commodity volume distribution percentage.
4. Awareness-to-trial.
5. The probability of first repeat purchase.
6. The probability of multiple repeat purchases.

Each of these six parameters were then increased and decreased by 15 percent, 35 percent, 55 percent, and 80 percent. These values correspond approximately to the quintile scores for each parameter observed while applying the model since its inception. Of the total set of possible combinations, eight were randomly selected, which, with the two base cases, yielded nine new product plans and nine established product plans.

Media Weight and Media Timing

For each of these eighteen different marketing plans, we then systematically varied the media timing patterns and media weights. We selected three different media timing patterns and three different media weight levels. The three different media timing treatments were (1) a front-loaded schedule; (2) a flighted schedule; (3) and a sustained schedule.

The front-loaded schedule allocated the entire media budget to the first three months of the year. This schedule assigned 30 percent of the budget to the first month, 40 percent to the second, and the remainder to the third.

The flighted schedule allocated the media budget equally to every other month—16.67 percent to the first month, 16.67 percent to the third month, and so forth. The sustained schedule divided the media budget equally between every month.

The three spending levels for media weight were (1) a light media plan consisting of 600 gross rating points; (2) an average budget of 1,200 GRPs; and (3) a very heavy budget of 2,400 GRPs. These three different GRP levels correspond to advertising spending for thirty-second commercials on prime time television of approximately $8.3 million, $16.1 million, and $31.7 million, respectively. Since we did not examine media mix, we chose prime time so that we could compare the plans.

Purchase Cycle

Joseph Ostrow has suggested that the purchase cycle—the average time between buys—for various products would influence the effectiveness of various media schedule and weight combinations.[2] If the consumer buys the product every other week and the advertising runs weekly, the consumer has the opportunity to see the advertising two times before buying the product. If, however, the consumer buys the product once a month and the advertising runs once every six months, she may not see any advertising at all during a period in which she buys the product five times.

We incorporated four different purchase cycles into each of the nine media schedules and weight combinations to determine whether the purchase cycle affects the media weight and schedule combination effectiveness. These purchase cycle lengths were twice a month, once a month, once a quarter, and once every six months.

Marketing Parameter Combinations

The data base development process yielded a total of 648 different variable combinations. These product scenarios resulted from the combination of nine marketing plan variations for each of three media weight variations (heavy, average, and light), three media schedule variations (front-loaded, flighted, and sustained), four purchase cycle variations (twice a month, monthly, quarterly, and twice a year), and two product types, new and established. Thus we employed a 3 x 3 x 4 x 2 experimental design, each cell containing nine observations. We then used each of the resulting 648 combinations as simulated test market model inputs.

Measures of Consumer Awareness and Market Share

As the dependent variables in the simulation study, two different measures of consumer awareness and two different measures of share were used as the model's output to see how the model's predictions would vary as a result of media weight and media timing variations. For the purposes of making predictions from the model, a one-year period was used. The four dependent variables this study examined were (1) average awareness, (2) end-of-year awareness, (3) average market share, and (4) end-of-year market share. Since media timing was one of the independent variables the study investigated, consumer awareness and market share for two different time periods—the average for the year and the forecast for Month Twelve—were used.

Because the appropriate definition of product awareness depends upon whether the product is new or established, the study retained this distinction to maintain a high degree of realism in the research. As we discussed in Chapter 8, experience shows that total brand awareness serves as the most appropriate consumer awareness measure for a new product or service; tracer element penetration is the most appropriate awareness measure for an established product or service.[3]

How We Analyzed the Data to Assess Media Weight and Timing

Analysis of variance (ANOVA) was employed to determine the influence of media weight, media timing, purchase cycle, and product type on the model's predictions of awareness and market share. To identify important trends in the data, we used the 0.05 level of statistical significance, and as a measure of each experimental factor's importance, we also used the percentage of the total sum of squares contributed by each main and interaction effect. In those instances in which the ANOVA identified statistically significant main or interaction effects, we also analyzed the cell mean figures.

Consumer Awareness and Market Share

The results of the ANOVA runs indicated that several different main and interaction effects were statistically significant. Exhibit 9–1 shows that the study found significant main effects for media weight and type of product on all four dependent variables. Therefore, media weight and type of product each affected average and end-of-year awareness, and average and end-of-year share of market. The media timing pattern influenced average awareness, end-of-year awareness, and average market share. The length of the purchase cycle affected the end-of-year awareness figure.

The research also found statistically significant interaction effects. There were interactions between media weight and type of product on both awareness measures, between the media timing pattern and type of product on average awareness, and between media timing and purchase cycle on end-of-year market share.

Examining the percentage of total sum of squares explained by the independent variables indicates that media weight and media timing exert, as one might intuitively expect, more influence on awareness than on market share. The main effect of media weight explains 29.4 percent of the total sum of squares for average awareness and 21.3 percent of the total sum of squares for end-of-year awareness. However, media weight explains only 5.5 percent of the total sum of squares for market share and 6.5 percent of the total sum of squares for end-of-year market share.

Similarly, the main effect of media timing explains 2.3 percent of the total sum of squares for average awareness and 4.9 percent of the total sum of squares for end-of-year awareness. Yet the media timing pattern explains only 1.7 percent of the total sum of squares for market share and 0.1 percent of the total sum of squares for end-of-year market share.

Comparing the relative importance of media weight and media timing in determining consumer awareness and market share indicates that media weight was considerably more important than

Exhibit 9–1

Summary of Analysis of Variance Results

Source	df	Average Awareness		End-of-Year Awareness		Average Market Share		End-of-Year Market Share	
		F-Value	Percent of Total Sum of Squares	F-Value	Percent of Total Sum of Squares	F-Value	Percent of Total Sum of Squares	F Value	Percent of Total Sum of Squares
Media Weight (W)	2	163.83[c]	29.37	129.22[c]	21.30	28.69[c]	5.51	31.69[c]	6.45
Media Timing Pattern (T)	2	12.92[c]	2.32	29.58[c]	4.88	9.07[c]	1.74	0.59	0.12
Purchase Cycle (C)	3	1.15	0.31	4.93[b]	1.22	0.19	0.05	0.88	0.27
Product Type (P)	1	94.36[c]	8.46	217.56[c]	17.93	331.49[c]	31.83	312.70[c]	31.80
W x T	4	0.58	0.21	3.13[a]	1.03	0.25	0.09	0.26	0.11
W x C	6	0.43	0.23	0.23	0.11	1.00	0.57	0.23	0.14
W x P	2	22.78[c]	4.09	27.88[c]	4.60	0.81	0.16	2.21	0.45
T x C	6	0.58	0.31	0.37	0.18	1.97	1.13	2.22[a]	1.35
T x P	2	7.08[b]	1.27	2.80	0.46	2.26	0.43	0.24	0.05
C x P	3	1.56	0.42	1.36	0.34	1.74	0.50	1.33	0.40
W x T x C	12	0.38	0.41	0.11	0.11	0.63	0.72	0.13	0.16
W x T x P	4	0.56	0.20	0.35	0.11	0.47	0.18	0.60	0.02
W x C x P	6	0.43	0.23	0.24	0.12	0.88	0.51	0.83	0.05
T x C x P	6	0.36	0.19	0.08	0.04	0.64	0.37	0.40	0.02
W x T x C x P	12	0.33	0.35	0.09	0.09	0.75	0.87	0.03	0.04
Error	576		51.64		47.47		55.32		58.57

[a] $p < .05$
[b] $p < .005$
[c] $p < .001$

media timing. Across all four measures, media weight explained 62.6 percent of the total sum of squares for awareness and market share while media timing explained only 9.1 percent of the total sum of squares.

The main effect of media timing had no effect on end-of-year market share since it was not significant at the 0.05 level. Thus, media weight was nearly seven times more important in explaining the total sum of squares for the four dependent measures of market response than was media timing. Or, to put it another way, the number of media dollars is more important than when the company spends them. This is not all that surprising in light of the whopping differences in media weight tested in the study. The high level of spending was four times greater than the light level.

How Media Weight Affects Awareness and Market Share

An analysis of cell mean figures provides a more complete interpretation of the influence of the various determinants of market response. Exhibit 9–2 presents the means for each of the four dependent variables for each media weight level. These data indicate a monotonically increasing trend for each measure of market re-

Exhibit 9–2

Effects of Media Weight on Measures of Market Response

Dependent Variable	Level of Media Weight		
	Light	Average	Heavy
Awareness:			
Average	15.4%	23.2%	36.2%
End-of-Year	16.7%	26.0%	37.4%
Market Share:			
Average	6.2%	7.3%	9.3%
End-of-Year	5.7%	7.1%	8.8%

sponse as the level of media weight increases from a light budget (600 gross rating points), to an average budget (1,200 GRPs), and finally to a heavy budget (2,400 GRPs).

For example, as we increase media weight, the mean forecast of average awareness rises from 15.4 percent to 23.2 percent and then to 36.2 percent. For average market share, the mean forecast rises from 6.2 percent to 7.3 percent to 9.3 percent as media weight increases. As gross rating points increase, the mean forecasts for end-of-year market share show similar rises.

What the Analysis of Means Reveals

Exhibit 9–3 shows the means for each type of media timing pattern. These data confirm that timing's influence is not as great as that of media weight. For example, the front-loaded pattern realizes average and end-of-year awareness mean forecasts of 28.3 percent and 21.1 percent, respectively; the flighted pattern produces means of 23.3 percent and 28.5 percent; and the sustained pattern turns out means of 23.2 percent and 30.5 percent.

The average and end-of-year market share forecasts are 8.6 percent and 6.9 percent, respectively, for the front-loaded pattern, 7.2

Exhibit 9–3

Effects of Media Timing Pattern on Measures of Market Response

	Type of Media Timing Pattern		
Dependent Variable	**Front Loaded**	**Flighted**	**Sustained**
Awareness:			
Average	28.3%	23.3%	23.2%
End-of-Year	21.1%	28.5%	30.5%
Market Share:			
Average	8.6%	7.2%	7.0%
End-of-Year	6.9%	7.3%	7.3%

percent and 7.3 percent for the flighted pattern, and 7.0 percent and 7.3 percent for the sustained pattern. Exhibit 9–3's results illustrate that a front-loaded media pattern is likely to generate the highest average awareness levels and market shares. On the other hand, a sustained pattern is likely to generate the highest end-of-year awareness levels and market shares.

These findings are consistent with those Hubert A Zielske and Walter A. Henry reported in the *Journal of Advertising Research* and Julian Simon discussed in the *Journal of Marketing Research*.[4] They found that a front-loaded pattern causes large market response increases early in the year but subsequent market response trails off rather drastically later in the year.

Purchase Cycle and Media Timing

Exhibit 9–4 presents end-of-year market share forecasts for the three media patterns by purchase cycle length. These show that for a product consumers buy frequently (twice a month or monthly), the front-loaded approach is the most effective.

For products consumers buy quarterly, the flighted media pattern produced the highest end-of-year market share forecasts. For products consumers buy twice per year, the sustained media pattern overwhelms the other two patterns with an 8.4 percent mean end-

Exhibit 9–4

**Effects of Purchase Cycle and
Media Timing Pattern on End-of-Year Market Share**

Purchase Cycle Length	Type of Media Timing Pattern		
	Front Loaded	**Flighted**	**Sustained**
Twice per Month	7.3%	6.9%	6.5%
Monthly	7.9%	7.6%	7.2%
Quarterly	7.1%	7.6%	7.3%
Twice per Year	5.6%	7.1%	8.4%

of-year market share forecast; the flighted pattern obtained a 7.1 percent share; the front-loaded pattern a 5.6 percent.

This study's results suggest that purchase cycle length can affect the media timing pattern's effectiveness considerably. For products that turn rapidly—that have short purchase cycles—companies want to motivate consumers to try the product and then repeat their purchase soon after the campaign's launch. For products consumers buy infrequently, a front-loaded campaign is a large advertising expenditure when consumers may not be in the market to buy.

These findings are consistent with two decades of in-market testing undertaken by package goods marketers to assess the effects of different media variables on advertising performance. The inconsistency of the findings from study to study is now revealed for the first time to be partially a function of purchase cycle. Given the discovery here that purchase cycle has a clear effect on the measured effects of advertising, and that purchase cycle has rarely—if ever—been systematically taken into account in designing and analyzing in-market test results, the bewildering, inconsistent patterns of past research findings should have been expected.

Product Type and Media Timing

Exhibit 9–5 shows that, for new products, a front-loaded media pattern produced a higher average awareness level, 35.4 percent,

Exhibit 9–5

**Effects of Product Type and
Media Timing Pattern on Average Awareness**

	Type of Media Timing Pattern		
Type of Product	**Front Loaded**	**Flighted**	**Sustained**
New	35.4%	26.4%	26.8%
Established	21.2%	20.1%	19.6%

than either the flighted or sustained patterns, which achieved 26.4 percent and 26.8 percent, respectively.

For new campaigns for established products, the effects of media timing are not statistically significant. Thus, while this analysis suggests that a front-loaded media schedule produces a significant advantage in generating above-average awareness for new products, no media timing pattern produced a comparable advantage for established products.

For end-of-year consumer awareness, the interaction effect between the type of media timing pattern and the type of product did not meet the 0.05 criterion for statistical significance. It was significant at the 0.06 level, however, which suggests that these results are "significant" from a managerial perspective. Here, the front-loaded pattern showed a smaller mean forecast of end-of-year awareness for new products than either the flighted or the sustained patterns. The front-loaded pattern's mean end-of-year awareness levels were 27.2 percent, the flighted pattern's were 37.5 percent, and the sustained pattern's were 38.7 percent.

For new campaigns of established products, the end-of-year consumer awareness mean scores were 15.1 percent, 19.4 percent, and 22.4 percent, respectively. These results confirm Exhibit 9–3's results that the front-loaded media pattern produces some early advantages in building awareness, but the high levels diminish over time unless the media schedule maintains the high awareness level.

Product Type and Media Weight

For both consumer awareness levels, media weight demonstrates a powerful effect on new product awareness as well as a strong effect on new campaigns for established products (Exhibit 9–6). For example, the mean level of end-of-year awareness for new products increased 153 percent as media weight increased from 600 GRPs to 2,400 GRPs. For established products, end-of-year awareness increased 80 percent.

As media weight increases from light to heavy, the average awareness measure also follows this pattern showing a 171 percent increase for new products and a 91 percent increase for established products.

Exhibit 9–6

**Effects of Product Type and
Media Weight on Average and End-of-Year Awareness**

Dependent Variable	Product Type	Level of Media Weight		
		Light	Average	Heavy
Average Awareness	New	16.6%	27.0%	45.0%
	Established	14.3%	19.4%	27.3%
End-of-Year Awareness	New	19.8%	33.5%	50.1%
	Established	13.7%	18.5%	24.7%

Media Weight and Media Timing

Increasing media weight generates the largest gains in end-of-year consumer awareness from the sustained media pattern (Exhibit 9–7). Increasing media weight from light to heavy produces a 105 percent rise in end-of-year awareness for the front-loaded media pattern, a 121 percent rise for the flighted pattern, and a 140 percent rise for the sustained pattern.

Exhibit 9–7

**Effects of Media Weight and
Media Timing Pattern on End-of-Year Awareness**

Level of Media Weight	Type of Media Timing Pattern		
	Front Loaded	Flighted	Sustained
Light	14.0%	17.9%	18.3%
Average	20.7%	28.0%	29.4%
Heavy	28.7%	39.5%	44.0%

Further, when we compare end-of-year consumer awareness for each media weight level, we find the sustained media timing pattern accomplishing the strongest results. The sustained pattern yields the most productive results as the advertiser increases media weight. When a marketer believes it important to have strong year-end consumer product awareness, the sustained timing pattern is most productive.

Management Implications

This study found that media timing and media weight effects depend largely on whether a product is new or established and whether consumers buy it frequently or infrequently. Further, the effects depend on whether we measure consumer awareness or market share and report either as an average over the year or a total at year's end.

Some readers may question this research's appropriateness or relevance. After all, the research purports to analyze data from 648 different simulations. The results, one could charge, are simply a reflection of the model used to make the forecasts. And there is some truth to this argument.

On the other hand, the modelers did not create the model to produce the outcomes presented in this chapter. Rather, they developed a model to describe the reality of the world and tested model validity by comparing model performance against reality in hundreds of cases, improving it annually as discrepancies between forecast and real-world performance appeared. Thus we think of the LITMUS model as being similar to the physical models used in wind-tunnel experiments to experiment with the effects of different automobile or sail or aircraft designs. These models are designed to capture current knowledge and predict the future. Similarly, the LITMUS model has been designed to do the same.

Perhaps the best testimony to the validity of the simulation exercise came from a senior marketing research executive at Procter & Gamble, a company that has probably done more in-market testing than any other. His response to an earlier draft of this work was simply, "This study does more to explain decades of in-market tests at P&G than anything else I've seen. The main effects and interactions reported here are right on with our experience. Indeed, if we'd had the results of this simulation earlier, we would have undertaken far fewer tests and designed them very differently."

Management can use these findings (and models such as those reported here) to improve the media budget's effectiveness on a case-by-case basis. For example, we found that for a given media weight, a front-loaded plan generates the highest *average* consumer awareness and market share. However, a sustained media plan generates the highest *end-of-year* consumer awareness and market share. Management objectives for average and end-of-year awareness targets dictate which media timing pattern is best for a given situation.

Most important, the results clearly demonstrate the need to take the product purchase cycle into account in planning and implementing marketing campaigns for new and established products and services. Front-loaded schedules always seem to work best for *fast turnover* new products (one to four or more purchases per month). They invariably fail for *slow turnover* brands (those purchased twice a year or less frequently) whether they are new or established.

The reason is simple: a front-loaded campaign will fire up awareness when people are not yet ready to buy. It's like heating the furnace on a warm day. When people are ready to buy because they've used up whatever the new product is designed to replace, they've already forgotten that the new brand exists. The fuel burned in summer does nothing to warm the house in winter.

10

Modeling Competitive Response

A Critical Issue of the '90s

Simulated test marketing research is the best tool that management has today to forecast the likely success of a new (or restaged) product or service. However, there is at least one area in which most current systems could be improved considerably and that is modeling competitive response.

Most simulations today assume one level of competitive response—the norm, the level of competitive activity that is normal or typical in the product category. In the real world, of course, there is no way to predict for certain what competitive response will be. What we do know is that it is increasingly greater than what marketers observed in the past.

As a result, sales can fall well below the simulated test market research's forecast. To improve our ability to forecast sales volume correctly, marketing managers must include more realistic assumptions about competitive response. As we pointed out in Chapter 2 with "The Case of the Annihilated Brand," a competitor who increases advertising spending in test markets astronomically can overwhelm the new introduction.

But does a new product have to fail, and how can a marketer improve the likelihood of a new product's success—always aware that it may provoke massive competitive response? The marketing manager must anticipate the competition's defensive reaction and then develop and test offensive strategies designed to overwhelm those competitive defenses. To do so without spending millions of dollars in the marketplace, marketers can simulate the effects of offensive and defensive strategies through simulated test marketing research.

During the past few decades, the tools available to marketing managers have improved dramatically. Simulated test marketing models discussed in this book routinely churn out volume forecasts and diagnostic insights that should improve the likelihood of marketplace success. One would expect as a result that new product survival rates would have improved. But as we've noted, new product failure rates are rising; 80 to 99 percent of all new product launches are failures today.

Several hypotheses attempt to explain why the new product success rate has not improved over the past three decades. One theory is that as more sophisticated marketers employ increasingly sophisticated research, competitors quickly neutralize a corporation's planned advances. In a so-called zero-sum game played by firms with rising levels of expertise, the result is market share equilibrium, and constant new product failure rates are the norm.

A second hypothesis is that advertising today, in terms of media weight and copy, isn't strong enough to launch a new product successfully. Proponents of this hypothesis point to advertising's falling share of marketing budgets, while consumer and trade promotion's share is rising. In the 1960s, for example, companies allocated seven out of ten dollars in the marketing budget to advertising. Today the average corporation allocates three of ten marketing dollars to advertising with trade and consumer promotion taking the rest.

The escalating cost of media and advertising clutter are also taking their toll. Although A. C. Nielsen tells us that the time people spent viewing television per day has been relatively stable for ten years (it averaged six hours, thirty-eight minutes in 1980; six hours, fifty-five minutes in 1990; and peaked at seven hours, ten minutes in 1986), the cost of commercial time has continued to skyrocket, and the absolute number of commercial messages has increased as stations add commercial seconds and companies run two fifteen-second spots in the place of one thirty-second spot. As a result, a company has to spend more money to reach the same number of prospects than it had to spend just five years ago, and when it does spend the money, the cacophony of clutter drowns out its message.

The problem with clutter might be overcome if advertising in the mid-'90s was stronger, with greater impact than advertising in, say, the 1970s or '80s. But there is no evidence that this is the case. Indeed, there is anecdotal evidence that advertising is becoming less effective rather than more over time. As discussed in *Marketing Myths that Are Killing Business*[1], we've met privately with a number of research or media heads of America's biggest advertising spenders and with some of the heads of their biggest research suppliers. To a person they said they no longer had any proof that the great bulk of advertising worked.

One said, "We don't measure one medium against another because we don't think either will work." Said another, "We stopped doing effectiveness research years ago."

Our research among a cross-section of marketing executives is also discouraging. Less than a quarter of our respondents expressed a belief that:

- Most in-market tests of advertising weight produce significant differences in sales (only 20 percent believe this).
- Most campaigns designed to increase sales of established products or services are successful (17 percent).
- Most in-market tests of advertising copy are successful in producing significant differences in sales (13 percent).

A third hypothesis is that the marketing battleground of the mid-1990s are very different from those of the 1960s, '70s, and '80s. If the earlier period was the age of the offensive strategy, then the 1990s represents the age of the defensive strategy. In the past, corporate strategy was to earn incremental market share points; current corporate strategy is to keep competitors from winning incremental share points.

In an earlier and more gentle time, marketing managers relied more on hunch, judgment, and creativity to launch the occasional new product. If a new product achieved an early success, competitive response was often too little and too late to influence the launch. In 1990s, competitive response to new products and to new campaigns is both swift and sure. Soon after launch, the products the new brand was supposed to dislodge hammer it unmercifully.

Since all three hypotheses are plausible, which one is true? They all are. More sophisticated marketers *are* using more sophisticated new product development and testing tools. And in a zero-sum game played by firms with increasing expertise, market share equilibrium *is* the result. Also, companies make success more difficult for themselves when they cut back on advertising and shift the money to promotion.

In our view, shared by some and argued by others, advertising works better than promotion to position and launch new products. Although promotion can be very efficient in generating new product trial, it fails to provide consumers with the buying rationale necessary to warrant repeat and sustained purchasing. So the shift to promotion has hurt new product efforts.

At the same time, marketers *are* increasingly defensive-minded. One firm's offensive thrusts are countered by another company's often massive levels of defensive activity—advertising, promotion, price cuts, trade deals, and more. They've seen this pressure in test markets, in regional roll-outs, and in national introductions. As the arsenal of defensive weapons becomes more powerful, it reduces the likelihood of a successful new product introduction (Exhibit 10–1). Companies deploy five kinds of weapons with increasing levels of destructive power to crush new brands. These are:

Exhibit 10–1

**The Relationship Between
Destructive Power and Difficulty of Implementation**

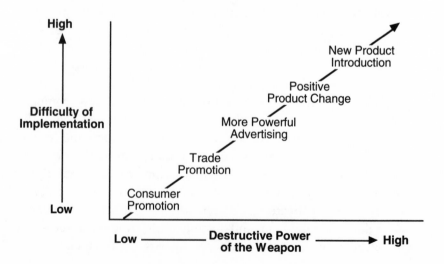

- Consumer promotion, mainly coupons.
- Trade promotion, discounts, special displays, co-op advertising, and so forth.
- More powerful advertising, including rebates, price ads.
- Positive product changes.
- A new product.

Each has a positive effect for the competitor who uses them and a clear negative effect on anybody else's new product. The competitor who uses any of these today can inflict substantial damage on a new product, leading to the typical new product failure. A company that employs the entire arsenal can produce a major disaster for a competitor, and companies are using these weapons more and more (Exhibit 10–2). Our recent survey of marketing directors at Fortune 100 companies found three out of four saying that competitive defenses are tougher today than ten years ago.

Between the neutralization that takes place in the marketplace with rising sophistication levels, the marketing budget's shift to promotion, and the competition's defensive activity, it's no surprise that new prod-

Exhibit 10–2

The Relationship Between
Weapon Deployment and New Product Damage

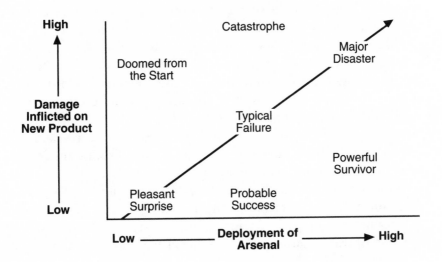

uct success rates have not improved. But does that mean companies should stop introducing new or re-positioned products and services?

Hardly. It *does* mean that companies have to plan even more carefully and employ all the marketing tools available. Companies need to rethink how they structure their marketing efforts—making sure the marketing people obtain and use cost information, for example—and evaluating thousands . . . hundreds of thousands of alternatives on the basis of profitability.

STMs Can Measure Competitive Response

Happily, sophisticated simulated test marketing systems today can take competitive response into account, thereby adapting to the new marketing realities. All that's required is the will to use them for this purpose. The marketing manager can evaluate any plan's offensive tactics by using sensitivity analysis (Chapter 7) to explore the effects of different components in the marketing mix on sales and profit performance. Some systems can even recommend an optimal plan (Chapter 11). In addition to testing the effects of various offensive strategies, sensitivity analysis can also examine what will happen to trial and repeat figures given different competitive responses.

To capture the impact of competitive activity on market response, a good laboratory simulation can incorporate a number of competitive promotional factors. For example, as we described in Chapter 6, smart systems are able to measure the effects of feature pricing strategies on behavioral response in the simulated store. This means that the effects of price can be validly measured in the simulation experiment.

Other competitive response factors, such as coupons, require a combination of the store experiment and consumer responses to the interview. Most consumers do not use coupons for most purchases. To measure the effect of consumer promotion, therefore, smart systems must estimate the probability that a consumer would use a coupon in the real world and then observe that consumer's behavior in the laboratory environment. Such a forecast employs a combination of attitudinal and behavioral responses.

Some competitive variables require a "decision calculus" approach based on real-world data and on the marketing manager's judgment. For example, a company obtains its share of store shelf facings as a function of trade deals. Since researchers have discovered that laboratory experiments do not measure the impact of shelf dominance on sales well (the research environment is too artificial), the research must use management judgment and historical relationships to make a forecast. One way to make this judgment is called decision calculus.

In decision calculus the marketing manager first plots current sales and share of store shelf facings on a sheet of graph paper. The X axis indicates sales, the Y axis indicates shelf facings. Next, based on the manager's experience, she guesstimates what sales level the company would obtain if it doubled the shelf facings. Third, she guesstimates the sales level if the company were to increase the shelf facing level well beyond that achieved by any competitor. Finally, she guesstimates the sales level if the shelf facings shrank almost to zero.

The graph now has four data points: sales with almost no shelf facings; sales with current shelf facings; sales with double shelf facings; and sales with the store shelves dominated by the new product. The manager then "fits" or has her computer's statistical program fit a line (usually a non-linear one) through those four points using standard statistical estimation techniques. She can then solve for the optimal shelf facing level. While decision calculus is a judgmental approach, it's a lot more rational then simply picking a number out of the air.

When a company engages a simulated test marketing system to capture competitive effects, it uses a multi-step procedure to forecast sales and profits. First, the marketing manager creates alternative competitive scenarios such as the most likely case, a more serious case, a life-threatening case, and even a doomsday case. Researchers then employ a combination of laboratory simulation, measurement, and decision calculus approaches to estimate the effects of each scenario on each market response parameter. For each scenario, the model is run to forecast awareness, sales, and profits.

Once a system generates a base forecast for each scenario, sensitivity analyses can be undertaken to assess what effect the competition's consumer and trade promotion will have on the new or restaged brand. Finally, with the objective of countering competitive response, the marketing manager then formulates alternative plans, and the system develops awareness, sales, and profitability forecasts for each of them.

Marketing managers take a number of common strategies to neutralize the competition. They often adjust each marketing plan component to combat the threat. Another tactic is to evaluate each component and make adjustments, such as changing advertising copy to improve its effect among the target audience. Marketers may modify a product introduction's schedule. For example, they may replace an "Accretion Strategy" with a "Big Bang Strategy." Finally, they analyze short run losses versus long run profits when they examine the "hold" versus "fold" position. Simulated test market research to evaluate the effect of competitive response before expensive, risky, real-world introductions is one way marketers can improve their own new product success rate.

Management Implications

The purpose of this chapter was to discuss the problem of competitive response in the mid-'90s and to suggest ways in which simulated test market systems can begin to take competitive response into account. The issue today is that STMs do not address the problem of competitive response very well at all. When it occurs in massive doses—and this is increasingly the case during the new product launch—the resulting forecasts can be off by a significant margin and the autopsy points to unanticipated aberrations in the marketplace. This is a mistake.

In this new age of defensive strategy, managers should expect and plan for unusual levels of competitive response. And simulated test marketing studies can be designed to take this changing marketing condition into account. Laboratory STMs can do a fair job of measuring market response to the new entry in the context of a less-than-hoped-for share-of-voice, diminished copy effectiveness, or price cuts by the market leaders. With some clever tinkering, simulated test market research can also incorporate the effects of competitive couponing, shelf facings, and other weapons in the competitive arsenal.

Our own perspective is that new product marketers should spend almost as much time thinking about what competitors might do to prevent their product from becoming successful as they do about their own offensive strategies. It is then a matter of converting competitive STM plans into the simulation study design and modeling exercise to identify the best plans for overcoming likely competitive moves.

11

Toward Marketing Plan Optimization

Marketing managers ultimately want to know, "Which marketing plan is best?" Unfortunately, as we discussed in Chapter 2, there can be literally billions of possible plans for any product or service. How is an executive to evaluate such a surfeit in a single lifetime? Sadly, many marketing managers, using traditional test marketing, develop and test only one or two plans among the possible billions—and they pick those they decide to test based on experience and instinct. The result is rising rates of new product failure.

Consider the following example of a new soft drink recently taken national.

Because the manager wasn't sure what level of ad support was appropriate, he considered budgets that ranged from $2 million to $26 million in $100,000 increments. That's 250 advertising options.

Because distribution possibilities ranged from 10 (distribution in only one chain in the market) to 90 percent (distribution in all chains that sold soft drinks), there were eighty-one distribution options.

Because the company could deliver coupons to any percentage of the population—from 0 to 100 percent—it had 101 coupon reach options. And because it could deliver as many as five coupons per household, it had six coupon frequency options.

Finally, because it might sample no one, everyone, or any percentage in between, it had 101 sampling options (Exhibit 11–1). These options represent 1,239,421,500 possible plans[1] of which

Exhibit 11–1

Marketing Options for a New Soft Drink

Marketing Mix Component	Range	Options
Advertising	2 - 26 Million	250 (Hundreds of Thousands)
Distribution	10 - 90%	81 (Points)
Couponing (% Population)	0 - 100%	101 (Points)
Couponing (# of Coupons per HH)	0 - 5	6 (Numbers)
Sampling (% Population)	0 - 100%	101 (Points)

the company evaluated two. The result, as one might expect considering the 1 in 619,625,750 odds, was failure.

Another case that we reviewed involved an international air carrier. The corporation's marketing plan for a new service consisted of eighteen strategic and tactical decisions, each of which offered five to 10,000 possibilities. The total number of possible plans was more than a trillion. The corporation assessed only a few—those that seemed to make the most sense in management's best judgment—and the new service failed.

Toward the Development of Optimal Marketing Plans

Simulated test marketing research models offer marketing executives two different approaches to optimizing a marketing plan. In one, the modelers deploy a formal optimizing algorithm that seeks the best possible solution to the problem. We'll provide a few examples of this approach in a moment. In the other approach, the marketing executives take the results of the STM research and modify the plan to improve the predicted results, and we'll conclude this chapter with a case showing how this approach can help.

The success of a new product launch or an existing product's re-launch is only limited by the number of marketing plans the marketer tests. Marketing mix models such as the ones used most by simulated test marketing modelers have proven that it is possible for simulated test marketing research to evaluate a marketing plan (any plan) and forecast the probable results if the company takes the plan into the market.

Today's challenge is to generate improved marketing plans. There are two broad approaches to the issue. The first approach employs technical and sophisticated mathematical algorithms to evaluate countless marketing plans and identify and describe a financially optimal one. The second approach uses research tools that help evaluate a limited number of marketing plans in order to find one which is better. A simulated test market, for example, can easily evaluate five different advertising spending levels, three different distribution levels, seven different prices, and so forth. In the following sections we will present case studies of how researchers have used the LITMUS and DESIGNOR models to address this optimization question.

The Optimization Procedure

In the LITMUS model, there are two ways to guide the optimization procedure. With a budget optimization, the marketing manager fixes a budget level and the model produces a plan that maximizes share and profits within those financial constraints. With a share optimization, the marketing manager sets a market share objective and the model establishes the minimum marketing budget necessary to meet that goal.

In one sense, the optimal solution is the same for both problems. That is, if maximum sales for a $10 million budget are, say, 100,000 cases, the minimum budget necessary to attain sales of 100,000 cases is $10 million. Moreover, the marketing mix that generates the maximum sales is the same as the one that minimizes the budget.

The optimization procedure moves through four stages (Exhibit 11–2). The first phase of the optimization procedure applies the sensitivity analysis we described in Chapter 7 to the manager-prepared plan. This identifies the relationship between changes in each marketing tool (e.g., thirty-second commercials, distribution level, coupon-

Exhibit 11–2

A Four Stage Optimization Approach

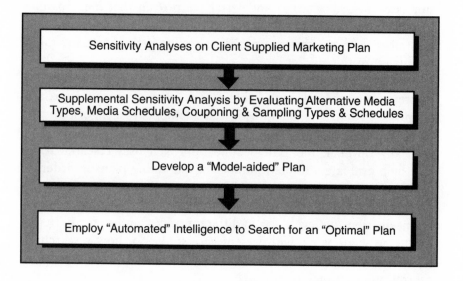

ing, etc.) in the manager-prepared plan and sales or profits or both. This phase identifies the plan's more and less cost-efficient vehicles.

The second stage applies sensitivity analysis to evaluate marketing vehicles that the manager's plan did not include. This allows the model to examine the effectiveness of all possible marketing vehicles—different advertising media, media schedules, coupons, samples, and their types and schedules.

The third stage develops a model-aided plan. A manual selection of a starting plan is based on the most efficient performance of media, media schedule, coupon type and schedule, and sample type and schedule subject to management constraints based on corporate policies and judgment. Management constraints may include things like no more than ten commercial spots a month in daytime television; no more than one full page per monthly magazine per month; or total gross rating points no fewer than twenty per month during the campaign's last four months.

The fourth stage is the formal optimization analysis that uses a hill-climbing procedure and manipulates four components in the marketing mix: advertising expenditures, coupon costs, sample costs, and distribution costs. The hill-climbing procedure is an adaptation of a standard mathematical algorithm in which the third stage defines the starting point. From the starting point, the model uses sensitivity analysis to determine the direction of most improvement in the marketing plan. After hundreds of small changes in the variables, and hundreds of runs, the model reaches the top of the hill, the optimal marketing plan.

Exhibit 11–3 depicts a view of a mathematical hill-climbing problem posed by optimization. Since the number of dimensions it can depict limits this figure, we assume for this example that the

Exhibit 11–3

Surface Mapping to Find an Optimal Plan

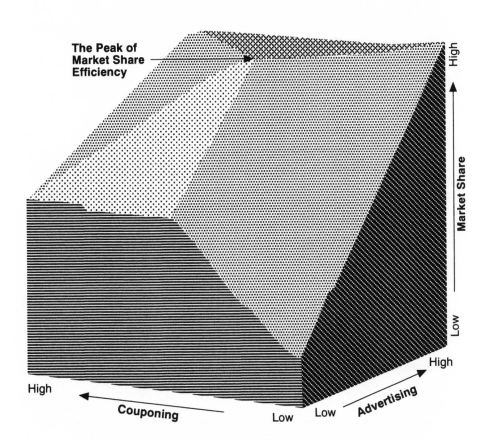

company has fixed sampling expenditures and distribution costs. Further, we assume that we want to optimize share with respect to a coupon and advertising budget. The goal is to search along the two dimensions—advertising and couponing—seeking the maximum share point. The share values form a surface, as Exhibit 11–3 shows. The objective is to find the highest point on the surface.

Case Histories of Optimization at Work

To understand the benefits of optimization, we will examine two case histories, each a new food product. The first case shows the result of guiding the optimization procedure by minimizing cost based on a share goal constraint—a share optimization. In this case management imposed no constraints on the optimization process.

The second case shows the result of maximizing share subject to a marketing budget constraint—a budget optimization. Although these examples show that optimization's benefits are great, the number of optimization applications remains small because they are time-consuming, costly, and because many marketers are unnerved by advanced technology.

A Share Optimization

Exhibit 11–4 shows the LITMUS projection for an optimization case guided by cost minimization. The original manager-prepared

Exhibit 11–4

Optimization Case for a New Food Product

	Manager-Prepared Plan	Model-Generated "Optimal" Plan
Cost of Plan	$27 Million	$19 Million
Forecasted Share of Market	13.7%	14.2%
Expected Gains/Losses (End of Year 1)	-7.9 Million	+0.2 Million
Pay Out Period	38 Months	16 Months

plan, based on a $27 million marketing budget, forecast a 13.7 percent market share with an expected loss in the first year of about $8 million. The model-generated plan, based on a $19 million marketing budget, forecast a 14.2 percent market share with an expected profit of $200,000—a much more efficient marketing plan. Instead of a first year loss, the system projected the product to finish the year in the black, an unusual result for a new product.

Exhibit 11–5 indicates the ways in which the optimal marketing plan differs from the manager-prepared plan. Neither plan allocated funds to samples. The model-generated plan allocates $1 million to distribution, which increases the average all commodity volume distribution in Year One to 78 percent, up from 65 percent in the manager-prepared plan.

The manager-generated advertising and coupon strategies are significantly different from the model-generated plans. The model pared advertising by $5 million; it recommended spending less on television and adding magazine advertising. Moreover, it increased the front loading of the gross rating point pattern. With coupons, the model changed the pattern slightly and recommended spending 30 percent less than the manager's plan. The net result was a more efficient use of promotion dollars to achieve a slight share gain.

A Constrained and Unconstrained Budget Optimization

The second optimization case is a budget optimization. In this case, the model produced two optimizations because management set media constraints, and we based one on these; the other had no constraints. Constraints limit the optimization procedure by eliminating marketing plans that could generate potentially higher sales. In this case, management chose to keep distribution expenditures constant and optimize media and consumer promotion expenditures.

Exhibit 11–6 shows the media constraints, the allocations in the constrained optimal plan, and the allocations in the unconstrained optimal plan. The constrained optimal allocation of gross rating points by the model is the management constraint for cable television and daytime television. However, the unconstrained optimal allocation of gross rating points by the model is above the management constraint for the relatively cost-efficient cable television and daytime television vehicles. Both the constrained and uncon-

Exhibit 11–5

$27 Million Manager-Generated Plan vs.
$19 Million Model-Generated Optimal Plan

	$27 Million Manager-Generated Plan	$19 Million Model-Generated Plan
Marketing Plan		
Media/Promotion	**$27.2MM**	**$19.0MM**
Advertising	13.9MM	8.8MM
Couponing	13.3MM	10.2MM
Distribution	–	1.0MM
Selected Plan Characteristics		
Advertising		
Media Types		
TV	Early Morning,Prime, Day, Early/Late Fringe	Prime, Day, Early/Late Fringe
Magazines	None	Good Housekeeping, Ladies Home Journal, Woman's Day
Total GRPs	**3,778**	**3,021**
April	611	330
May	1,234	1,371
June	244	990
July	508	330
Aug	342	–
Sept	242	–
Oct	454	–
Couponing		
Promotion Types	On Pack, FSI, Contact, BFD	FSI, Contact with Fill-in, BFD (Newspaper)
Households Reached	**306%**	**283%**
April	56	47
May	71	67
June	35	53
July	48	62
Aug	48	27
–	–	–
January	48	–
Sampling	None	None
Distribution	65% ACV April 72% Peak August 71% Off Season	78% ACV April Max 88% Aug/Sept Dropping to 84% Off Season

Exhibit 11–6

Media Constraints and Optimal Allocations

Parameter	Parameters for Management Constraints Optimization Maximum Allocation	Allocation Based on Constrained Optimization	Allocation Based on Unconstrained Optimization
GRPs Allocated to Months 1-4	69%	66%	55%
Broadcast GRPs Allocated to :15 Ads	43%	35%	30%
Broadcast GRPs to Daytime TV	35%	35%	45%
Percent of Total Dollar Spending Allocated to Cable TV	10%	10%	12%

strained optimal plans are under management's limit for gross rating points allocated to the first four months and for fifteen-second ads, which are relatively less cost-efficient media choices.

The budget optimization yielded significantly better results than the manager-prepared plan. The constrained plan forecast a 14.8 percent sales increase over the manager-prepared plan's forecast; the unconstrained optimization forecast an 18.2 percent sales increase (Exhibit 11–7).

The allocation of dollars between advertising and consumer promotion is about the same in all three plans. Reallocating advertising vehicles for the constrained optimization increased the relative proportion of day, syndication, and cable gross rating points (Exhibit 11–8). The constrained optimal plan reduced early morning, prime, late fringe, and print's allocation of gross rating points as a percentage of total GRPs.

The unconstrained optimal plan further increased the relative proportion of day and cable gross rating points (Exhibit 11–8). Moreover, the allocation of gross rating points in late fringe was increased relative to the constrained plan, where fringe was excluded. This plan further reduced prime time and print advertis-

Exhibit 11–7

Baseline, Constrained, and Unconstrained Forecasts

	Baseline Forecast*	Constrained Optimization Forecast	Unconstrained Optimization Forecast
Total Expenditures	$10.3MM	$10.3MM	$10.3MM
Media Expenditures	7.4MM	7.4MM	7.4MM
Promotion Expenditures	2.9MM	2.9MM	2.9MM
GRPs	**1,687**	**1,901**	**2,066**
Awareness			
Year/Range	18 - 38%	26 - 41%	30 - 43%
Average	32%	36%	38%
Penetration			
% Ever Tried at End of Year 1	10.0%	10.6%	10.7%
Volume			
Units (MM)	25.02	28.75	29.68
Cases (MM)	2.09	2.40	2.47
Percent Change			
In Cases from Baseline Forecast	–	14.8%	18.2%

*In 92% of cases, sales are within +/- 10% of forecasted levels.

ing, as well as cutting the proportion of gross rating points allocated to syndication.

A Different Kind of Optimization Case Study

The other way to improve the marketing plan is to take the simulated test marketing research's results and adjust weak elements of the marketing mix to improve the product's chances for success. This is

Exhibit 11–8

Baseline and Optimal Marketing Plans

$7.4MM Media Spending

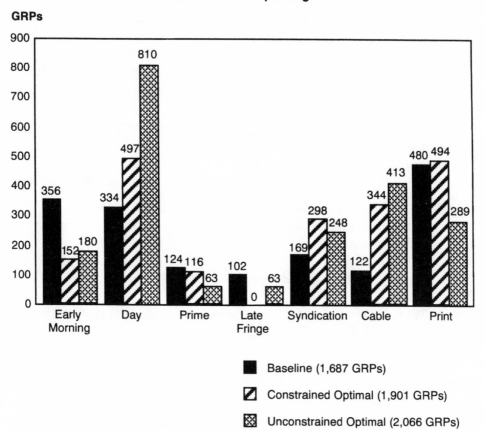

GRPs

■ Baseline (1,687 GRPs)
▨ Constrained Optimal (1,901 GRPs)
▧ Unconstrained Optimal (2,066 GRPs)

not really optimization in its true, mathematical sense, but rather represents a common lay interpretation of the word. It means using the results of the simulated test market to help build the best possible plan, the objective of the work we described in Chapter 7.

The following, based on a DESIGNOR consulting project for a major multi-national client, illustrates that kind of optimization. We report this case in considerable detail to show how new wrinkles on simulated test marketing can help improve a marketing plan.

The client corporation had developed a new product in a category that was still growing but in which the corporation did not currently have a product. The new product was a line extension; the corporation was taking its existing brand name into a different category of personal product.

The advertising agency developed four alternative television commercials, "A," "B," "C," and "D."

The corporation wanted to test six prices with a 50 percent total price variation. For the research, Novaction, the research company, split the sample into separate price cells and each consumer saw only one price level.

In other words, the product's price in cell 1 was 10 percent higher than the average price in the category, the price in cell 2 was 18 percent higher, and so forth.

The study's main objectives were answers to three questions:

1. How much? The study was to assess accurately the new product's sales potential and how this varied by price and advertisement exposed.
2. Why? The study was to understand the performance of each element of the mix and how it contributed to overall sales potential.
3. What if? How could the corporation maximize the new mix's potential?

Exhibit 11–9

Price Index
(Relative to Category Average)

Price Cell 1	110
Price Cell 2	118
Price Cell 3	125
Price Cell 4	133
Price Cell 5	140
Price Cell 6	148

The study was done among a random sample of women, the quota controlled for age and product category usage so that it represented the potential target audience. The sample contained about 60 percent product users. Because the parent corporation's category penetration is greater than 95 percent, virtually all of the 40 percent non-users were aware of the parent's brand name.

During the field work, the researchers interviewed respondents concerning their current product usage habits and the brands with which they were familiar. The respondents watched one of the four ads for the new product in a clutter of competitive television commercials. They then had an opportunity to buy the new or competitive products with a voucher, and those who bought the new product were interviewed after they had used it in their homes.

What were the results?

Addressing the first question—how much?—three sales forecasts were developed: sales from advertising without sampling; sales with a sampling campaign; and a combination sales forecast. The best commercial—"A"—and best price—an 18 percent premium price over the market average—moderate advertising support (1,300 GRPs; with commercial "A," simulations showed that a large sampling campaign was more effective than high advertising expenditure); and 76 percent distribution gave the following results:

Trial rate	17.5%
×	
Long-term repeat	38.7%
= Sales potential	6.8%
(at full awareness and distribution)	
×	
Awareness	37.0%
×	
Distribution	76.0%
= Sales potential	1.9%
(at expected awareness and distribution)	

The best case involving a large sampling campaign—a 19 percent hit and use—with the same distribution gave the following results:

Hit and use	19.0%
×	
Distribution	76.0%
×	
1st repeat after sampling	41.0%
×	
Non-overlap with advertising	93.2%
= Additional penetration	5.5%
×	
Long-term repeat	38.7%
= Additional share from sampling	2.1%

The overall sales forecast (users and non-users) under the best case scenario shows the following:

Users

Share from advertising	1.9%
Share from sampling campaign	2.1%

Non-users

Share from advertising	0.4%
Share from sampling campaign	1.0%

The best case, in other words, showed that the new product's total sales potential was only a 5.4 percent share of the category. Over half of all sales (3.1 percent) would come from the large sampling campaign. Around a quarter of this small sales volume was represented by current non-users drawn into the category. It is very rare for a new product to attract a significant number of new users into a product category (in our experience, 10 percent is a remarkably high figure), although marketers frequently make this unfortunate assumption. In this case, however, target category penetration was still growing, and the response among the research sample's non-users showed that the new product would indeed gain significant volume by attracting new users.

In considering the second question—*why* the new product would obtain such a relatively small market share—Novaction looked at several issues: product quality, advertising originality and relevance, advertising content, brand identification, trial rate, and price elasticity. To take them in order:

Product Quality. The new product's formulation was significantly better than consumers' usual products, showing well above "average" performance for a new brand. It obtained a new product usage score of 31 percent. This score equals the percentage of the sample who rated the product "better" or "much better" than their usual brand minus the percentage who ranked it "worse" or "much worse." This performance could be understood by its strong post-use image on two key perceptual dimensions of the market (numbers 1 and 3 in Exhibit 11–10). Due to this good in-use performance, a sampling program was shown to be very efficient.

Exhibit 11–10

Phase I: Test Product Before and After Use

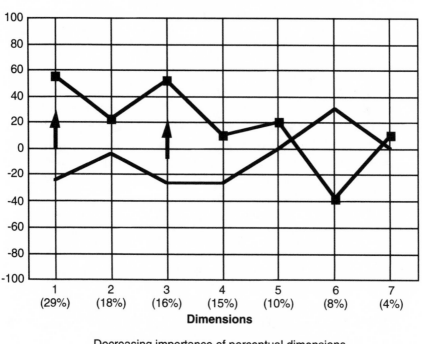

Originality and Relevance. The best performing television commercial projected average on originality (with an index of 115) and slightly above average on relevance (103 index). The index is calculated relative to the category leader's advertising performance. Respondents rate the advertising's uniqueness and relevance on a seven-point scale. The other three commercials did not achieve above-average scores.

Advertising Content/Takeout. Consumers' content recall (the themes they could remember spontaneously after viewing the commercials) focused on an aspect shown to be of only minor importance (dimension number 6 in the exhibit). Analysis of the market showed that this dimension explained only 8 percent of consumers' preference between brands. Given the strength of the product after-use, our recommendation was to focus much less on this area and more where the product actually delivered better performance. These areas also corresponded to more important consumer needs (dimensions 1 and 3). Exhibit 11–10 shows respondent perceptions of the test product before and after use on the key dimensions consumers use to differentiate brands.

Identification. The test product's second clear weakness related to its "stretch" from the parent category. The difficulty in establishing its own identity away from the parent brand was a weakness both in the advertising, with only half the respondents able to identify the brand name correctly after viewing the commercials, and in the packaging, again with low level of shelf identification compared to DESIGNOR'S standards.

Trial Rate. Even for the best advertisement, the average trial rate was a very low 17.5 percent at full awareness. This was much lower than the expected trial for the average new entrant into this category, which based on the system's norms would be 24.7 percent. These norms are grounded on twenty years of experience—over 2,000 STM projects and 6,000 tested mixes—to show the expected trial and repeat levels for an average new entrant to the market.

Price Elasticity. The optimal price for the new product was in price cell 2. Above the second price cell (18 percent above the category average), trial for the new product fell off rapidly, as illustrated in Exhibit 11–11.

It is in fact not common for the lowest price cell to correspond to the best trial for a new product because price often has a direct influence on the product's perceived quality. For this reason, Novaction believes in separate price cells rather than price "games" varying the

Exhibit 11–11

Trial Response to Price

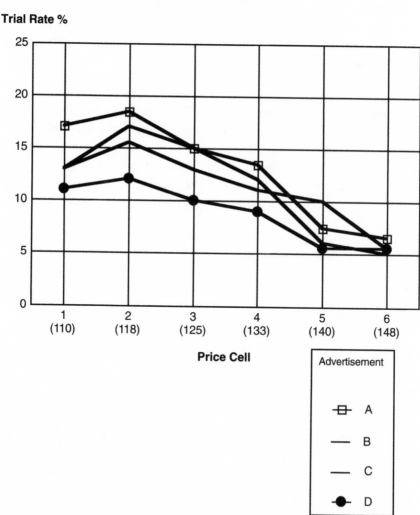

price to each consumer. The change in repeat rate as the price increased was much less; the repeat declined from slightly under 40 percent in price cell 1 to just over 30 percent in price cell 6.

This research led Novaction to make recommendations to the corporation's management to improve this new product's sales potential and profitability.

Pre-use Perception Improvement. Eliminate the mismatch between the advertising communication and product reality. Focus on communicating the now-discovered strengths of the actual product, which are also more important to consumers than other features. Simulations showed that a trial increase of as much as 40 percent was possible if the pre-use perception of the product could be made to match that achieved post-use.

Identification Improvement. This is a frequent weakness of brand extensions into different categories. We have, however, seen many cases in which companies overcame this weakness. Novaction's list of specific areas to improve covered packaging design, labeling, package shape, and better identification of the new brand name and product type in the advertising. Simulations showed that the product could achieve up to three extra market share points through these changes.

Price Elasticity. From its experience, Novaction researchers knew that the brand's inability to differentiate itself perceptually (that is, dominate a perceptual dimension pre-use) resulted in a strong trial elasticity to price. However, after the customers used the product, the brand was in a very different situation. With its strong after-use performance, it was then far less price sensitive. If the corporation could successfully implement improvements, it could hope for a better trial price response.

Sampling Program. The effectiveness of any sampling program led Novaction to simulate the effect of and to recommend even higher sampling levels than those the client had been considering.

It was concluded that while the new product had shown a strong in-use performance, its disappointing advertising did not support it. Elements of the packaging were also questionable. Novaction warned the client about the vulnerability of such a brand to any changes in the competitive environment and recommended that rather than launch the product with the tested marketing program the corporation should improve the mix to increase the sales potential and to improve the "robustness" of the mix relative to competitive reaction.

The corporation made several revisions to the test product mix. These included two new television commercials ("F" and "G") and revised packaging. Novaction conducted a second study that included three price points, corresponding to cells 2, 3, and 4 of the first study (indexes of 118, 125, and 133 relative to market average price). The sample definition was the same, and the question flow was similar but without product placement.

The best case now included advertising "F" (the other spot did not present a significant improvement); a higher price level (price cell 3 with an index of 125); a large sampling campaign (39 percent hit and use); moderate advertising support (sampling was still more effective than high advertising); and 76 percent distribution.

Under this scenario, the new product's sales potential rose to 8.1 percent at a higher price.

Why the improvement? The revised television commercial was more successful in conveying its message to consumers on the first key perceptual dimension of this market, although it did not manage to improve on the other dimensions.

Product identification, however, remained a weakness. The client managed to improve correct name recall and shelf visibility levels only marginally by package and advertising changes, but they were still below standard for a new brand. This is a common problem with line extensions of this type, and the client had not found a full solution.

The trial rate improved 26.5 percent in price cell 3 (a 25 percent premium). The previous trial rate in this cell had been 14.6 percent. The new rate was better than the average successful new product introduction in the category—24.7 percent.

Trial response to price improved, and the brand now supported a premium of up to 25 percent. Sales predictions for the three price cells (under the same assumptions as previously) became 8.4 percent for price 2 (an 18 percent premium); 8.1 percent for price 3 (25 percent premium); and 6.3 percent for price 4 (33 percent premium).

Considering the "what if?" question, Novaction consultants knew from the first study that the product's high quality justified the use of sampling to increase penetration. The forecast showed even greater sales by doubling the sampling levels:

	19% *hit & use*	38% *hit & use*
Price 2	8.4%	11.9%
Price 3	8.1%	11.3%
Price 4	6.3%	9.5%

It would be very difficult, however, to reach 38 percent of the population effectively.

The new product now represented a very strong opportunity for the client. With high sampling levels, the client could anticipate an 8 to 11 percent share of category volume. One of the two new ads was significantly better than all others and offered the most robust mix and lowest price elasticity. The new mix would now support a price premium of 25 percent over the market average. The new brand's identification in both the advertising and the packaging still needed improvement, and the consultant made some suggestions. And finally, the client could obtain very strong brand leverage from an efficient sampling program.

The client launched the product nationally shortly after the second study. Sales tracked very closely to the study's predictions. Shortly after the launch, a competitor introduced a similar product, but because the test product had been "optimized," the new entry did not affect its sales and the competitor was not a success.

Management Implications

The purpose of this chapter was to demonstrate the benefits of an optimization approach to marketing planning. Using new and evolving tools like those discussed here and in Chapter 7, marketers are learning that simulated test marketing firms can go far beyond conventional volume forecasts to help improve marketing plans significantly.

This chapter reported two different approaches the industry uses to accomplish this end. The first is the type of formal, mathematical optimization modeling represented by the work done by Blackburn and Clancy for the Yankelovich organization; the second is the less technical but equally valuable approaches of the more sophisticated simulated test market modeling organizations represented here by Novaction's DESIGNOR. Both approaches show the marketing manager how best to allocate a marketing budget based on the market response the product generates and on the cost and effectiveness of the marketing vehicles available to launch the product.

We have found over and over that applying optimization modeling leads to forecast sales increases ranging from 3 percent to 50 percent over manager-prepared plans. At the same time, optimizing the marketing plan means cost reductions of as much as 30 percent for a given sales goal. It can also mean, as we'll see in a moment, the difference between a successful new product launch and a likely failure. The edge that this optimization measure provides a marketing manager varies by case. Also, as marketing managers use the system and learn from the optimization results, the system's superiority over manager-prepared plans declines.

At the same time, optimization's margin of superiority over the first plan submitted by a marketing manager has averaged 30 percent. In one application for a new food product, a case presented and discussed at two different management science conferences, optimization identified a $19 million marketing plan that performed slightly better in terms of market share than the product manager's $27 million plan and overwhelmed the manager's plan in terms of forecast profitability.

We have found that marketing managers and their advertising agencies usually concur with the optimization recommendations after they have had time to discuss, debate, and digest them. Sometimes this digestion process becomes charged with tension, even acrimony. In one case involving one of the country's largest advertising agencies, the optimization procedure recommended *against* the agency's $11 million spot television plan as part of a new product launch. The agency's reaction was a declaration of war. Diplomacy, however, averted actual combat.

The diplomatic efforts showed there was no difference between spot and non-spot markets in terms of advertising response as measured by the simulated test market research. Moreover, while product usage was 30 percent greater in spot markets than in non-spot markets, spot television cost 40 percent more per gross rating point. The optimization sensibly recommended against the spot schedule and, in time, the agency concurred.

12

Simulated Test Marketing
and Expert Systems

Over the past three decades simulated test marketing technology has evolved from a reliable and valid sales volume forecasting tool into a collection of tools that provide targeting and positioning guidance, cannibalization analysis, marketing plan diagnostics, competitive response analysis, and even optimal marketing plans. Marketing plan optimization is at the forefront of existing marketing intelligence, the edge that leads to expert marketing systems.

Although simulated test marketing technology offers marketing managers the tools they require to launch successful new products and new campaigns, most fail to use the tools to their full potential—one reason why most new products do not achieve the company's sales and profit objectives and why nine out of ten attempts to re-launch, re-stage, or turn around dying products and services fail to reverse share declines.

New developments and trends, however, are pushing back marketing's frontiers, and one of the most important is the development of expert systems. This technology offers exceptional promise with the transition to "expert managers," executives who will lead the way to exceptional marketing programs.

The purpose of this chapter is to provide a non-technical introduction to expert systems in marketing. Our objective is to ignite our readers' enthusiasm for this emerging technology and to encourage them to seek out more in-depth information from other sources.

The Need for Better Tools

Every marketing manager in America sits down once a year to write a marketing plan for his brand. The first section of the plan is often called a "Fact Book." It consists of data from various sources that represent a dry description of where the brand stands relative to the competition. The manager shows figures on market penetration, brand share, competitive usage rates, and brand profiles, often comparing the current year against some earlier period such as three or five years ago.

In many cases, the marketing manager provides detailed profiles of key target groups within the product category such as heavy users. The manager profiles these targets in terms of demographic variables, and, in some cases, attitudinal and media behavior patterns as well. No targeting analysis is complete, however, without a comparison of how the company's brand is performing in terms of these key targets compared to competitors.

Often, writing this Fact Book consumes a few weeks of a brand manager's (or an assistant's) time and often—and this is the sad part—the resulting document is poorly written, costly, underanalyzed, and not based on timely or, in some cases, useful information.

Today there are services available employing automated intelligence programs that work with one or more years of client data that search for, analyze, and write a report featuring critical, timely data key to developing an annual marketing plan. Our own work on Brand Guidance Systems is one example. The report is a finished document complete with data tables, statistical analyses, and narrative interpretation.

Another example: not long ago we sat through a company's day of media advertising planning. The firm was not sure that its target market—executives in high-tech industries—watched television or actually read the field's specialized business publications. The advertising agency brought rough estimates of cable and network television reach for this group, but they had only circulation—not readership—figures for the twenty top trade publications they were considering. They did have roughly comparable readership scores for *Business Week* and some of the general audience publications, such as *Time, Esquire,* and *GQ.* In other words, they had incomplete data and what they had was not generally comparable.

We found it appalling that in 1993 executives of a major advertising agency were leafing through loose-leaf research books to find cross-tabs of media exposure patterns for men, forty years of age and older, in high-technology industries. One ought to be able to sit at a computer and tell it: "I have a budget of $25 million. My target group consists of these kinds of people. Give me a profile of the media these folks watch, read, and are exposed to."

The computer could ask questions such as: "How many times do you have to reach a person each month to be successful? Do you have one campaign going or several?" Once the company answered the questions, the computer would analyze its data bases and make a recommendation. A relatively primitive expert system could provide a recommendation. But if companies buy media in terms of 18-to-49-year-old women instead of buying more subtle target groups—like people most responsive to the firm's marketing efforts—even a primitive expert system is probably overqualified.

The last five years have seen tremendous growth in computerized marketing decision support systems (MDSS) that are outgrowths of corporate sales data bases. The latest technology matches near real-time sales tracking information, which means that marketing executives obtain sales data almost as fast as sales occur, with sophisticated market modeling. For the first time, we are able to study marketing input-output relationships in depth.

The complaint of most practitioners who are struggling with implementing a marketing decision support system is that they are drowning in data and have no information. Which is why companies are creating automated intelligence, or expert systems, on top of the MDSS systems. These systems can absorb the huge data stream pouring into corporate data bases, winnow through the flood to find the critical trends and advertising sales effects, and emerge with recommendations for action.

Tools now exist, some in the form of expert systems, that vary considerably in terms of sophistication. A device that simply takes a load of data and analyzes it to ferret out the key findings is a very primitive version of automated intelligence technology. But the fact that a technology may be primitive does not make it uninteresting or useless. Something may be very useful without requiring a great deal of technological polish.

The most advanced of these programs incorporates the best thinking of inspired analysts with the tireless patience of the computer. In the future, these systems will use sophisticated modeling and decision rules to identify marketplace opportunities, such as local competitive vulnerabilities, long-term share-gain opportunities, or optimal price/deal tactics.

In the near future, it will be possible for most brands to "parse out" the effects of short-term sales promotions and local store activity to uncover direct short-term effects of advertising. For those who take a longer-term view, the promise of single-source panel data is the ability to track the longer-term effects of advertising on purchasing loyalty and deal sensitivity.

Not only will these expert systems work with the data that exists, they will permit human managers to study the world that could be. They will integrate marketing science modeling, automated-intelligence technology, historical marketplace relationships, and marketing mix models. These systems will take the mathematics and merge it with the knowledge of marketing experts: the experience, the rules of thumb, and the insights experienced marketing practitioners now use.

True single-source data, which merges household media exposure information with sales data for the same household, is increasingly available. Many companies are merging this new data source into their overall structure for evaluating advertising and, in the process, fundamentally changing the advertising evaluation system.

Some marketing people react to these changes by throwing up their hands and looking away. They say in essence, "So what? I don't need more and faster data. I don't know what it tells me anyway." If they don't know what the data tells them, and if they're not willing to learn, they're right. They don't need more data, they need compassion.

Because if a company is an astute, smart, and aggressive competitor, and its managers take the time to understand and use these new information systems, they can gain a tremendous competitive advantage. Especially if the competitors are sitting back and saying, "So what?"

We do not really believe the day will arrive when a computer can become a marketing department in a box. The world, human beings, and reality will remain too complex. We do believe, however, that an expert manager guided by an expert system will be a formidable competitor. Companies that adopt this emerging technology early will enjoy an edge over competition, an edge that will be difficult to overcome. Perhaps total product failure rates, on average, will remain the same. But they will certainly decline for the firms employing expert managers and systems, as they will increase for the companies that do not.

An Introduction to Expert Systems

To imagine how an expert system works, think of how a skilled mechanic makes a diagnosis of a car's problem. He asks questions to establish symptoms, history, and indications: "What kind of noise? When did it start? Do you only hear it on cold mornings?" On the basis of experience, the mechanic runs the tests that seem indicated. He applies his accumulated expertise selectively and by trial-and-error, testing for one thing, then another to rule out possibilities. He may consult with other mechanics or refer to repair manuals to learn more. Out of all this comes a diagnosis.

Expert systems typically follow a similar process. The systems represent knowledge in symbolic form, with numeric values reflecting the subjective probability of the information's likelihood, or its truthfulness. The expert system's general reasoning strategy (the so-called inference engine) is separate from the domain-specific trial-and-error attempts, models, and facts (the so-called knowledge base). The domain-specific knowledge includes some combination of facts—in a marketing system these might be something like, "All shipments to Europe originate from our New York office"—rules—"*If* the marketing objective is to stimulate primary demand, *then* the advertising objective is to stimulate category need"—and models and their interrelationships—"To calculate sales-response coefficients, first run a regression of sales on marketing variables."

This separation between inference and knowledge allows the system to use knowledge in a variety of ways. It can select particular elements in the knowledge base and request additional information to solve a specific problem. An expert system can explain the reasoning behind its questions and recommendations by reporting the trials it has attempted and the facts it used to investigate hypotheses and to draw conclusions.

Expert systems will, we believe, lead to expert marketing managers, managers who will institute exceptional marketing programs. An expert system is like having a consultant beside the desk, one smarter than most consultants, more expert than most consultants, and one who doesn't charge $3,000 a day.

The Link Between Expert Systems and Artificial Intelligence

Artificial intelligence represents general intelligence while expert systems represent specialized intelligence in a particular field such as geology, neurology, or marketing. An expert system, moreover, depends upon an artificial intelligence subsystem to do its thinking. But, the artificial intelligence subsystem needs to be integrated with the knowledge of an expert or experts and, often times, specialized data bases as well (Exhibit 12–1).

A whole new class of "knowledge engineers" captures the expert's knowledge—the skilled mechanic or experienced marketing executive. The knowledge engineer's contribution is to create a computer

Exhibit 12–1

An Expert System

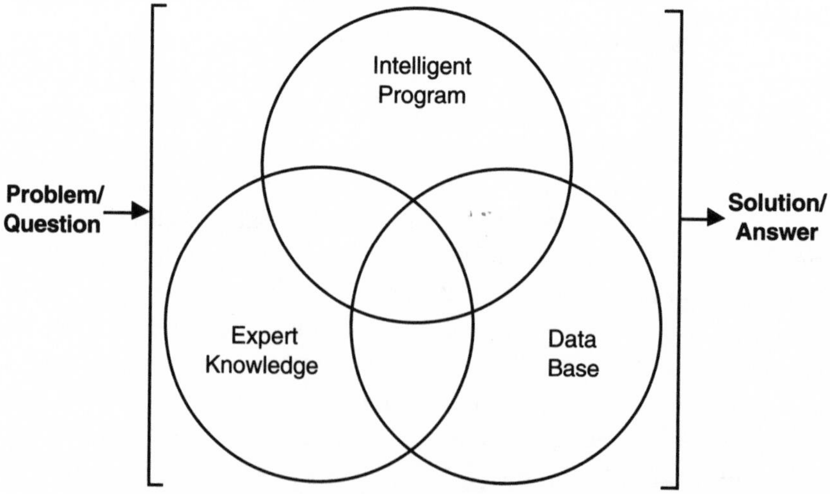

program that reflects the knowledge, experience, rules of thumb, insights, heuristics, and judgments of a particular field's experts.

A good expert system thinks through a problem or question—given the available intelligent program, expert knowledge, and data base—to arrive at a solution, an answer, or a decision. In an expert system, as in real life, the higher the intelligence of the program or person, the greater the expert's knowledge, and the more sophisticated the data bases, the better the solution, answer, or decision.

Such a system can use two forms of intelligence: the form that has dominated the field of computer-based intelligence thus far is called "artificial intelligence," while our own term, "automated intelligence," describes an alternate approach (Exhibit 12–2). The difference between the two is similar to the orthodox ethnological distinction between human and animal thinking. Until recently, researchers almost universally held that humans think creatively. We reason. We make choices. Birds and animals cope with the challenges they face solely by following the hard-wired behavioral instructions determined by their genetic heritage. Humans think; animals follow complex command structures. Birds build essentially the same nest year after year; humans build an endless variety of homes.

Artificial intelligence programs differ from the common programming languages such as COBOL, FORTRAN, and SPSS. They operate like human thinking processes. They seem to reason. They employ logical rules to manipulate words and phrases in languages such as "Lisp" and "Prolog."

Exhibit 12–2

Two Forms of Computer-Based Intelligence

Characteristics	Artificial Intelligence	Automated Intelligence
Simulates	Creative Thinking	Flexive Reacting
Manipulates	Non-Numerical Symbols	Numerical Values
Based On	Rules of Logic	Algorithms, Equations
Program Languages	A.I. Natural Languages	Contemporary Languages

Automated intelligence programs, on the other hand, can follow complex orders. They do what they're told to do. But they do no reasoning. They manipulate words and numerical characters, using algorithms and equations written in mathematical languages such as "PL-1" and "C." Expert systems can employ both types of intelligence in the same system.

Early and Recent Examples of Expert Systems

In the 1950s, the mathematician Alan Turing posited a test for true thinking machines. Imagine you are sitting at a computer screen; you type a question and an answer appears on the screen. Either a person reading your question has typed the answer or a computer has. If you hold a fifteen-minute "conversation" with such a system and cannot tell that you are talking to a computer, Turing would say the machine is truly thinking.

Expert systems go beyond artificial intelligence by seeming to clone the knowledge and decision-making ability of an expert in a particular field.

Liza was an early example of an expert system; popular at universities in the late 1960s, it was a main-frame-based program that simulated a psychiatrist. Liza talked to thousands of graduate students each year about everything from problems with their mothers to procrastinating on term papers. Other pioneering examples included computerized chess games and video games.

During the past two decades many firms have gained experience in using artificial vision and robotics technology. These automated-intelligence-based machines have successfully increased manufacturing efficiencies. The firms using such technologies are looking forward to a time when expert systems technology may supplement or even replace professional managers.

There are a number of publicized expert systems that do everything from diagnosing infectious diseases to identifying the structure of unknown compounds (Exhibit 12–3). MYCIN, for example, is a computer program written by Edward Shortcliffe, a Stanford computer scientist and physician. Using tools developed for artificial intelligence research, Shortcliffe combined everything he knew about diagnosing infectious blood diseases and meningitis into about 500 "if-then" rules. Rule 27, for example, says, "*If* an organism found in

Exhibit 12–3

Examples of Expert Systems

Mycin	Infectious Diseases
Caduceus	Medical Diagnosis
Prospector	Geological Exploration
Xcon	Configuring VAX Computers
Genoa	The Structure of Unknown Compounds

a patient's blood is rod-shaped, gram-negative, and able to survive in the absence of oxygen, *then* there is a strong likelihood that the organism is a type of bacteria called *Bacteroides*." In tests that applied these rules to cases reported in the medical literature, MYCIN was eventually able to diagnose as well as or better than most doctors.

The ability to diagnose makes MYCIN a very intelligent system; however, there is no evidence the system can learn from its experience. Humans operating the system may learn and, when they do, they can add more rules or data or modified algorithms to their electronic assistant. Thus, even though current expert systems such as MYCIN are able to perform their decision-making tasks, they have not cloned the human thought process.

Another criticism of current expert systems is that the knowledge the designers build into structure is relatively shallow. A psychologist might refer to an expert system as an "idiot savant." Randall Davis, a professor at MIT's Artificial Intelligence Lab, says on this point, "If you brought MYCIN a bicycle with a flat tire it would do its best to find you an antibiotic."

Finally, expert systems are expensive. Given the ratio of current benefits to high costs, some observers have questioned this technology's return on investment.

Expert Systems in Marketing

Although a survey done in 1986 by Clancy at Boston University among nineteen of the top marketing scientists in the United States concerning artificial intelligence and expert systems suggested much interest in the topic, a few proposals, but no on-line systems, a number of expert systems have been developed and introduced since that time.

Robot Researcher, a now-abandoned test program, was developed by Yankelovich Clancy Shulman in the mid-1980s to work with a marketing research data base. It wrote the first draft of a research report based on an awareness tracking study, a copy test, or a sales analysis, a tedious, repetitive kind of analysis. The technology behind Robot Researcher, a computer program written in PL-1, attempted to clone how a senior researcher would address such a problem.

Robot Researcher selected the appropriate statistical test and integrated it with pre-programmed text with words and phrases randomly modified the way a good analyst would. Finally, Robot Researcher printed the report in MultiMate, a popular word processing package at that time. An analyst could read the report, edit it, and add a title page and background section to complete it. Robot Researcher turned out such a report in a few hours; research departments across the country typically take a week or more to develop one.

One of the early applications of Robot Researcher was to take a basic marketing research study data base and analyze whether awareness, attitude, and usage scores were significantly higher or lower among different groups in the population. The report might open with Robot Researcher saying, "In our national, projectable sample, 30 percent of the population is aware of our new line of condensed soups. This figure is significantly higher among college educated consumers, where the score is 46 percent and significantly lower among high school educated or grade-school educated consumers, where the awareness drops to 14 percent. Looking next at the relationship between income and awareness, we see a similar pattern. Awareness scores are higher among high-income people (37 percent) and significantly lower among people with incomes of less than $10,000 (21 percent). Turning to region of the country, we see that scores are much higher in the Eastern region (42 percent) than they are in the Midwest (38 percent) and most of all on the West Coast (29 percent). . . ." The report was tedious and the more variables introduced for Robot Researcher to examine, the more difficult it was for an intelligent human to read without wanting to scream, "Help! We need someone who can write!"

That was not the only problem. Although Robot Researcher was very efficient at producing reports tracking multiple variables, it had drawbacks. For example, each time a questionnaire changed, the human researcher needed to modify the program. Moreover, Robot Researcher's stock of descriptive phrases for talking about data was boring and repetitive or, when taken out of context, hilarious, and the project was abandoned in 1989.

By 1990, however, many marketing scientists, researchers, and consulting firms and corporations were building and using first-generation expert systems. Perhaps the best known examples are programs that employ automated intelligence technology to make the marketing research task easier. Such programs help a researcher design a conjoint study, aid the interview process, assist the report writing, or facilitate the analysis.

In 1988 Information Resources introduced CoverStory, a software product that assists consumer packaged goods marketing executives to investigate, analyze, and present IRI's syndicated scanner data.[1] CoverStory automatically analyzes the data and writes an English language memo such as, "During the four weeks ending 11/18/94, volume in the Total Frozen Pizza category stood at 31.1 million consumer units—up 0.7% from the prior year. Pillsbury's share of the category was 29.1, which is an increase of 5.7 share points from last year but a loss of 3.1 points since last period. . . ."

Developed by Professors John Little of MIT and Leonard Lodish of Wharton, CoverStory extracts the most important information, as defined by the user, from the IRI data base and delivers it in memo format, supported by tables and graphs. For a specific product category, CoverStory produces headlines for category volume and trends, describes how the company's brands are doing in sales and share, while extracting and presenting major geographic shifts in brand performance. It identifies major shifts in price, merchandising, and distribution associated with share gains and losses. It also identifies competitors who are gaining and losing share.

Dr. Little said at the time that since consumer packaged goods manufacturers buy 1,000 times more syndicated data than they have in the past, and although fourth generation computer languages and workstation software solve the basic problem of easy retrieval and analysis of information, CoverStory was the first software to automatically search for the key news items in a scanner data base, report them in easy language on the screen, and produce them in presentation-quality copy. CoverStory reports provide a coherent picture of who's gaining, who's losing, where, and why.

In 1994 A. C. Nielsen plans to release the Nielsen Solution System, which, using Windows-based software, will allow users to track and analyze market performance in new ways using all channels, markets, and data, including Monitor, Media/Coupon, and basic Household in one data base. According to Serge Okun, president and chief executive officer of Nielsen and IMS International, "Nielsen Solution System allows you to slice and dice through a data base in a twinkling, changing product groupings, geography, and history without having to reprogram." The company's literature says that for the first time, Nielsen customers will be able to:

- Analyze data in real time geared to issue-driven concerns rather than pre-existing UPC categories.
- Use retailer department definitions or non-traditional cross-store views to analyze data.
- Access real-time complete information to compare against tracking data.
- Integrate Nielsen Household and media data across categories for sophisticated analyses.
- Create new data bases on the fly and in real time tailored to individual client needs.

System I.Q.

Like Robot Researcher, CoverStory, and—we assume—the Nielsen Solution System, most smart programs or primitive expert systems available in marketing today do their assigned chores efficiently, displaying a modest level of intelligence but little marketing expertise. We can think of such systems as marketing novices, trainees with a reasonable I.Q., a background in statistics, and a modest amount of experience (Exhibit 12–4).

We can explain the I.Q. of a program or system in two dimensions: quantitative ability and verbal ability. Quantitative ability refers to analytical power, graphic capabilities, and a facility with

Exhibit 12–4

Expert Systems Today

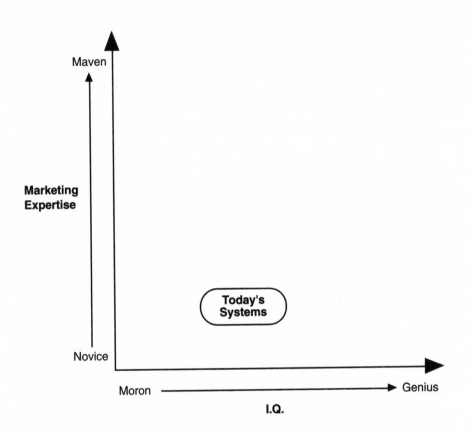

numbers. Verbal ability refers to the program's power to articulate. The higher a program's quantitative and verbal ability, the higher its I.Q. (Exhibit 12–5). If the program is low in both, it is a moron. If it is high in both, it is a genius.

Similarly, we can express marketing expertise in two dimensions: expert knowledge and the complexity of the marketing program the system is designed to address. The greater the marketing knowledge programmed into the system and the bigger, more complex problems it can handle, the greater the system's expertise. We would call a system that has in-depth knowledge about all the mar-

Exhibit 12–5

The Relationship Between Verbal and Quantitative Capabilities and System I.Q.

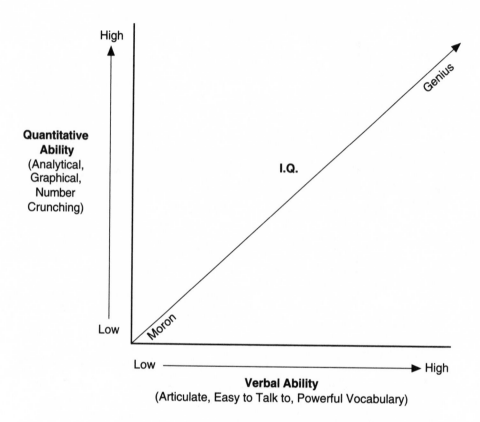

keting mix components—for example, it can describe a total marketing plan as optimal or close to optimal—a maven since it would be high on both expert knowledge and complexity (Exhibit 12–6).

A Smart Marketing System

To illustrate a simple expert system, we will use AdTester, a hypothetical straightforward application of the Robot Researcher technology. It has an average I.Q., but displays little marketing savvy. AdTester analyzes copy test results, as the following example will demonstrate. Assume that your company has tested three ads,

Exhibit 12–6

**The Relationship Between Expert Knowledge and
Problem Complexity and System Marketing Expertise**

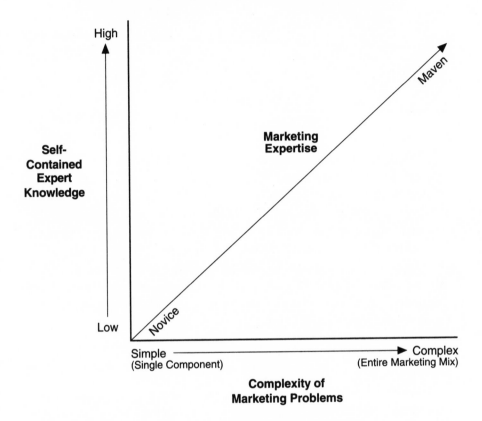

"Fast," "Value," and "Reliable," using one of a number of commercially available copy testing systems such as ARS, ASI, Burke, or McCullom-Spielman. In the test, 250 buyers of the product category saw the ads, and the research obtained five key advertising response measures for each: attention-getting power, message communication, credibility, attitude change, and persuasion.

When the marketing manager loads the copy test data into the computer's appropriate data base and executes the AdTester program, the screen asks the manager whether it should display the results, and if so which criteria it should use. If the manager tells the machine that "persuasion" is the criterion, AdTester reports the test

Exhibit 12–7

An Example of Ad Tester Output

	Three Ad Treatments		
	"Fast" (N=156)	**"Value"** (N=148)	**"Reliable"** (N=151)
Pre-Post Change in Predicted Behavior	+13%	-5%	+22%

used and the results. In this case, the "Reliable" ad message is the winner because it achieved the strongest pre-post change in predicted behavior (Exhibit 12–7).

After presenting the results, AdTester informs the marketing manager that other analyses are possible, and asks what the manager wants to do next. AdTester has a reasonable I.Q., but little marketing expertise. It is like having an assistant who has memorized all the details of an ARS or Burke report and can instantly cite the numbers, findings, and conclusions in response to any question. Such an assistant, while helpful, is not an expert.

An Expert Marketing System

During the late 1990s, the state-of-the science expert system in marketing will have advanced considerably (Exhibit 12–8). To illustrate the improvement, compare AdTester, which can be offered today, to the hypothetical AdViser.

AdViser is an advanced version of AdTester in terms of brain power and expertise. AdViser is not only very smart, it also knows a great deal about marketing generally and about advertising and advertising research in particular. AdViser, like AdTester, helps select advertising copy; it can listen to the manager's verbal commands, talk, and display information on a screen all at the same time.

Using the same three ad tests we used for the AdTester example, the session with AdViser begins with a statement of the mission and a question concerning which of the five criteria the marketing manager would like analyzed—attention-getting power, message communica-

Exhibit 12–8

Expert Systems Today and Tomorrow

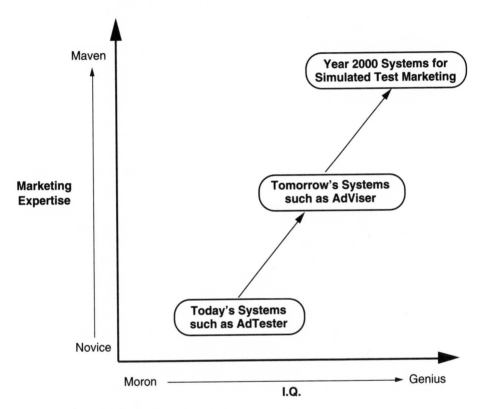

tion, credibility, attitude change, or persuasion. However, rather than making a choice, which was necessary with AdTester, the marketing manager can say that he or she is unsure and tells AdViser that the company's primary interests are sales effects and profits.

AdTester uses its marketing knowledge to inform the marketing manager that market share in this particular product category is very sensitive to changes in attitudes and persuasion. The marketing manager tells AdViser to use its judgment in weighting the criteria, and AdViser requests information concerning the media weight and mix.

With this data, AdViser calculates the share of voice the marketing plan will generate and shows the statistical and mathematical operations it has performed. Although AdTester found that "Reliable" was the winner in terms of pre-post change in predicted behavior, AdViser's more sophisticated analysis discovers that the "Fast" campaign is superior in terms of projected sales. Further, AdViser predicts that a $7 million investment in the "Fast" campaign will produce a $2 million profit within 16 months.

AdTester and AdViser are prototypes of copy selection tools. Designers will develop many other expert systems for marketers, systems that will do everything from design media schedules, products, and services, to laying out an entire marketing plan. Although AdViser is not available now, it is a system that it will be possible to build in the near future.

The best systems today, however, do not yet listen or talk. They require trained analysts to add and interpret detailed marketing information. As a result, impressive as the system's marketing knowledge and quantitative ability may be, it is years from performing like AdViser. Yet, the promise for evolving simulated test marketing systems is bright indeed.

The previous chapters showed that simulated test market technology has been evolving. A smart optimization system (Chapter 11) combines expert judgments, proprietary data bases, and automated intelligence algorithms to search through billions of possible marketing plans to find the one plan forecast to be the most profitable.

Consider as an illustration that a company has undertaken a simulated test marketing study, has armed a 486 PC with all of the marketing plan and marketing response information from the study, and integrated this information with even smarter models than the DESIGNOR, LITMUS, ASSESSOR, BASES, and other systems currently available. Now take this a step further. All of this data and expertise is linked to an expert system as smart with respect to new product marketing planning as AdViser is with advertising.

This new expert system would automatically undertake the targeting, positioning, pricing, sensitivity, and other analyses we discussed in Chapters 7 and 11 in order to make sophisticated recommendations for improving the product and its marketing program. Conceivably, the printed output from such a program would be re-engineering recommendations for the white coats in the R&D labs and detailed marketing recommendations for advertising and promotional planners, packaging and sales managers, and everyone else responsible for making key decisions for the new product.

Management Implications

The purpose of this chapter was to provide a non-technical introduction to expert systems in marketing. Expert systems, as we have described them, represent the integration of marketing data bases, the judgments of marketing experts, and automated or artificial intelligence programs—the result of which is a tool designed to make the manager's life and work easier. Today primitive versions of this rapidly evolving technology write research reports, help an interviewer work her way through a difficult questionnaire, and help design new products and more effective advertising.

In the years ahead, expert systems will be developed to address every marketing problem from targeting and positioning to media selection and scheduling to distribution and pricing.

The most exciting application of expert systems, however, from our standpoint will occur when they are designed to help marketers create more effective marketing plans. When this happens, it is hard to imagine that simulated test marketing of new and restaged products and services will not play a major role. Earlier chapters in this book have described the tools that STM systems currently offer for improving, if not optimizing, a marketing plan. When these tools are integrated with the thinking of marketing experts and intelligent programming algorithms highlighted in this chapter, marketing will have reached a new era of efficiency.

13

Recent Discoveries
Based on Autopsies
of New Product Failures

Simulated test market research is a tool that can help marketers dramatically improve the odds that their new and re-staged products and services will be successful. But, valuable as the tool may be, it is only one element in an outstanding marketing effort.

In fifteen years of new product and re-staging research we have observed many failures in both the laboratory and the real world. Often we've been invited by marketers to undertake an autopsy of what went wrong to figure out if the patient is really dead, if so why, and if not how it can be resuscitated. In this chapter, we will identify and describe ten of the most common discoveries that we have made based on this autopsy, discoveries that are relevant whether the organization is large or small, marketing to consumers or to businesses, selling goods or services. We thank our friends and former colleagues at Yankelovich Partners, particularly Walker Smith, Doug Haley, and Lisa Carter, for their contributions to our evolving thinking.

The lessons include:

1. Failure begins when marketers assess the marketing climate inadequately.
2. The wrong group is targeted.
3. A weak positioning strategy is employed.
4. A less-than-optimal (and here we're being kind) "configuration" of product or service attributes and benefits is selected.

5. A questionable pricing strategy is implemented.
6. The advertising campaign generates an insufficient level of new product/new service awareness.
7. Cannibalization depresses corporate profits.
8. Overoptimism about the marketing plan leads to a sales forecast that cannot be sustained in the real world.
9. Seemingly minor modeling issues (like Achilles' heel) lead to poor forecasts and sometimes fatal decisions.
10. The marketer believes that the new product and its marketing plan has died and cannot be revived.

Assessing the Marketing Climate

If you were planning to sail between New York and England, you would like to take advantage of wind, wave, and current. If you could sail with optimal knowledge, you would arrive quickly, comfortably, and safely.

If, on the other hand, you chose to go against the wind and the waves and the currents, you would arrive exhausted. You would be wet, bruised, late, and perhaps—like poor Mike Plant who drowned in November 1992 on his Atlantic crossing—you would not arrive at all.

Many marketing plans are fraught with problems because the navigator failed to assess climatic conditions correctly. Smart marketers track the marketing weather before they embark on their voyage through time. This is not to say there aren't some brands that can fight the weather and do something unusual.

Take the sailboat analogy. Sometimes a Dennis Conners is able to note the course, estimate there may be a better wind someplace else, and sail off to the amazement of more conservative skippers who would stick with the weather report. And Conners may win. But the number of counter-weather performers who win is small, and their successes have as much to do with luck as skill—and luck can be capricious.

The marketing weather takes many, many forms. One form has to do with changing population characteristics, with demographic variables. Another has to do with consumer values. Americans, for example, are gradually losing discretionary time. They are streamlining their lives and are more interested in substance than in style. They expect more service and their attitudes toward the environment have changed. With changed attitudes, changed behavior will follow.

Conventional status symbols are fading, a change that began to occur before the most recent recession. Americans are beginning to sense that what you know and how you spend your leisure time is more important than what you have. The idea that, as the bumper sticker said, "The Person Who Dies with the Most Toys Wins" has been discredited.

Personal, customized, individual accomplishments—writing a book, climbing Mt. Everest, learning Japanese—will be much more powerful in the mid-1990s than the conventional symbols of success—a 6,000-square-foot home, a Rolex watch, or a gas guzzling power boat.

Twenty years ago many Americans thought that a woman wearing a full-length sable coat and a three-carat diamond and driving a Ferrari convertible represented the pinnacle of success. (Not every single person thought so, of course, but enough to set the country's mood.) More and more, these external signs of wealth and status are a sign that you're a jerk.

Such display is not the only behavior diminishing. Smoking a pack of cigarettes before breakfast, belonging to two clubs, drinking three martinis at lunch, lining up four trash containers at the curb, and raising five children were conventional behavior for social trend-setters in the 1950s; today they are increasingly socially embarrassing.

Conspicuous consumption is decreasing, and it's not clear whether it will come back or not. This is not because people cannot afford to consume conspicuously. Rather, people feel they have other, more important things to do with money than to spend it frivolously. Consumers also display an increasing need for deeper social connections, particularly with one's family; a need for greater emotional enhancement; a desire for more meaningful social commitments and community involvement; and living what is increasingly called a "self-examined" life.

This yearning for the simple life has wide-ranging consequences for marketers. Consumers no longer feel the need to buy the "best" or most expensive products; they are saying there are better things to do with their time and money. Status and prestige are decreasingly seen as surrogates for quality while convenience, reliability, and price value are in the ascendancy.

People don't want to be deeply involved in the buying process any more; they don't want to take time to find the highest quality, the lowest price. As a result of the decreased involvement, branding is becoming a dominate factor in consumer decision making. Branding offers consumers a shortcut to identify high value products and services. Yet too many marketers are killing their brands with promotions, line extensions, and decreased advertising spending. New product introductions are at record heights although few consumers are interested.

These, of course, are only a few of the climatic changes that are taking place. Attudinally, behaviorally, psychographically, demographically, and sociographically American society is changing. Only a marketer who keeps up with the latest weather reports will enjoy smooth sailing.

Some marketers are very proud of their efforts to keep track of the national climate. We were recently involved in an autopsy during which the marketer showed us that his new service "fit" perfectly with the attitudinal changes that were taking place in America today. Two different reports from social value trend research companies were presented to support his contention. Interestingly, when we completed our autopsy, we had discovered that the marketer was wrong for reasons that were not very clear at the time the new service was launched. This marketer, like most dealing with marketing climate data, treated it as a backdrop for the development of the marketing plan rather than as a critical input into strategic decisions. Although the marketer had good data on what was happening *nationally* (i.e., across a cross-section of *all* Americans), the social trends were not occurring among the specific target group the marketer had selected. This is a little bit like watching the weather channel for a national report when what you really need to know is whether it's sunny or snowing outside. This suggests that marketers should investigate climatic trends, not just for the population as a whole, but for the specific targets in which they have an interest.

Targeting the Wrong Group

The first decision in the marketing plan is who to go after: Who should be the marketing program's target? Although this is a key decision, many companies devote little time—or no time—to it. Executives think they know who the target should be and they go after it without much research or evaluation.

Autopsies often reveal that the marketer has selected the wrong group.

The fact is that marketers are impulsively choosing targets such as 18-to-49-year-old women, heavy users, big customers, new customers, people who look like current customers, non-users, without any research or analysis. And often they are wrong!

We differentiate between two different targets: the product's buyers and non-buyers. In other words, between customer targets and prospect targets. Industrial marketers, business-to-business marketers, and direct marketers tend to distinguish between current customers and prospects, tailoring their efforts for one or the other, rather than focus on a general target (that is, on both customers and prospects). Packaged goods marketers, in contrast, often develop an overall strategy that covers both. They want the heavy consumers of, say, beer, and they don't differentiate between their own customers and the competition's. Their challenge is to persuade non-buyers to try their brew and to encourage current buyers to remain loyal.

What are typical targets that companies choose without thought? The all-time most popular packaged goods target is 18-to-49-year-old women. The second most popular is heavy users. Service marketers love frequent buyers. Increasingly marketing managers for durable goods are attempting to bring non-users into a category. And business-to-business and direct mail prospectors commonly focus on people who "look just like our best customers." Every one of these targets can be a mistake.

Eighteen-to-49-year-old women are relatively easy to reach with media, but typically 25 to 50 percent of a new brand's volume comes from consumers outside of the media target; that is, they use the product but do not watch the television shows or read the magazines in which the brand advertises. Heavy users are a less profitable target group than moderate users (and sometimes light users) because the cost of attracting them often far exceeds their sales contribution. Typically heavy users are very similar to light users in everything other than consumption or family size or both (big families do tend to buy more spaghetti sauce, toothpaste, detergent, television sets, and long-distance services than individuals living alone). Heavy users are often price conscious, deal prone, and disloyal to the brands they buy. Winning them with an offer they cannot refuse today is no great feat because the company will lose them to a competitor's deal tomorrow. Other heavy users are psychologically locked to a competitive brand. They are somebody else's best customers and very difficult to move.

What about expanding the category, bringing non-users into the tent? The Yankelovich Partners test market data base contains many examples where the firm interviewed a general population sample because marketing management expected (or hoped for, or prayed for) significant trial interest from current category non-users. Yet in most cases, non-users contributed no more than 5 to 10 percent to the sales volume. Unless the product category is brand new and growing rapidly, a new product will attract few non-users to the category.

What about the prospects who look like the company's best customers? Direct mail companies go wild for this group. Yet the fact is that these are people who are often your competitor's best customers and they are very difficult to move. Someone who looks and acts, as an illustration, like an American Express high roller but has rejected AmEx in favor of Visa Gold is not really a great prospect for AmEx.

In summary, autopsies find that targeting is a contributor to the death of new product plans: a large number of new products fail because the companies have not selected an optimal target group. Traditional target selection tactics no longer work. To evaluate an optimal target, a company must measure candidates on seven profit-directed criteria:

1. *Responsiveness.* The more a target group responds to a company's marketing efforts, the greater its value to the company.
2. *Sales potential.* A target group that buys or uses more of the company's product is more valuable than one that buys less.
3. *Growth potential.* A growing target is more desirable than a static or shrinking group.

4. *Common motivations.* The more homogeneous and preemptible a target's needs are, the greater its value.
5. *Decision-making power.* The more responsibility the target prospects have for making a buying decision, the more significant they are to the company.
6. *Retention potential.* The more likely it is that a target can be economically sustained and, therefore, retained over time, the greater its value.
7. *Media exposure patterns and media costs.* These are important because it usually makes little sense to define a target a marketer cannot reach through media or that is impossibly expensive to reach (for example, looking up every prospect's number in the phone book).

If the company evaluates each potential market on these criteria, it can improve its success dramatically.

A Weak Positioning Strategy Is Employed

Sometimes a marketer has correctly assessed the climate, picked the right target, built reasonable awareness levels, and achieved high distribution levels and yet the new (or re-staged) product fails because an insufficient number of people have been motivated to try it. Companies need to scrap concepts that do not motivate consumers early and to make good concepts even better. Many marketers believe that new products and services are based on positioning strategies for which they have an advantage in highly motivating features or benefits or both.

Yet if most new products and services were based on powerful pre-emptive strategies would the new product failure rate be as high as it is? No. Autopsies of new product/services failures suggest that three out of ten times the cause of death is a weak positioning.

This could not have been more clear to us than when we examined the strengths and weaknesses of new products and services run through the LITMUS system. Each new product study we did included consumer ratings of how the new product compared to its competitors on ten to twenty product attributes and benefits in the product category and how motivating each of these attributes and characteristics were to buyers. What we discovered is shown in Exhibit 13–1.

Exhibit 13–1

The Recent History of New Product Introductions

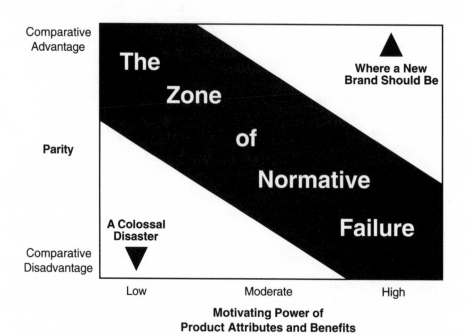

Most new products fell into what we labeled "the zone of normative failure." Consumers perceived them as offering attributes and benefits that (a) were not terribly motivating and (b) were not much different from those of competitors.

Weak positioning strategies arise from death wish marketing and death wish research. Such research includes focus groups, gap and grid analysis, perceptual mapping, importance ratings, and problem detection. Focus group research can only be exploratory and cannot be projected. Perceptual mapping can be difficult to interpret and describes the past, not the future. Importance ratings, derived importance ratings, and desirability ratings alone are inappropriate. Gap analysis and choice modeling can steer a company in misleading directions.

Many new product/re-staging failures can be traced to a weak positioning strategy. This is evident when the new concept fails to ignite much interest on the part of the prospective buyer. In many product categories, for example, a "laboratory trial" rate of 20 percent or less suggests that the product concept or its advertising could be described as a soporific: It was so uninteresting that it put people to sleep. Yet, we know of cases where marketers, aware of poor trial scores, let inertia lead the way and took the product into a real-world test.

These low levels of trial are not surprising given the prevalence of death wish research on which the strategy is based. To achieve success, a company must develop a strategy based on highly motivating claims that pre-empt competitive assertions; must apply research tools that correctly assess the power of many attributes and benefits; and must recognize the potential of intangible or emotional themes.

Selecting a Less-than-Optimal Configuration of Concept and Product Features—The Need for Better Products

Assuming the marketer has done everything else "correctly," the company needs to determine the product offering—the "configuration" of attributes, benefits, promises, package, name, price, and performance that is close to being financially optimal . . . yet companies rarely do this. Usually, they test relatively few alternatives, and as a result they introduce products that do not perform as well as hoped. Some are more expensive to manufacture and market than they need be. Other products and services are maximally appealing and therefore not as profitable as they can be. But, in the most common situation, they design products which meet, but do not exceed, customer expectations and competitive performance. In other words, "me too" products.

Where do product configurations come from? The most common source is concept and product testing, which are plagued with problems. Such tests often raise as many questions as they answer and have several failings. Concept and product test research companies generally employ small (seventy five to 200), non-projectable samples of men and women accosted in shopping malls by an interviewer who promises them a small payment for thirty minutes of their time.

Worse, researchers sometimes use purchase intention scales with no known reliability or validity. The scales miscarry because researchers don't know (a) if they repeated the study among the same respondents they would they obtain the same results, or (b) whether the results actually reflect what they want to learn—the percentage of people who would really buy the product if it were available and they became aware of it. It is like measuring I.Q. by wrapping a rubber tape measure around a person's head; the results vary with every test and they do not show intelligence anyway.

Few concept or product test researchers are able to ask "what if" questions concerning variations in concept features and benefits efficiently. What if the packages is red? Green? Teal? What if the price is 98¢? $1.98? $2.98? These tests by their nature cannot handle many alternative possibilities. Also, marketing managers seldom know a product's fixed and variable manufacturing and marketing costs. But without knowing costs a marketing manager cannot estimate profitability.

Finally, few concept and product test research companies offer a valid model of the marketing mix into which to feed research scores to predict sales and profitability. They present numbers to management as if they were discrete pieces of information in themselves: "This one got a 33 percent top box score, beating the control product by almost six points." That may be good news, but will the product sell? And if it sells, will it be profitable?

Companies can overcome these problems with several changes. Begin with a larger (300 to 500), more projectable sample of prospective buyers in more locations than the ones such tests typically employ. The sample should be serious respondents, people recruited via random digit dialing to a central location, not the first bodies willing to answer questions in a shopping mall. Expose this sample to a full description of the concept, complete with the name, positioning, packaging, features, and price. Present the concept with competing products sold in the market at their actual prices. Experience shows that the more a test simulates, models, or mirrors reality, the more accurate the forecast.

Have consumers rate the new product before and after in-home use in terms of purchase probability using measuring instruments with known reliability and validity. We recommend the eleven-point scale discussed in Chapter 3 that couples word meanings with probability estimates to stimulate serious thinking by respondents.

Here's another way to develop a powerful concept. In the mid-1970s, Professor Paul Green of the Wharton School of Business at the University of Pennsylvania pioneered a new research methodology that made the task of evaluating many concepts more efficient—one of the major scientific advances in marketing during the past twenty years. This technology, called multiple trade-off analysis or conjoint measurement, enables researchers to evaluate many different concepts using approaches borrowed from experimental psychology.

Essentially, the researcher designs an experiment to test several factors—name, positioning, key benefits, size, shape, color, price, and more—by showing different combinations to different people. By applying multiple trade-off analysis, a researcher can capture the main effects of, say, seven different factors by exposing consumers to a relatively small set of concepts (sixteen or fewer).

In practice, this means the research can evaluate thousands of potential concepts at a price comparable to a traditional test of perhaps five concepts. Marketing research's real hurdle in using conjoint analysis has been company management. Managers don't understand the procedure and often don't *want* to understand. Also, trade-off studies have their own problems. They produce unreal measures of sales potential because of a questionable track record in predicting real-world sales. Moreover they tend to be limited; they measure several hundred combinations, but today marketers have, not hundreds, but hundreds of thousands of options—and the standard trade-off analysis cannot handle them well.

More seriously, traditional trade-off studies tend to be misleading because they focus on the *most appealing* product. But the most appealing product is never the most *profitable* product. Offering the most appealing product concept is like offering a three-scoop ice cream cone with chocolate sprinkles for a dime. The product has enormous consumer appeal, but one cannot make money with it. That may be an extreme example and one managers grasp immediately. Unfortunately, they often do not understand that their new or re-positioned product is an appealing money-loser, or—a more common situation—that it will not actually lose money, but will not earn what it might.

Neither purchase probability nor multiple trade-off analysis utility scores address the marketer's key question: Will the new product or service be *profitable*? And that's what smart managers want to know.

Fortunately there is an alternative in *computer-assisted new product design*. This unique trade-off analysis helps marketers design optimal products and services. The optimizer itself has several features: It predicts real-world behavior and sales; it covers millions of concepts; it identifies the most profitable concepts and products; the marketer can personally play out "what if?" scenarios; and it offers targeting and positioning guidance. The model is able to estimate trial (and repeat if product alternatives are tested) for more than 100 million different product configurations. Combine this information with a company's knowledge of its market and the computer can convert the trial figures into demand estimates.

To use this optimizer, the company gives its estimates of consumer demand to a non-linear optimization computer model, and the machine selects the "optimal" product. Company management tempers the estimates by judgments about the marketing plan and cost considerations.

Take a home-baked soft pretzel as an example. Assume that we tested eight different factors by exposing respondents to a carefully selected set of 16 scenarios. The factors include two positionings (serious bakers/non-bakers), three benefits (nutritious/fast/fun), four product attributes (salt nuggets/mix type/vitamin content/Old German Recipe), and five price points ($1.09/$1.19/$1.49/$1.79/$1.99).

To forecast demand, the company must provide an estimate of the target group's size. Let's assume that the company has learned that 22 million households are prospects for Home Baked Pretzels. Demand for any *one* configuration is then equal to the base level—22 million—plus or minus the effects of each individual factor, plus the interactions between factors. The demand (in total number of households) multiplied by the price equals total dollar demand.

Conjoint analysis permits us to address the question of which factors have the greatest effect on behavior. Couple the behavior forecasts with manufacturing cost information and, for the Home Baked Pretzel, the computer found that the optimal concept was to "appeal to occasional bakers as a great-tasting, fast baking snack made from an Old German Recipe including the baker's own fresh milk and eggs. Offer it with European salt nuggets in the eight-pretzel size at $1.19." The market share potential was 9.5 percent; the profit potential was $16 million.

To develop the most profitable product (or service) at an "optimal" price, a company must look at four things: the product's tangible features, its intangible benefits, price sensitivity, and the return on investment. Today, the computer can manipulate the raw data fast enough and inexpensively enough to give marketing executives the information they need to make intelligent decisions.

While the traditional methods—concept and product testing—remain the most common way to develop and test new products they are not necessarily the best approach to new product/new service development. A company can improve on its concept and product testing, but the techniques remain limited if only because they cannot test a large number of configurations economically.

Trade-off analysis was an enormous improvement over concept and product testing. But in general, the goal remained the same as traditional testing's: find the product that produces the highest level of consumer appeal, the highest level of purchase probability.

And that, of course, is not what a company really needs. What it really needs is the most *profitable* product. We've found the difference in profitability between the optimal product and management's favorite product to be as much as 575 percent. This means that a marketing managers cannot, flying by instinct and gut feel, simply pick the most profitable product or service from among all the—often literally—billions of possible combinations.

Questionable Pricing Strategies

"Correct" pricing is becoming ever more important, but unfortunately marketers are not taking pricing strategy and research as seriously as they should. We do not argue "right" or "wrong" pricing strategies. A strategy may be appropriate or not, and a company may—and probably should—change strategies as circumstances evolve, as products and markets change or mature.

We *do argue* that a company should have some pricing strategy. A conscious, deliberate plan will always be better than expediency or following a dumb rule of thumb. We are regularly surprised, however, when we visit a major American corporation and find no pricing strategies. We became interested enough that we did some small scale research to learn whether this lack of strategy was just among the companies we knew or if the situation was widespread.

Our research looked at all American businesses as fitting into one of four boxes, referred to as The Strategy/Research Pricing Matrix:

	Serious Strategy	*Little or No Strategy*
Serious *Research*	Sophisticated Players	Radical Empiricists
Little or *No Research*	Gamblers	Losers

The companies in the top left box, the Sophisticated Players, are those that conduct serious pricing research (that is, primary research, not secondary analysis) and follow a serious pricing strategy. The Losers, at the lower right, do little or no research and have little or no strategy.

Our research found:

- Only about 8 percent can be considered Sophisticated Players with both a pricing strategy and research to support it.
- Only about 4 percent are Radical Empiricists with research but no strategy.
- Some 47 percent are Gamblers; they do have a serious pricing strategy but do little or no research to support it.
- These results leave a sobering 41 percent of all companies with neither strategy nor research—the Losers.

In other words, we estimate that more than half—55 percent—of all American companies *do* have a pricing strategy, but only 12 percent perform any serious pricing research to support the strategy.

What kind of pricing research are companies doing? "How much would you pay" studies; concept testing; statistical analysis of non-experimental data; multi-attribute modeling; multiple trade-off analysis; and in-market experiments. Not all these are equally valid; we just pointed out the problems with concept tests. The theory behind multi-attribute modeling is that the sum of importance ratings times brand ratings across all attributes for a given brand equals the brand's "value." A brand's price should be proportionate to its value. That is, if the value of a new product is 90 percent of the "value" of the market leader, it should be priced at 90 percent of the market leader. It leads to findings found in Exhibit 13–2.

This table says on the most important attribute, "great taste," respondents gave both Pepsi and Zippy Cola a 5. Multiply the impor-

Exhibit 13–2

Zippy Cola Evaluated Against Pepsi and Coke

Attribute	Importance	Evaluation		
		Pepsi	Coke	Zippy
Great Taste	5	5	4	5
Right Amount of Carbonation	4	4	5	5
Popular Brand	4	4	5	2
Not Too Sweet	3	4	2	5
Deep Rich Color	2	4	5	5
Weighted Sum		**77**	**76**	**78**

tance ratings by the evaluations and add them up and you reach the preposterous conclusion that Zippy Cola should be priced comparable to or higher than the market leaders.

While the example is deliberately extreme to illustrate the point, companies currently engage in such faulty research to establish prices. The research is flawed because it assumes that it captures all attributes, both tangible and intangible, which it does not. It assumes that importance ratings really measure "motivating power," which they do not. And it assumes the company can ignore the price of entry into the category, which it cannot. Zippy Cola would not be competing only against the taste of Pepsi and Coke; it would be competing against decades of advertising.

To discover the optimal price, we believe that companies should use simulated test marketing plus trade-off analysis, a dynamic duo which we discussed in Chapter 7.

Insufficient Awareness Levels

Every new product (or re-staged brand) needs to achieve a reasonable level of product or campaign awareness. Yet awareness levels are declining, a function of drops in advertising spending, media clutter, and unexciting creative. Since advertising is a far more important determinant of awareness than promotion, advertising "fixes" are an important part of the solution.

We have been collecting data for two decades that suggest that new product awareness and penetration—both the result in large part of advertising—are increasingly difficult to achieve. Therefore, performance per dollar is slipping. The consumer's increasing inattention to advertising explains, in part, why copy test and persuasion scores have been dropping by 1 to 2 percent a year for more than a decade. And this drop explains, in part, why advertising awareness and new product awareness scores have also been dropping.

In 1976 the three television networks accounted for 91 percent of the prime time viewing. It's been downhill since. By 1986 the figure had fallen to 74 percent; by 1990 to almost 61 percent. David F. Poltrack, senior vice president of research for CBS, said at the end of 1990 that the networks have to think about a share in the mid-50s by 1995. Meanwhile, costs have continued to rise, so advertisers are paying more while getting less.

Today, consumers are far more likely to ignore or forget an advertising execution than remember and act on it. These me-too message strategies fail to tap consumer needs and, consequently, fail to motivate the prospects to buy the company's product or service. It's not unusual to see different brands in the same category using the same message strategy, and often a not very good one at that.

Since insufficient new product or campaign awareness is an increasing problem, a new product or campaign must break through the "clutter barrier" or remain invisible. Companies need to take steps to improve awareness despite declines in advertising expenditures. If only 2 percent of all advertising campaigns are terrific, testing only one or two executions almost guarantees mediocrity. Because the ARF and IRI studies[1] suggest that recall and persuasion do not predict sales, de-emphasize these criteria in copy testing. Consumer attitude toward advertising is the most important and most often neglected predictor of market response. Testing that takes place in simulated natural conditions yields more valid responses and, ultimately, better copy.

Recent evidence suggests the cost per thousand (CPM) viewers varies from the cost per thousand impacted (CPMI) viewers, and that media planners would make different decisions depending on which criterion they use. While our study[2] measured many vari-

Exhibit 13–3

**Advertising Response for Four Key Commercials
(By Program Involvement)**

	Program Involvement		
	Low	**Moderate**	**High**
Unaided Recall	18.4%	21.0%	22.2%
Aided Recall	34.0%	48.0%	54.0%
Copy Point Credibility	24.0%	37.0%	41.0%
Purchase Interest	13.2%	15.7%	17.0%
Pre-Post Behavioral Change	6.4%	12.6%	14.4%

ables, the five key ones were unaided recall, aided copy point recall, credibility for each message recalled, purchase interest using the industry's favorite five-point rating scale, and pre-post changes in buying intentions on a constant sum scale. We found that under simulated-natural environment conditions, "program involvement" exhibits a significant positive effect on all measures of ad response.

The figures indicate that, as program involvement rises, all five measures also rise. The bottom figures are perhaps the most important measure, the pre-post change in behavior. Among people low in program involvement, the average change was 6.4 percent. Among people high in involvement, the figure was more than twice as large, 14.4 percent.

If program involvement enhances advertising response, and if involvement means more than simple viewership, then cost per thousand people involved or impacted should replace cost per thousand exposed as the tool of choice for media selection decisions. Although marketers have purchased media based on CPMs for the last thirty years, we say there is now a better way to buy.

Media vehicles do differ considerably in terms of involvement or impact—even holding audience size or rating constant. If media impact determines ad response, it can aid or impede a campaign's success. The question is how closely related are the CPM and the

CPMI for the same set of programs? Would a company make the same or a different media buy if the decision were based on impacted viewers rather than the total number?

We were able to estimate "advertising effectiveness" scores for 40 different prime-time and news/current events programs. Exhibit 13–4 shows the comparison between the CPM and the CPMI for the ten programs in the top quartile, that is those that rated highest in both the CPM and the CPMI.

The average cost per thousand for these ten shows is $13.07; the average cost per thousand impacted, however, is $11.03, a significant 18.5 percent cost savings. In seven of these ten cases, the CPMI index value is greater than the CPM index value. In two cases the indexes are identical, and in only one is the CPM index greater than the CPMI. Cost per thousand impacted figures therefore offer higher levels of predicted effectiveness as well as lower costs. To demonstrate

Exhibit 13–4

CPM/CPMI Comparison for the 10 Top Programs

Programs in Top Quartile	CPM	Index Value	CPMI	Index Value
1	$10.92	.96	$8.17	1.67
2	$12.07	1.08	$9.29	1.39
3	$12.43	.67	$9.80	1.53
4	$12.78	1.08	$11.18	1.08
5	$12.91	1.39	$11.60	1.47
6	$13.19	.99	$11.81	1.40
7	$13.51	.67	$11.84	1.08
8	$13.67	1.67	$11.99	.96
9	$14.08	.90	$12.12	1.30
10	$14.52	1.16	$12.52	1.16

their potential overall superiority over cost per thousand, we divided the average predicted efficiency scores by their respective average cost per thousand for each approach. The resulting "efficiency ratio" for CPM was 8.1; for CPMI it was 11.8—a 46 percent improvement.

Our findings indicate that television program involvement *does* appear to be positively, causally linked to advertising effectiveness. Program involvement, attitudes, or "impact" varies significantly by program—and corporate media decisions should take those variations into account.

Line Extensions Cannibalize Profits

In the 1990s many marketers, eager for quick success, routinely introduced line extensions to a major brand. The pattern has become fairly standard. The line extension manager launches his or her new brand, diverting resources away from the parent. The extension achieves its sales objectives and the manager is rewarded. The parent goes into slow decline and the diagnosis reveals that cannibalization is the disease.

At one time, line extensions may have been an almost risk-free way to introduce new products. Corporations felt that line extensions are easier to develop and introduce than completely new brands, they are the most profitable. This may still be true in certain special circumstances. Brand extensions sometimes offer great market potential—a strong brand name can give immediate recognition to an extension, thereby saving advertising and promotion expense. Extending the brand (Liquid Tide, Diet Coke, or Gillette Sensor for Women) is a way to ensure brand/market continuity and maintain sales and profit levels as the core brand matures.

On the other hand, a brand extension can be extraordinarily risky. Dangers include a product that disappoints loyal consumers and damages the core brand's reputation. The core name may be inappropriate for the new product (and vice versa) even if the new product is well made and performs as intended. The core name may lose its unique positioning in the consumer's mind through overuse, leaving a loosely connected bunch of brands, with the appearance of being in the same general category.

Line extensions tend to cannibalize the parent brand. A company should evaluate a line extension on the basis of its net incremental profits—not sales. The issue is not how much volume the new product generates but how much *additional* profit. When a company looks at net incremental profits, line extensions often prove to be far more risky than most marketers have been led to believe.

To study the impact of a line extension, we have employed the three-phase convergent validation approach to determine the potential cannibalizing impact of a new entry on the existing brand franchise. This was the process we discussed in Chapter 7.

Overoptimism Can Be Dangerous

While new product managers should be optimistic, overoptimism is dangerous; it's the most frequent cause of discrepancies between STM projections and actual new product performance. The average sales volume prediction is 88 percent greater than first year sales; 80 percent of this overage can be attributed to overstated marketing plans.

Exhibit 13–5

STM Plan vs. Real-World Delivery

	Simulated Test Market Plan	Actual Real-World Delivery
Advertising		
Spending	$26MM	$21MM
Share of Voice	24%	18%
Arresting Power	Above Average	Average
Motivating Power	Well Above Average	Average
Promotion		
Reach	56%	44%
Redemption	6.2%	4.1%
Distribution		
ACV	73%	67%
Number of Products	3.1	2.5
Competitive Response	Nothing Unusual	Full Court Press

By far the biggest source of errors are unrealistic media, promotion, and trade plans. Modeling errors, as we will see, also contribute to disappointing marketplace performance. On the other hand, consumer response is a reasonably valid predictor of marketplace performance. Buyer behavior can be predicted.

Exhibit 13–5 shows an example of the slippage that can occur between plan and reality.

Marketing managers need to be very careful when they provide marketing inputs to simulated test market researchers. The inputs drive the output. A manager who is overly enthusiastic about what he or she can get in terms of advertising support, promotion, and distribution will unconsciously poison a volume forecast hyping the numbers to yield a "go" decision when in reality the plan should be junked. One approach that we recommend is to create a "worst case" marketing scenario. Use the lowest advertising support level, the dumbest advertising, negligible distribution, and the strongest competitive response and test this case in the STM. At worst you'll learn what the lowest level of performance might be. But you might also learn that this worst case scenario better resembles what you take into the real world than the overoptimistic plan you plan to give to the STM research staff.

Small Modeling Issues Create Major Problems

Even if overoptimism is not the problem, not every new product forecast yields a successful outcome. Sometimes seemingly small modeling issues can create major forecasting problems. Many systems, for example, are unable to forecast awareness accurately. Some do not take the purchase cycle into account. Others ignore the effect of distribution on sales in the absence of advertising, as well as ignoring the relationship between consumer involvement in the product category and effective distribution.

Let's briefly discuss some of these issues. In all pre-test market research systems, total brand awareness has a linear effect on trial and, in most systems, on total volume as well. Alternate approaches to estimating awareness include client-provided estimates of year-end awareness, simple GRP models, complex GRP models, and the kind of sophisticated model employed by LITMUS and DESIGNOR. These latter take into account many determinants of awareness including gross rating points (reach times frequency); GRP allocation by period (media schedule); impact of each media type; advertising impact (within each media type); share of voice; ceiling effect (maximum awareness); product category effect; forgetting effect (in the absence of advertising); pre-level (prior to launch); dissimulation/confusion factor; couponing reach per period; couponing impact; sampling reach per period; sampling impact; quantity of distribution effect; shelf facings effect (number and share); and word-of-mouth.

As discussed in Chapter 8, the more determinants included in the model, the better the forecast.

Another modeling issue is the shortfall in effective product distribution. Manufacturers are finding it increasingly difficult to obtain adequate breadth of distribution for multi-item product lines. Retailers are "cherry-picking" the lines, which means that often one-third of one-half of the new items are sparsely distributed. Increasingly, forecasting the impact of item distribution is critical to an accurate sales projection. In our work we've found that reduced item availability typically results in a 5 to 20 percent sales reduction.

In one case, the simulated test market research forecast $33.7 million in sales during the first year. The brand was a five-flavor line and the marketer assumed a 73 percent ACV. In actual in-store presence, Flavor A obtained a 75 percent ACV, Flavor B 64 percent ACV, Flavor D 32 percent ACV, and Flavors C and E obtained no distribution whatever. As a result, the actual sales were $16.8 million, just about half what was forecast.

Another critical issue that we have discussed at several points in this book is the important role played by the product purchase cycle in the marketing process. Advertising and promotion need to be tied to the product purchase cycle. A heavily front-loaded campaign, as an illustration, might work well for a fast-turnover package goods, but it could be a disaster for toilet bowl cleaner purchased a few times a year or a PC which might be purchased once every four years. Many simulated test marketing models don't and can't differentiate between slow and fast turnover products in this respect and thus could produce dangerously misleading forecasts.

Two other marketing issues that need to be addressed by simulated test marketing services are consumer promotion and public relations. Consumer promotion, reflected in the coupons that consumers bring to the supermarket, has been a foundation of many marketing plans for new products for the past decade. Yet most STMs approach this tool in a very unsatisfactory way without the kind of serious thinking and modeling which has gone into capturing the effects of advertising. Few STMs formally consider the effects of promotions on awareness and repeat purchase, and with the possible exception of LITMUS, none micro-model its effects on even consumer trial on a monthly basis.

Public relations is another understudied tool. Since an effective PR campaign is often less expensive than its advertising or promotional counterparts, watch for PR to become an increasingly important component of the marketing communications mix. This is particularly true for breakthrough products and for new services and durables. Interestingly, academic marketing modelers have for three decades talked about the role of "word of mouth" and in many instances have explicitly captured word of mouth in their models. Marketing practitioners, particularly simulated test market researchers, have chided this obsession as being irrelevant to most new product introductions. Practitioners claim that it's difficult enough to get people to watch a commercial for the new product and get them to remember anything about it let alone worrying about people discussing it over backyard fences or at cocktail parties. Public relations, on the other hand, is a managed, controlled form of communications which is important and which both academic researchers and STM modelers have largely ignored. This imbalance of effort needs to be corrected in the mid-'90s and beyond.

The New Product Only Appears to Be Dead: It Can Be Revived

In Chapters 7 and 11, we discussed how simulated test marketing technology can be used to improve a new product or re-staged brand's marketing program. Although most new products still fail, the types of tools and methods discussed in those chapters can take an adequate product with a less-than-optimal marketing plan and make it succeed. We've found that improved marketing plans can increase sales by as much as 70 percent. The key is to study consumer behavior in as close to real-world conditions as possible and to use a model that is skilled in evaluating the advertising media and promotional tools used to introduce new products.

Targeting, positioning, pricing, advertising, distribution, promotion—all are among the elements that contribute to new product success or failure. Each of these components and more can be studied and improved prior to and following a simulated test marketing study. Although it's unlikely that a guy who only a mother could love will be transformed into someone with drop dead good looks, in marketing, as in the real world, surgery and cosmetics can go a long way toward making an ordinary person appear handsome. This is not to suggest that we recommend that marketers bring more ordinary products to life. The fact is that in every product category, brand proliferation has become a problem. We need fewer rather than more brands.

We do mean to suggest and to emphasize, however, that smart marketing is a lot more than just a good product or service. A marketing manager is charged with the responsibility of investigating and fine-tuning every decision in the marketing mix. And when everything is done right, the product is likely to be successful. The days of searching for just a better mousetrap are coming to an end. Today, we need the better mousetrap, but we also need the more serious study of the marketing climate, the more thoughtful target group, a powerful pre-emptive positioning, attention-getting, likable advertising, an attractive price, a sufficient level of distribution, and all the other elements that contribute to new product success.

Management Implications: Marketing Must Be at the Center of a Business

American business is experiencing serious problems. Led by financially oriented managers during the 1980s and early '90s, a frenzy of mergers and purges, acquisitions and divestitures, expansion and downsizing have resulted in zero growth in sales, profitability, and productivity. Finance has been the center of the business solar system for too long. It should not have been there in the first place.

Just as the Copernican Theory placed the sun at the center of the solar system and eclipsed the Ptolemaic Theory, a revolution will occur in the mid- to late-1990s that will place marketing at the center of business. Marketing, after all, is what drives business. Marketing is responsible for finding, serving, and keeping customers, and that's what every business is about. As Regis McKenna has said, "Marketing is everything, and everything is marketing." Marketing keeps everyone in the organization afloat. Without marketing, the business would not exist.

A revolution is coming not simply because marketing must replace finance as the focus of business's attention but because marketing doesn't work as well as it should. Companies large and small are spending money with little knowledge of what they produce. With more than $500 billion invested annually in media advertising and trade and consumer promotion, more money passes through the hands of American marketing managers than the gross national products of most nations.

Yet when asked "What do you get for your marketing investment?" or "What level of ROI did you achieve?" most managers don't know. And, interestingly, they even admit that they have grave doubts. In one recent survey more than half report that they "don't believe that most marketing programs produce a return on investment."

We do know that few advertising campaigns appear to have any effect on sales. If you increase the advertising or change the copy for an established product or service, most of the time nothing happens. If you develop an entirely new marketing program for an established product that's losing share—sliding downhill—nine out of ten times nothing happens. And if you launch a new product or service, whether a food product, automobile, financial service, medical testing device, or television program, eighty to ninety-nine times out of a hundred it will fail.

They fail because managers are not using the marketing tools currently available and because they believe things that simply aren't true. This is part of the "death wish marketing" syndrome. Yet, marketing—no matter what practitioners thought in the past—is more science than art. It is no longer necessary to rely exclusively on hunch, hope, mythology, and divine illumination. The data and the tools currently exist to improve a company's marketing success rate dramatically. All that's required is the will to use them.

This is not to advocate abandoning such essential inputs of great marketing as creativity, sound management judgment, and experience. These are absolutely essential. And no one should think we believe in slavish obedience to the numbers alone. On the contrary, we are increasingly convinced that American business needs to *balance* science and subjective insight in marketing.

Effective marketing is serious business. Before the organization invests a single dollar in the annual marketing program, it should challenge the marketing manager to demonstrate the profit-directed thinking that went into each critical decision in the plan. It should demand to see the anticipated return on the organization's investment in the plan as a whole.

Starting with a perfectly clean slate, managers must analyze the environment, the target, the positioning, the product design, the pricing strategy, the advertising—everything. And each of these alternatives can be—should be—evaluated in terms of criteria related to profitability.

The time is over for choosing target groups because they are women between 18 and 49; for choosing positioning strategies because of meaningless "gaps" or even more meaningless focus groups; for choosing product designs because they produce the highest "top box" scores. The time is over for selecting ad executions because of high recall stores; for selecting media plans based on experience at roulette tables; for setting prices based on neither strategy nor research; and for setting consumer-service levels based on the intent to satisfy everyone. The time is over for marketing plans that are based on picking one out of billions of possible plans out of a hat.

American industry can no longer tolerate such a waste of our economic resources. We can no longer countenance routine marketing failure. We can no longer accept marketing management-led light brigade charges into oblivion as the order of the day. If all you do is what you've done, then all you'll get is what you've got. Most companies haven't gotten much in terms of new product/new service success during the past decade. Companies need to do something different.

The time is *now* for simulated test marketing and other new technologies designed to improve the performance of marketing programs for new and re-staged products and services. The marketing equivalent of the Copernican revolution is here. Those of our readers who embrace it will experience improved marketing programs, more profitable businesses, and help ensure a stronger America.

Notes

Chapter 1

1. Donahue, Christine. "How Procter & Gamble Fumbled Citrus Hill," *Adweek's Marketing Week*, 29, No. 12, March 7, 1988, p. 1.
2. Ibid. p. 6.
3. The Procter & Gamble Company, *Annual Report*, 1990.
4. "Proctor & Gamble to Eliminate Line of Juice," *The New York Times*, September 18, 1992, p. D3(L).
5. Ibid.
6. "New Product Totals," *Gorman's New Product News*, January 4, 1994, pp. 12–13.
7. Friedman, Marty. "Hard Questions, Soft Answers," *Gorman's New Product News*, July 7, 1989, p. 8.
8. Achenbaum, Alvin. "How to Succeed in New Products," *Advertising Age*, June 26, 1989, p. 62.
9. Ogiba, p. 23.
10. If a family loyally buys only Skippy peanut butter, Skippy represents 100 percent of the family's share of requirement for peanut butter. If the family switches between Skippy and Jif, Skippy may represent only a 50 percent share of requirement.
11. Freeman, Laurie. "Colgate Misfires in U.S.," *Advertising Age*, June 5, 1989, p. 3.
12. Fitzgerald, Kate. "Why Sears' McKids Failed," *Advertising Age*, January 14, 1991, p. 8.
13. Carey, David. "Bob Barney's Last Hurrah," *Financial World*, October 20, 1987, p. 31.
14. Whitton, Lynn S., "Juxtaposition: Financial Services and Packaged Goods Research in the New Product Arena." A paper presented at the ARF Pre Test Market Research Workshop, Chicago, June 1988.
15. Ogiba, p. 18.
16. Friedman, "Hard Questions, Soft Answers," p. 10.
17. Malhotra, Rakesh. "Behavioral Research & Single Source Data." A paper presented at the ARF Behavioral Research and Single Source Data Worship, New York, June 1990.
18. Cited by Rakesh, ibid.

Chapter 2

1.   Aaker, David A. and George S. Day, *Marketing Research*, New York: John Wiley & Sons, 1983, p. 680. This section draws upon Aaker's and Day's overview, which in turn draws on Alvin A. Achenbaum's "Market Testing: Using the Marketplace as a Laboratory," in Robert Ferber, ed., *Handbook of Marketing Research*, New York: McGraw-Hill, 1974.

2.   Sawsy, Alecia, "Diaper's Failure Shows How Poor Plans, Unexpected Woes Can Kill New Products," *The Wall Street Journal*, October 9, 1990, p. B1.

3.   Kindel, Stephen, *Financial World*.

4.   Aaker and Day, ibid., p. 684.

5.   Brennan, Leslie, "Quick Study: So Fast Are Today's Testing Techniques That Marketers Can Evaluate a Product Before Competitors Get Wise—Usually," *Sales & Marketing Management*, March 1988, p. 50.

6.   Lanznar, Gail A., "The Pendulum Swings." A paper presented at the ARF Behavioral Research and Single Source Data Workshop, New York, June 1990.

7.   Brown, Jane, "Test Marketing Trends—1976–1990." A paper presented at the ARF Behavioral Research and Single Source Data Worship, New York, June 1990.

8.   Brand and category indices are commonly used bases for evaluating different markets. An index of 100 indicates that a brand or category is "average" within a market. An index of 80 indicates a level of only 80 percent of average (or 20 percent below average).

9.   Clancy, Kevin J. and Robert Shulman, *The Marketing Revolution: A Radical Manifesto for Dominating the Marketplace*, New York: HarperBusiness, 1991, p. 204.

10.   Malhotra, Rakesh. "Behavioral Research & Single Source Data." A paper presented at the ARF Behavioral Research and Single Source Data Worship, New York, June 1990.

11.   Stalk, George Jr. *Competing Against Time: How Time-Based Competition Is Reshaping Global Markets*, New York: The Free Press, 1990, p. 21.

Chapter 3

1.   Charnes, Abraham, William W. Cooper, James K. DeVoe, and David B. Learner, "DEMON: Decision Mapping via Optimal GO-NO Networks—A Model for Marketing New Products," *Management Science*, 12, July 1966, pp. 865–88.

2.   Edward I. Brody. "When and How to Use New Product Models: General Issues and a Personal View." A paper presented to the ARF Pre Test Market Research Workshop, Chicago, June 2, 1988.

3.   Pringle, Lewis G., R. Dale Wilson, and Edward I Brody. "NEWS: A Decision-Oriented Model for New Product Analysis and Forecasting," *Marketing Science*, 1, Winter 1982, pp. 1–29.

4.   Gerald J. Eskin, "Setting a Forward Agenda for Test Market Modeling." A paper presented at the ARF Pre Test Market Research Workshop, Chicago, June 2, 1988.

5.   For a description of the model, see Eskin, Gerald J. "Dynamic Forecasts

of New Product Demand Using a Depth of Repeat Model," *Journal of Marketing Research*, 10, May 1973, pp. 115–29.

6. Eskin, "Setting a Forward Agenda for Test Market Modeling."

7. Ibid.

8. Blackburn, Joseph D. and Kevin J. Clancy. "LITMUS: A New Product Planning Model," in *Proceedings: Market Measurement and Analysis*, Robert P. Leone (ed.), Providence, RI: The Institute of Management Sciences, 1983, pp. 182–93.

9. ACV, or all commodity volume, is the percentage of all sales for that product category captured by the stores in which the new product is distributed. Assume a new soft drink is distributed only in Kroger Stores. The manufacturer failed to get distribution anyplace else. As it turns out, that's not that bad because—to make up a number—16 percent of all U.S. soft drink sales are in Kroger supermarkets. So the marketer is in stores that represent 16 percent of all the sales. In other words, a 16 percent ACV.

10. Burger, Philip C., Howard Gundee, and Robert Lavidge (1981), "COMP: A Comprehensive System for the Evaluation of New Products," in *New Product Forecasting: Models and Applications*, Yoram Wind, Vijay Mahajan, and Richard N. Cardozo, eds. Lexington, MA: Lexington Books, pp. 269–83.

11. Pringle, Lewis G., R. Dale Wilson, and Edward I Brody (1982), "NEWS: A Decision-Oriented Model for New Product Analysis and Forecasting," *Marketing Science*, 1, Winter, 1982, pp. 1–29.

12. For a review of some of the features of these STMs, see Robinson, Patrick J. (1981), "Comparison of Pre-Test-Market New- Product Forecasting Models," in *New-Product Forecasting: Models and Applications*, Yoram Wind, Vijay Mahajan, and Richard N. Cardozo, eds. Lexington, MA: Lexington Books, pp. 181–204.

13. Baldinger, Allan, L. "Trends and Issues in STM's: Results of an ARF Pilot Project." A paper presented at the ARF Pre Test Market Research Workshop, Chicago, June 2, 1988.

14. Baldinger, Allan L. "The State of Test Marketing: Results of an ARF Survey." A paper presented at the ARF Behavioral Research and Single Source Data Workshop, New York, June 26–27, 1990.

15. Baldinger, Allan, L. "Trends and Issues in STM's: Results of an ARF Pilot Project."

Chapter 4

1. Examples of these approaches include the discussions of ASSESSOR in Lilien and Kotler (1983), pp. 728–34; Urban and Hauser (1980), pp. 393–417; Urban, Hauser, and Dholakia (1987), pp. 218–31; and Wind (1982), pp. 422–27.

Chapter 5

1. Clancy, Kevin J. and Thomas T. Nagle, "Pricing Research: Theory and Measurement with Clear Management Implications." A paper presented at the American Marketing Association's Annual Attitude Research Conference, Newport Beach, CA, January 1990.

Chapter 8

1.   Percy, Larry and John R. Rossiter. *Advertising Strategy: A Communication Theory Approach.* New York: Praeger Publishers, 1980.

2.   Burke, William L. and Ruth G. Newman. "Brand Awareness and Profitability," *The PIMSLETTER on Business Strategy.* Cambridge, MA: The Strategic Planning Institute, No. 24, 1980.

3.   Haley, Douglas F. "Advertising Tracking Studies: Packaged-Goods Case Histories," *Journal of Advertising Research*, 25, February/March 1985, pp. 45–51.

4.   Golanti, Dave. "American Express Goes for the Platinum: Cardholders Invited to Exclusive Club," *Advertising Age*, 55 August 3, 1984, pp. 42–43.

Chapter 9

1.   See, for example, Blackburn, Clancy, and Wilson 1988; Blattberg and Golanty 1978; Claycamp and Liddy 1969; Pringle, Wilson, and Brody 1982; and Urban and Hauser 1980.

2.   Ostrow, Joseph W. "Setting Frequency Levels: An Art or a Science?" *Journal of Advertising Research*, 20, August 1984, pp. 39–44.

3.   Blackburn, Joseph D., Kevin Clancy, and R. Dale Wilson. "Forecasting Awareness of New Products and Penetration of New Campaigns for Established Products: Applications of LITMUS II," Boston University School of Management Working Paper, 1990.

4.   Zielske, Hubert A. and Walter A. Henry. "Remembering and Forgetting Television Ads," *Journal of Advertising Research*, 20, April 1985; pp. 7–13; Julian L. Simon. "What Do Zielske's Real Data Really Show About Pulsing?" *Journal of Marketing Research*, 16, August 1979; pp. 415–20.

Chapter 10

1.   Ibid., p. 141.

Chapter 11

1.   The formula is 250 x 81 x 101 x 6 x 101.

Chapter 12

1.   This discussion of CoverStory is based on company information.

Chapter 13

1.   Haley, Russell and Al Baldinger, "The ARF Copy Research Validity Projects, *Journal of Advertising Research*, Vol. 31, No. 2, April/May, 1991, pp. 11–32.

2.   Clancy, Kevin J. and David Lloyd, "CPMs Versus CPMIs: Implications for Media Planning," *Journal of Advertising Research*, Vol. 31, No. 4, August/September 1991.

Bibliography

Aaker, David A. and George S. Day, *Marketing Research*, New York: John Wiley & Sons, 1983.

Armstrong, J. Scott. *Long-Range Forecasting: From Crystal Ball to Computer*, 2nd ed., New York: John Wiley & Sons, 1985.

Baldinger, Allan L. "Trends and Issues in STM's: Results of an ARF Pilot Project." A paper presented at the ARF Pre Test Market Research Workshop, Chicago, June 2, 1988.

Baldinger, Allan L. "The State of Test Marketing: Results of an ARF Survey." A paper presented at the ARF Behavioral Research and Single Source Data Workshop, New York, June 26–27, 1990.

Blackburn, Joseph D., Lisa E. Carter, and Kevin J. Clancy. "LITMUS II: A New Model to Help Optimize Marketing Plans for New Products and Services," in *Are Interviews Obsolete? Drastic Changes in Data Collection*. Amsterdam: European Society for Opinion and Marketing Research, 1984.

Blackburn, Joseph D. and Kevin J. Clancy. "LITMUS: A New Product Planning Model," in *Proceedings: Market Measurement and Analysis*, Robert P. Leone, ed. Providence; RI: The Institute of Management Sciences, 1980.

Blackburn, Joseph D. and Kevin J. Clancy. "LITMUS: A New Product Planning Model," in *Marketing Planning Models*, A. A. Zoltners, ed. Amsterdam: North Holland Publishing Company, 1982.

Blackburn, Joseph D. and Kevin J. Clancy. "LITMUS II: An Evolutionary Step in New Product Planning Models from Market Plan Evaluation to Marketing Plan Generation," in *Advances and Practices of Marketing Science 1983*, Fred S. Zufryden, ed. Providence; RI: The Institute of Management Sciences, 1983.

Blackburn, Joseph D. and Kevin J. Clancy. "Awareness Forecasting Models Comment," *Management Science*, Vol 3, No. 3, Summer 1984.

Blackburn, Joseph D., Kevin Clancy, and R. Dale Wilson. "Forecasting Awareness of New Products and Penetration of New Campaigns for Established Products: Application of LITMUS II," Boston University School of Management Working Paper, 1990.

Blackburn, Joseph D., Kevin Clancy, and R. Dale Wilson. "The Effects of Media Timing and Media Weight on Market Response for New and Established Products," Boston University School of Management Working Paper, 1990.

291

Brody, Edward I. "When and How to Use New Product Models: General Issues and a Personal View." A paper presented at the ARF Pre Test Market Research Workshop, Chicago, June 2, 1988.

Brown, Jane, "Test Marketing Trends—1976–1990." A paper presented at the ARF Behavioral Research and Single Source Data Worship, New York, June 1990.

Burger, Philip C., Howard Gundee, and Robert Lavidge. "COMP: A Comprehensive System for the Evaluation of New Products," in *New Product Forecasting: Models and Applications*, Yoram Wind, Vijay Mahajan, and Richard N. Cardozo, eds. Lexington, MA: Lexington Books, 1981.

Burke, William L. and Ruth G. Newman. "Brand Awareness and Profitability," *The PIMSLETTER on Business Strateg.* Cambridge, MA: The Strategic Planning Institute, No. 24, 1980.

Carey, David. "Bob Barney's Last Hurrah," *Financial World*, 156, No. 21, October 20, 1987.

Charnes, Abraham, William W. Cooper, James K. DeVoe, and David B. Learner, "DEMON: Decision Mapping via Optimal GO-NO Networks—A Model for Marketing New Products," *Management Science*, 12, July 1966.

Clancy, Kevin J. and David Lloyd, "CPMs Versus CPMIs: Implications for Media Planning," *Journal of Advertising Research*, Vol. 31, No. 4, August/September 1991.

Clancy, Kevin J. and Robert Shulman, *The Marketing Revolution: A Radical Manifesto for Dominating the Marketplace*, New York: HarperBusiness, 1991.

Clancy, Kevin J. and Robert Shulman, *Marketing Myths that Are Killing Business: The Cure for Death Wish Marketing.* New York: McGraw-Hill, 1993.

Donahue, Christine. "How Procter & Gamble Fumbled Citrus Hill," *Adweek's Marketing Week*, 29, No. 12, March 7, 1988.

Eskin, Gerald J. "Dynamic Forecasts of New Product Demand Using a Depth of Repeat Model," *Journal of Marketing Research*, 10, May, 1973.

Eskin, Gerald J. "Setting a Forward Agenda for Test Market Modeling." A paper presented at the ARF Pre Test Market Research Workshop, Chicago, June 2, 1988.

Eskin, Gerald J. and John Malec. "A model for Estimating Sales Potential Prior to the Test Market," in *Marketing: 1776–1976 and Beyond*, Kenneth L. Bernhardt, ed. Chicago: American Marketing Association, 1976.

Fitzgerald, Kate. "Why Sears' McKids failed," *Advertising Age*, January 14, 1991.

Fourt, Louis A. and Joseph W. Woodlock, "Early Predictions of Market Success for New Grocery Products," *Journal of Marketing*, 25, October 1960.

Golanti, Dave. "American Express Goes for the Platinum: Cardholders Invited to Exclusive Club," *Advertising Age*, 55, August 3, 1984.

Golanti, John L. "Clarification of the TRACKER Methodology and Limitations," *Marketing Science*, 3, Summer 1978, p. 203.

Haley, Douglas F. "Advertising Tracking Studies: Packaged-Goods Case Histories," *Journal of Advertising Research*, 25, February/March 1985.

Haley, Russell and Al Baldinger, "The ARF Copy Research Validity Projects, *Journal of Advertising Research*, Vol. 31, No. 2, April/May 1991.

Kalwani, Manohar and Alvin J. Silk. "Structure of Buying for New Packaged Goods," *Journal of Marketing Research*, 17, August 1980.

Lanznar, Gail A. "The Pendulum Swings." Paper presented at the Advertising Research Foundation Behavioral Research and Single Source Data Workshop, New York, June 1990.

Lilien, Gary L. and Philip Kotler (1983). *Marketing Decision Making: A Model-Building Approach*. New York: Harper & Row, Publishers, 1983.

Lin, Lynn Y. S., William J. McKenna, Reg Rhodes, and Steve Wilson. "New Product Analysis and Testing: How to Optimize Them," *Handbook of Business Problem Solving*, Kenneth J. Albert, ed. New York: McGraw-Hill, 1980.

Narasimhan, Chakravarthi and Subrata K. Sen. "New Product Models for Test Market Data," *Journal of Marketing*, 47, Winter 1983.

Ogiba, Edward F. "New Products: A View from the Top," *Food & Beverage Marketing*, November 1991.

Ostrow, Joseph W. "Setting Frequency Levels: An Art or a Science?" *Journal of Advertising Research*, 20, August 1984.

Percy, Larry and John R. Rossiter. *Advertising Strategy: A Communication Theory Approach*. New York: Praeger Publishers, 1980.

Pringle, Lewis G., R. Dale Wilson, and Edward I Brody. "NEWS: A Decision-Oriented Model for New Product Analysis and Forecasting," *Marketing Science*, 1, Winter 1982.

Robinson, Patrick J. "Comparison of Pre-Test-Market New-Product Forecasting Models," in *New-Product Forecasting: Models and Applications*, Yoram Wind, Vijay Mahajan, and Richard N. Cardozo, eds. Lexington, MA: Lexington Books, 1981.

Sawsy, Alecia, "Diaper's Failure Shows How Poor Plans, Unexpected Woes Can Kill New Products," *The Wall Street Journal*, October 9, 1990.

Shocker, Allan D. and William G. Hall. "Pretest Market Models: A Critical Evaluation," *Journal of Product Innovation Management*, 3, June 1986.

Silk, Alvin J. and Glen L. Urban. "Pre-Test-Market Evaluation of New Packaged Goods: A Model and Measurement Methodology," *Journal of Marketing Research*, 15, May 1986.

Simon, Julian L. "What Do Zielske's Real Data Really Show about Pulsing?" *Journal of Marketing Research*, 16, August 1979.

Stalk, George Jr. *Competing Against Time: How Time-Based Competition Is Reshaping Global Markets*. New York: The Free Press, 1990.

Urban, Glen L. and John R. Hauser. *Design and Marketing of New Products*. Englewood Cliffs, NJ: Prentice-Hall, 1980.

Urban, Glen L., John R. Hauser, and Nikhilesh Dholakia. *Essentials of New Product Management*. Englewood Cliffs, NJ: Prentice-Hall, 1987.

Urban, Glen L. and Gerald M. Katz. "Pre-Test-Market Models: Validation and Managerial Implications," *Journal of Marketing Research*, 20, May 1983.

Urban, Glen L., Gerald M. Katz, Thomas E. Hatch, and Alvin J. Silk. "The ASSESSOR Pre-Test Market Evaluation System," *Interfaces*, 13, December 1983.

Wilson, R. Dale, "Test Marketing Simulation Systems: A Review of Four Major STM Methodologies," Working Paper, The Eli Broad Graduate School of Management, Michigan State University, 1992.

Wilson, R. Dale and David K. Smith, Jr. "Advances and Issues in New Product Introduction Models," in *New-Product Development and Testing*, Walter Henry, Michael Menasco, and Hirokazu Takada, eds. Lexington, MA: Lexington Books, 1989.

Wind, Yoram J. *Product Policy: Concepts, Methods, and Strategy*. Reading, MA: Addison-Wesley Publishing Company, 1982.

Yankelovich Skelly and White, Inc. "LTM Estimation Procedures," in *New-Product Forecasting: Models and Applications*, Yoram Wind, Vijay Mahajan, and Richard N. Cardozo, eds. Lexington, MA: Lexington Books, 1981.

Zielske, Hubert A. and Walter A. Henry. "Remembering and Forgetting Television Ads," *Journal of Advertising Research*, 20, April 1985.

Index

About the Authors

Kevin J. Clancy and Robert S. Shulman are chairman and CEO, respectively, of Copernicus: The Marketing Investment Strategy Group, headquarted in Westport, Connecticut. Previously they held the same positions with Yankelovich Clancy Shulman, building it into one of the largest and most prestigious marketing, consulting and research firms in the world. They are authors of *The Marketing Revolution: A Radical Manifesto for Dominating the Marketplace* and *Marketing Myths That Are Killing Business: The Cure for Death Wish Marketing*, both business best sellers. Dr. Clancy is also a professor of marketing at Boston University and held positions in marketing and sociology at the Wharton School. Early in his career he was Vice President for Research Services at BBDO Advertising. Dr. Clancy is a graduate of the City University of New York and earned a Ph.D. in sociology and research methods from New York University. Following graduate studies in political science, Mr. Shulman rose through the ranks at Xerox Corporation to become National Accounts Manager. Later he joined the Yankelovich organization where he was a Vice President in the simulated test market division. Mr. Shulman is a recognized expert on marketing strategy, new product evaluation, and sales management. Mr. Shulman earned a B.A. from Eisenhower College and did doctoral work in political science at the University of Tennessee. **Marianne M. Wolf** is an Adjunct Professor at California Polytechnic State University in San Luis Obispo, and an Associate Director at Yankelovich Partners Inc. At Cal Poly she teaches marketing research, principles of marketing, and strategic planning. At Yankelovich Partners she is responsible for managing key West Coast accounts and for managing new product forecasting research products throughout the US and Europe. Dr Wolf received her Ph.D. in economics from The John Hopkins University.